# 2024

## Abitu

Original-Prüfur
mit Lösungen

Gymnasium · Gesamtschule NRW

## Englisch LK

**STARK**

© 2023 Stark Verlag GmbH
17. ergänzte Auflage
www.stark-verlag.de

Das Werk und alle seine Bestandteile sind urheberrechtlich geschützt. Jede vollständige oder teilweise Vervielfältigung, Verbreitung und Veröffentlichung bedarf der ausdrücklichen Genehmigung des Verlages. Dies gilt insbesondere für Vervielfältigungen, Mikroverfilmungen sowie die Speicherung und Verarbeitung in elektronischen Systemen.

# Inhalt

Vorwort
Hinweise zu den digitalen Zusätzen

## Hinweise und Tipps zum Zentralabitur 2024

| | |
|---|---|
| **Schriftliche Abiturprüfung** | I |
| Die zentrale Abiturprüfung in NRW | I |
| Wie ist eine Abiturprüfungsaufgabe aufgebaut? | III |
| Die Bewertung der Abiturprüfungsaufgabe | VI |
| Die Bearbeitung der verschiedenen Teilaufgaben | VII |
| Praktische Tipps zur Vorbereitung | XXI |
| Das Anfertigen der Prüfungsarbeit | XXIII |
| Die Arbeit mit diesem Buch | XXIV |
| **Mündliche Abiturprüfung** | XXVI |
| Der Aufbau | XXVI |
| Die Bewertung | XXVII |
| Tipps | XXVII |
| Die Arbeit mit diesem Buch | XXVIII |

## Übungsaufgaben: Leseverstehen und Schreiben

**Aufgabe 1:** "Developed nations have sown the wind, Vanuatu has reaped the whirlwind" ........ 1
Themen: Globalisierung – ökologische, ökonomische und politische Aspekte
Textsorte: Zeitungsartikel
Aufgabenfokus Analyse: *structure, argumentative technique, language*
Zieltextformate Textproduktion: *comment, opening statement*

**Aufgabe 2:** "Kill Bill: why we must take Shakespeare out of the classroom" ........ 12
Themen: Shakespeares Einfluss auf junge Menschen, Medien
Textsorte: Zeitungsartikel
Aufgabenfokus Analyse: *argumentative techniques, language*
Zieltextformate Textproduktion: *comment, letter to the editor*

**Aufgabe 3:** "The Other Britain Waiting to Surface" / "Turning Words into Action" ........ 21
Themen: Großbritannien nach dem Brexit, Verhältnis zu Europa, multikulturelle Gesellschaft

Textsorte: Blogartikel, Poster
Aufgabenfokus Analyse: *campaign poster and how it fits the article*
Zieltextformate Textproduktion: *comment, article*

**Aufgabe 4:** "Bernie Sanders: 58th Green Foundation Lecture" /
"Democracy Wear" .................................................................. 32
Themen: Amerikanischer Traum, Chancen und Risiken der Globalisierung
Textsorte: politische Rede; Bildmaterial: Cartoon
Aufgabenfokus Analyse: *effects of cartoon and speech; rhetorical devices*
Zieltextformate Textproduktion: *comment, blog post*

**Aufgabe 5:** *The Hunted* by Alex Shearer ............................................. 44
Themen: Visionen der Zukunft, Utopie und Dystopie
Textsorte: Romanauszug
Aufgabenfokus Analyse: *criticism of (a fictional) society*
Zieltextformate Textproduktion: *comment, dialogue*

**Aufgabe 6:** "Focusing on schoolgirl abductions distorts the view
of life in Nigeria" .................................................................. 55
Themen: Postkolonialismus, Nigeria
Textsorte: Zeitungsartikel
Aufgabenfokus Analyse: *writer's view, communicative strategies, language*
Zieltextformate Textproduktion: *comment, interview*

**Aufgabe 7:** *Oil on Water* by Helon Habila .......................................... 66
Themen: Postkolonialismus, Globalisierung, Nigeria
Textsorte: Romanauszug
Aufgabenfokus Analyse: *portrayal (of villagers/oil company), narrative technique, language*
Zieltextformate Textproduktion: *comment, article (school paper)*

### Übungsaufgaben: Sprachmittlung

**Aufgabe 1:** „Leitwölfe und Powerfrauen" / „Selbstinszenierung in den
neuen Medien" ...................................................................... 77
Themen: Frauenbilder in den Medien, Bezug zu Nigeria
Textsorte: Auszug Website, diskontinuierliche Texte; Zieltextformat: *email*

**Aufgabe 2:** „Pellkartoffeln mit Quark sind gutes Essen" ........................... 83
Themen: Visionen der Zukunft, Nahrungsmittelpreise, sozialer Zusammenhalt
Textsorte: Zeitungsartikel; Zieltextformat: *email to a friend*

**Aufgabe 3:** „Auch Einwanderungsländer bieten eine Heimat" .................... 87
Themen: Postkolonialismus, Heimatbegriff
Textsorte: Interview; Zieltextformat: *article*

## Übungsaufgabe: Mündliche Abiturprüfung

**Aufgabe 1:** "Shakespeare is too obscure for the stage, methinks" ................ 92
Themen (Prüfungsteil 1): Shakespeares Einfluss auf junge Menschen, Medien;
Textsorte: Zeitungsartikel
Themen (Prüfungsteil 2): Shakespeare, Visionen der Zukunft, Dystopie,
Globalisierung, Studieren und Arbeiten in einer globalisierten Welt

## Zentrale Abitur-Prüfungsaufgaben

### Abiturprüfung 2020 – Aufgabe 1
*(Inhalte: Amerikanischer Traum, Globalisierung, Zukunftsperspektiven junger Erwachsener)*
**Textaufgabe:** *4 3 2 1* by Paul Auster ............................................. 2020-1
Textsorte: Romanauszug
Aufgabenfokus Analyse: *point of view, language*
Zieltextformate Textproduktion: *comment, interview*

**Mediation:** „Wie sinnvoll wäre ein Pflichtdienst für junge Leute?" ......... 2020-3
Textsorte: Zeitungsartikel; Zieltextformat: *email*

### Abiturprüfung 2020 – Aufgabe 2
*(Inhalte: multikulturelle Gesellschaft, Großbritannien, Medien, Globalisierung)*
**Textaufgabe:** "Diversity in publishing is under attack" ..................... 2020-13
Textsorte: Zeitungsartikel
Aufgabenfokus Analyse: *communicative strategies, language*
Zieltextformate Textproduktion: *comment, debate statement*

**Mediation:** „Literatur als Brückenbauer in Frankfurt" ........................ 2020-15
Textsorte: Zeitungsartikel; Zieltextformat: *email*

### Abiturprüfung 2021 – Aufgabe 1
*(Inhalte: Postkolonialismus, Afrika, Nigeria; Bedeutung von Lyrik)*
**Textaufgabe:** "AFRICA" by Osayande Igbinedion .......................... 2021-1
Textsorte: Gedicht
Aufgabenfokus Analyse: *structure, language, poetic devices*
Zieltextformate Textproduktion: *comment, online article*

**Mediation:** „Wie der junge Goethe: Warum gerade ausgerechnet auf Instagram Gedichte ganz groß sind" ................................................. 2021-3
Textsorte: Zeitungsartikel; Zieltextformat: *email*

### Abiturprüfung 2021 – Aufgabe 2
*(Inhalte: multikulturelle Gesellschaft, koloniale Vergangenheit, Großbritannien, Amerikanischer Traum, Meinungsfreiheit)*
**Textaufgabe:** "The toppling of Edward Colston's statue is not an attack on history. It is history." ............................................................... 2021-13
Textsorte: Zeitungsartikel

Aufgabenfokus Analyse: *communicative strategies, language*
Zieltextformate Textproduktion: *comment, formal letter*
**Mediation:** „Die kolonialen Denkmäler und Straßennamen müssen weg" .................................................................. 2021-15
Textsorte: Interview; Zieltextformat: *online article*

**Abiturprüfung 2022 – Aufgabe 1**
*(Inhalte: Großbritannien, multikulturelle Gesellschaft, Rassismus)*
**Textaufgabe:** *Girl, Woman, Other* by Bernardine Evaristo ................. 2022-1
Textsorte: Romanauszug
Aufgabenfokus Analyse: *narrative perspective, use of language*
Zieltextformate Textproduktion: *comment, interior monologue*

**Mediation:** „Warum wir zu unserem Neo-Spießertum stehen sollten" ...... 2022-4
Textsorte: Zeitungsartikel; Zieltextformat: *email*

**Abiturprüfung 2022 – Aufgabe 2**
*(Inhalte: Rolle der Medien, Meinungsfreiheit, ethische Fragestellungen zu neuen Technologien, Globalisierung)*
**Textaufgabe:** "Teen Fiction and the Perils of Cancel Culture" .............. 2022-14
Textsorte: Zeitungsartikel
Aufgabenfokus Analyse: *line of argument, language*
Zieltextformate Textproduktion: *comment, online article*

**Mediation:** „Studie: Jugendlichen fehlt bei Nachrichten Alltagsbezug" ..... 2022-17
Textsorte: Artikel; Zieltextformat: *speech script*

---

**Abiturprüfung 2023** ................................... www.stark-verlag.de/mystark
Sobald die Original-Prüfungsaufgaben 2023 freigegeben sind, können sie als PDF auf der Plattform MyStark heruntergeladen werden (Zugangscode vgl. Umschlaginnenseite).

---

**Autorin**

**Birgit Holtwick** (Hinweise und Tipps, Übungsaufgaben, Lösungen zu den zentral gestellten Prüfungsaufgaben)

# Vorwort

**Liebe Schülerinnen, liebe Schüler,**

mithilfe der folgenden Informationen, Aufgaben und Lösungen haben Sie verschiedene Möglichkeiten, sich auf das Abitur im Fach Englisch vorzubereiten:

- Der erste Teil des Buches enthält viele **Hinweise und Tipps** zur schriftlichen und mündlichen Prüfung. Ich empfehle Ihnen, diese Seiten als Erstes zu lesen. Am Ende des Kapitels finden Sie zudem auch weitere Hinweise, wie Sie sinnvoll und gewinnbringend mit diesem Band arbeiten können.
- Im zweiten Teil finden Sie **Übungsaufgaben** im Stil der **schriftlichen Abiturprüfung**, genau abgestimmt auf die **aktuellen Vorgaben**. Im vorderen Teil können Sie den Bereich „Leseverstehen und Schreiben" intensiv üben, danach folgen noch einige Aufgaben zur „Sprachmittlung". Die dazugehörigen **Lösungsvorschläge** sind in drei Stufen aufgebaut. Zunächst erhalten Sie einige Denkanregungen und allgemeine Informationen zur jeweiligen Teilaufgabe. Danach finden Sie Stichworte, die wesentliche Lösungsaspekte benennen. Erst in einem dritten Schritt folgt die ausformulierte Musterlösung. So können Sie selbst entscheiden, wie viel Hilfe Sie bei der Bearbeitung der Aufgaben brauchen. Ganz am Ende des Übungsteils ist ein Beispiel für eine **mündliche Prüfung** enthalten.
- Im Anschluss folgt eine Auswahl von **Original-Prüfungsaufgaben** der letzten Jahre, ebenfalls mit ausführlichen Lösungsvorschlägen.
- Lernen Sie gerne am PC, Tablet oder Smartphone? Auf den nächsten Seiten finden Sie Hinweise zu den digitalen Zusätzen zu diesem Band.

Verwenden Sie das Buch ganz nach Ihren individuellen Bedürfnissen. Eine Hilfe dabei ist das ausführliche Inhaltsverzeichnis, aus dem Sie z. B. neben den Themen auch die Schwerpunkte der Analyseaufgabe oder die geforderten Zieltextformate ablesen können. So finden Sie leicht die Aufgabentypen, die Sie noch üben möchten.

Sollten nach Erscheinen dieses Bandes noch wichtige Änderungen im Zentralabitur vom Ministerium für Schule und Bildung in Nordrhein-Westfalen bekannt gegeben werden, finden Sie Informationen dazu auf der Plattform **MyStark**.

Schon jetzt wünsche ich Ihnen viel Erfolg bei Ihren zentralen Abiturprüfungen!

Birgit Holtwick

# Hinweise zu den digitalen Zusätzen

Auf alle digitalen Zusätze können Sie online über die Plattform **MyStark** zugreifen. Ihren persönlichen Zugangscode finden Sie auf der Umschlaginnenseite (vorne im Buch).

## PDF der Original-Prüfungsaufgaben 2023

Um Ihnen die Prüfung 2023 schnellstmöglich zur Verfügung stellen zu können, bringen wir sie in digitaler Form heraus. Sobald die Original-Prüfungsaufgaben 2023 freigegeben sind, können Sie sie über die Plattform MyStark abrufen.

## Lernvideos zur Textaufgabe

Textaufgaben sind Teil vieler Prüfungen und Klausuren – und machen oft einen Großteil der Prüfungsleistung aus. Mithilfe der **Lernvideos zum richtigen Umgang mit Textaufgaben** können Sie sich optimal auf die Anforderungen in diesem Bereich vorbereiten. Am Beispiel von zwei Texten mit je drei Aufgabenstellungen wird gezeigt, wie man an eine Textaufgabe herangeht und sie erfolgreich löst.

**Die Lernvideos beinhalten:**
- **Schritt-für-Schritt-Anleitungen** zum richtigen Vorgehen in der Prüfung
- **Sachtext** und **literarischer Text** als Grundlage
- nützliche Hinweise zu **häufigen Operatoren** und **Zieltextsorten**

## Video zur mündlichen Abiturprüfung

Teil Ihres Abiturs ist auch eine mündliche Prüfung. Für viele Schülerinnen und Schüler sind solche Prüfungen mit Unsicherheit und Nervosität verbunden. Aber keine Panik, denn auch hier gibt Ihnen eine gute Vorbereitung die nötige Sicherheit. Über diesen QR-Code bzw. in der Plattform MyStark können Sie sich ein Video mit vielen praktischen Tipps zum mündlichen Abitur ansehen – egal, in welchem Fach Sie ins mündliche Abitur gehen.

## Interaktives Training

Im **Online-Training** „**Basic Language Skills**" erhalten Sie Zugriff auf zahlreiche **interaktive Aufgaben** zu Grundlagen wie **Hörverstehen, Leseverstehen** und **Sprachverwendung im Kontext**. Dies sind ganz wichtige „Basics", die Sie für eine gute Sprachbeherrschung brauchen.

**Das interaktive Training bietet Ihnen:**

- „**Listening**" – authentische Hörtexte mit vielfältigen Aufgaben, die Ihr Hörverstehen testen
- „**Reading**" – abwechslungsreiche Lesetexte und dazugehörige Aufgaben
- „**English in Use**" mit gemischten Aufgaben rund um den Gebrauch der englischen Sprache
- Alle Aufgaben sind interaktiv, d. h., Sie können sie direkt am PC oder Tablet bearbeiten und erhalten sofort eine Rückmeldung zu Ihren Antworten.

## Web-App „MindCards"

Mit der Web-App „**MindCards**" können Sie am Smartphone Vokabeln lernen. Auf diesen interaktiven Lernkarten finden Sie hilfreiche Wendungen, die Sie beim Schreiben von Texten oder im mündlichen Sprachgebrauch einsetzen können.

Scannen Sie einfach die QR-Codes oder verwenden Sie folgende Links, um zu den „MindCards" zu gelangen:
https://www.stark-verlag.de/mindcards/writing-2
https://www.stark-verlag.de/mindcards/speaking-2

Writing          Speaking

# Hinweise und Tipps zum Zentralabitur 2024

## Schriftliche Abiturprüfung

### Die zentrale Abiturprüfung in NRW

In NRW findet die Abiturprüfung in allen schriftlichen Fächern in Form des Zentralabiturs statt. Das bedeutet, dass die Aufgaben für alle Fächer einheitlich vom Ministerium für Schule und Bildung (MSB) gestellt und jeweils am selben Tag und zur selben Zeit von den Prüflingen bearbeitet werden.

Die Abiturprüfung besteht aus zwei Teilen:
- Teil A: Leseverstehen und Schreiben (integriert)
- Teil B: Sprachmittlung (isoliert)

Im Klausurteil A werden Ihnen zwei Prüfungsvorschläge zur Auswahl vorgelegt. Sie entscheiden, ob Sie den literarischen Ausgangstext oder den Sachtext bearbeiten möchten. Schauen Sie sich dazu alle Aufgaben genau an und überlegen Sie in Ruhe, welche Kombination aus Text und Aufgaben Ihnen am besten zu bewältigen scheint. Im Klausurteil B wird Ihnen immer ein deutschsprachiger Sachtext als Grundlage für die Mediationsaufgabe vorgelegt. Sie haben hier also keine Auswahlmöglichkeit. Zwischen Teil A und B gibt es nicht unbedingt eine thematische Verknüpfung, sodass beide Teile wirklich ganz unabhängig voneinander bearbeitet werden können.

Die Abiturvorbereitung im Englischunterricht stützt sich auf den Kernlehrplan, in dem insbesondere die Ziele des Englischunterrichts festgelegt sind. Diese sind untergliedert in die Kompetenzbereiche:
- funktionale kommunikative Kompetenz (z. B. Leseverstehen, Schreiben, Sprachmittlung)
- interkulturelle kommunikative Kompetenz
- Text- und Medienkompetenz
- Sprachlernkompetenz
- Sprachbewusstheit

Innerhalb des Kompetenzbereiches „interkulturelle kommunikative Kompetenz" werden auch die Themenfelder, mit denen Sie sich in der Qualifikationsphase auseinandersetzen müssen, definiert. Zusätzlich werden die Themenfelder für jeden Abiturjahrgang weiter konkretisiert, sodass sich für die Abiturprüfung 2024 folgende Themen ergeben:

**Alltagswirklichkeiten und Zukunftsperspektiven junger Erwachsener:**
Ein Themenfeld im Lehrplan umfasst verschiedene Lebensentwürfe, das Studium, die Ausbildung und den Beruf – insbesondere auf internationaler Ebene – sowie Englisch in seiner Funktion als *lingua franca*. Für das Abitur wird hier ein Fokus auf die Bereiche **Studieren und Arbeiten in der globalisierten Welt** gesetzt.

**Politische, soziale und kulturelle Wirklichkeiten und ihre historischen Hintergründe:**
- **Das Vereinigte Königreich im 21. Jahrhundert – Selbstverständnis zwischen Tradition und Wandel**
  Bei Großbritannien liegt der thematische Schwerpunkt auf den **Traditionen und Veränderungen in Politik und Gesellschaft**. Dies bezieht sich insbesondere auf die **Stellung des Vereinigten Königreichs innerhalb Europas**. Auch Texte zur **multikulturellen Gesellschaft** können Bestandteil der Prüfung sein.
- **Amerikanischer Traum – Visionen und Lebenswirklichkeiten in den USA**
  Hier liegt der Fokus auf den Themen **Freiheit und Gleichheit** und darauf, inwiefern es sich hierbei um **Mythen** handelt, d. h., inwieweit die Ideale in den USA in der **Realität** umgesetzt sind.
- **Postkolonialismus – Lebenswirklichkeiten in einem weiteren anglophonen Kulturraum**
  Als Bezugsland wurde **Nigeria** ausgewählt, wobei dieses stellvertretend für den afrikanischen Kontinent gesehen werden soll.
- **Literatur und Medien in ihrer Bedeutung für den Einzelnen und die Gesellschaft**
  Im Bereich von Literatur und Medien steht **Shakespeare** im Vordergrund. Es geht insbesondere um seinen **Einfluss auf und seine Bedeutung für die heutige Jugend**. Für die Aufgaben werden Kenntnisse von **filmischen Umsetzungen** seiner Werke und von **Textauszügen** aus mindestens einer seiner Tragödien oder Komödien vorausgesetzt.
  Daneben können auch **Utopien und Dystopien**, also literarische **Visionen der Zukunft**, Thema der Abiturtexte sein. Dabei spielen insbesondere **ethische Implikationen** von Entwicklungen in **Wissenschaft und Technik** eine Rolle.

**Globale Herausforderung und Zukunftsvisionen:**
Hier stehen vor allem **ökonomische, ökologische und politische Herausforderungen** im Fokus des Interesses. Der **technische und wissenschaftliche Fortschritt** in der modernen Gesellschaft wird unter ethischen Aspekten beleuchtet. Chancen und Risiken der **Globalisierung** werden betrachtet.

Die Abgrenzung der Themen untereinander ist nicht eindeutig, sodass einzelne Schwerpunkte auch anderen Themenfeldern zugeordnet werden können. So kann der Fokus Nigeria beispielsweise neben „Postkolonialismus" auch dem Punkt „globale Herausforderungen" zugeordnet werden (z. B. ökonomische und ökologische Folgen der Erdölproduktion).

## Wie ist eine Abiturprüfungsaufgabe aufgebaut?

Die Abiturprüfung besteht aus zwei Teilen. In **Teil A** wird eine Textaufgabe behandelt, die immer aus den drei Teilaufgaben *comprehension, analysis* und wahlweise *comment* oder *re-creation of text* besteht. Ausgangstext ist ein englischsprachiger literarischer Text oder ein englischsprachiger Sach- und Gebrauchstext. Die Texte umfassen im Leistungskurs maximal 1 000 Wörter. Sie können außerdem durch Bilder (z. B. Cartoons) und diskontinuierliche Texte (z. B. Tabellen, Grafiken) ergänzt werden. In diesem Fall werden die Ausgangstexte angemessen gekürzt.

Sie können am Prüfungstag selbst entscheiden, ob Sie einen fiktionalen oder einen nicht-fiktionalen Ausgangstext wählen. Ebenso haben Sie im Anforderungsbereich III immer die Wahl zwischen einer evaluierenden und einer produktionsorientierten Teilaufgabe *(comment* bzw. *re-creation of text)*. Legen Sie sich aber besser nicht im Vorfeld auf eine Text- oder Aufgabenform fest, denn vielleicht wird in der Prüfung ein literarischer Text behandelt, der Ihnen bekannt ist, oder gerade die *comment*-Aufgabe erweist sich als besonders komplex. In jedem Fall ist es sinnvoll, wenn Sie flexibel reagieren können.

In Teil B haben Sie keine Wahlmöglichkeit, Sie erhalten einen deutschsprachigen Sach- oder Gebrauchstext, der eine Länge von 450 bis 650 Wörtern hat. Die Aufgabenstellung setzt den Rahmen für die Sprachmittlung und legt fest, welche Informationen Sie für wen in welcher Form wiedergeben sollen.

### Die Textaufgabe

In der Textaufgabe erhalten Sie drei Aufgaben zu einem Ausgangstext. Diese decken drei verschiedene Anforderungsbereiche ab, denen typische Arbeitsaufträge (Operatoren) zugeordnet sind.

Bei den Aufgaben im **Anforderungsbereich I** stellen Sie Ihr Leseverständnis unter Beweis, indem Sie die Inhalte des Ausgangstextes in eigenen Worten darstellen. Oftmals müssen auch nur Teilaspekte des Ausgangstextes wiedergegeben werden. Folgende Operatoren werden in der Aufgabenstellung typischerweise verwendet:

| Operator | Bedeutung | Beispiel |
| --- | --- | --- |
| *Describe* | eine genaue Beschreibung einer Person, einer Sache, einer Situation erstellen | "Describe the measures taken by the oil company to obtain the villagers' land." (S. 66) |
| *Outline* | Hauptmerkmale, wesentliche Elemente oder die Struktur einer Sache/eines Sachverhalts wiedergeben | "Outline the author's view on social media." (Video 1/Sachtext) |
| *Point out* | die in der Aufgabenstellung genannten Aspekte finden und erklären | "Point out what Amy and Archie are each occupied with." (S. 2020-1) |

| | | |
|---|---|---|
| *State* | die wesentlichen Aspekte eines Sachverhalts/eines Gesprächs o. Ä. kurz und präzise darstellen | "State why the author claims that Shakespeare does not belong in the classroom." (S. 12) |
| *Summarise/ Sum up* | eine knappe Darstellung der wesentlichen Aspekte oder Ideen eines Textes oder Themas anfertigen | "Summarise what happened in Vanuatu and why. […]" (S. 1) |

Die Aufgaben im **Anforderungsbereich II** zielen auf eine Analyse des Ausgangstextes unter vorgegebenen Gesichtspunkten ab. Hier geht es beispielsweise darum, **wie** eine Textaussage vermittelt, eine Aussageabsicht erreicht oder eine bestimmte Wirkung erzielt wird. Sie müssen für die Bewältigung der Aufgabenstellung selbstständig relevante Textstellen auswählen und vertiefend untersuchen. Häufig geht es dabei neben inhaltlichen vor allem um sprachliche Aspekte. Auch ein Vergleich verschiedener Aspekte des Textes ist denkbar. Operatoren in diesem Anforderungsbereich sind:

| **Operator** | **Bedeutung** | **Beispiel** |
|---|---|---|
| *Analyse/ Examine* | eine detaillierte Analyse des Textes erstellen | "Analyse the way the author presents his views. Consider communicative strategies and use of language." (S. 2020-13) |
| *Characterise (Give/Write a characterisation)* | eine Figur oder einen Sachverhalt detailliert charakterisieren | "Characterise the police officer as he is presented in this abstract." (Video 2/literarischer Text) |
| *Compare* | zwei Figuren oder Sachverhalte vergleichen und dabei Gemeinsamkeiten und Unterschiede aufzeigen | "Compare how the villagers as well as their situation and the oil company are portrayed. Focus on narrative techniques and the use of language." (S. 66) |
| *Explain* | einen Sachverhalt/eine Verhaltensweise verdeutlichen, indem Gründe, Details und einzelne Aspekte herausgearbeitet werden | Mögliche Aufgabenstellung: "Explain why the measure failed." |
| *Illustrate* | einen Sachverhalt anhand von Beispielen aus dem Text verdeutlichen | "Illustrate how this excerpt serves to criticise the fictional society depicted." (S. 44) |
| *Interpret* | die Bedeutung, die Funktion oder die Botschaft eines Textes/ Materials herausarbeiten | Mögliche Aufgabenstellung: "Interpret the cartoon." |

Im **Anforderungsbereich III** gibt es zwei Teilaufgaben, von denen Sie **eine** wählen müssen. Jeweils eine von beiden hat einen engen Bezug zum Ausgangstext, die andere nur einen Bezug zum Thema, aber nicht zum Text. Beide Aufgabenstellungen können durch zusätzliches Material (z. B. Cartoon, Werbeanzeige, Statistik, Zitat) ergänzt werden.

Eine dieser Teilaufgaben umfasst den Bereich der Evaluation und Bewertung. Hier sind Sie aufgefordert, unter Abwägung verschiedener Argumente zu einer **begründeten** Meinungsäußerung zu kommen. Typische Operatoren sind hier:

| Operator | Bedeutung | Beispiel |
|---|---|---|
| *Assess/ Evaluate* | eine fundiert begründete Meinung zu einem Sachverhalt zum Ausdruck bringen | "Judging from the excerpt, assess whether *The Hunted* might be called a dystopian novel." (S. 44) |
| *Comment (on)* | die eigene Meinung deutlich zum Ausdruck bringen und mit Begründungen und Belegen untermauern | "Comment on the present situation of girls and women in Nigeria." (S. 55) |
| *Discuss* | Argumente für und wider einen Sachverhalt darstellen und auf dieser Grundlage zu einer begründeten Meinungsäußerung kommen. | Mögliche Aufgabenstellung: "Discuss the impact oil reserves have on Nigeria." |

Die andere Teilaufgabe fordert jeweils eine **kreative** Leistung, in der Sie die Merkmale des vorgegebenen Zieltextes beachten müssen. Es kann auch sein, dass hier zusätzliches Material (z. B. ein Bild oder ein Zitat) vorgelegt wird, das den Schreibimpuls erweitert (vgl. Übungsaufgabe 3). Der Operator ist in der Regel *write* und wird durch die geforderte Textsorte ergänzt. Folgende **Zieltextformate** werden als bekannt vorausgesetzt:
– *letter/email: formal or personal letter/email, letter to the editor*
– *speech script: talk, public/formal speech, debate statement*
– *article: newspaper report, comment, internet article*
– *(written) interview*
– Ausgestaltung, Fortführung oder Ergänzung eines literarischen Ausgangstextes *(Erzähltext, Theaterstück, Drehbuch)*

---

Tipp

Auch wenn sich die Aufgabenstellung im Detail je nach Text unterscheidet, bleibt die grundsätzliche Vorgehensweise bei den jeweiligen Operatoren gleich. In den **Videos** auf der Plattform **MyStark** (Zugangscode vgl. Umschlaginnenseite) erklären wir Ihnen, wie Sie bei den wichtigsten Operatoren im Bereich Schreiben vorgehen müssen. Außerdem erfahren Sie etwas zu häufigen Zieltextformaten wie z. B. Leserbrief oder Blogartikel.

---

V

**Die Sprachmittlungsaufgabe**

Bei der Sprachmittlungsaufgabe geht es vordergründig um die Wiedergabe inhaltlicher Aspekte des deutschsprachigen Ausgangstextes auf Englisch. Bei genauerem Hinsehen ist diese Aufgabe aber noch sehr viel komplexer, denn Sie müssen zunächst die für die Aufgabenstellung relevanten Textinhalte auswählen und diese dann unter Berücksichtigung der vorgegebenen Situation und des angegebenen Adressaten in das geforderte Zieltextformat übertragen. Vor dem Hintergrund der interkulturellen Mitteilungssituation müssen Sie immer auch überlegen, welche Erläuterungen Sie zur Sicherung des Verständnisses ggf. noch ergänzen wollen. Mögliche Operatoren:

| Operator | Bedeutung | Beispiel |
| --- | --- | --- |
| *Explain* | einen Sachverhalt verdeutlichen, indem ggf. kulturspezifische Unterschiede berücksichtigt werden | Mögliche Aufgabenstellung: "Based on the information given in the article write an email in which you explain the project's goals." |
| *Outline/ Present/ Summarise/ Sum up* | eine knappe Darstellung der wesentlichen Aspekte oder Ideen eines Textes oder Themas anfertigen und dabei ggf. kulturspezifische Aspekte erläutern | "Based on the article write them an email in which you outline a current trend in Germany." (S. 2022-4) |
| *Write (+ text type)* | einen Text unter Beachtung der jeweiligen Merkmale produzieren | "Based on the interview […], write the article." (S. 2021-3) |

Folgende **Zieltextformate** werden für die Sprachmittlungsaufgabe als bekannt vorausgesetzt:
– *letter/email*
– *newspaper/internet article*

**Die Bewertung der Abiturprüfungsaufgabe**

Die Textaufgabe macht 70 % der Endnote aus, die Sprachmittlungsaufgabe 30 %. In beiden Aufgaben zählt der Inhalt 40 % und die sprachliche Leistung sowie die Darstellungsleistung zählen insgesamt 60 %. Im Einzelnen werden die Punkte wie folgt aufgegliedert.

**Textaufgabe**

| Inhalt | P |
| --- | --- |
| *Comprehension* (Anforderungsbereich I) | 12 |
| *Analysis* (Anforderungsbereich II) | 16 |
| *Comment/Re-creation of text* (Anforderungsbereich III) | 14 |

| Sprache | |
|---|---|
| Kommunikative Textgestaltung<br>• Relevanz der Aussagen für die Aufgabe<br>• Beachtung der Merkmale der Zieltextsorte<br>• Struktur des Textes<br>• keine Wiederholungen oder umständlichen Formulierungen<br>• relevante Textbelege korrekt zitiert | 21 |
| Ausdrucksvermögen/Verfügbarkeit sprachlicher Mittel<br>• Verwendung eigener Formulierungen<br>• differenzierter und stilistisch angemessener Wortschatz<br>• variabler Satzbau | 21 |
| Sprachrichtigkeit<br>• korrekte Verwendung des Wortschatzes, der Grammatik und der Orthografie | 21 |
| **Summe** | 105 |

## Sprachmittlungsaufgabe

| Inhalt | P |
|---|---|
| Zusammenfassung der wesentlichen Inhalte im Sinne der Aufgabenstellung und ggf. Erläuterung kulturspezifischer Aspekte | 18 |
| **Sprache** | |
| Kommunikative Textgestaltung<br>• Ausrichtung des Textes auf die Mittlungsabsicht und den Adressaten<br>• Berücksichtigung der vorgegebenen Situation<br>• Beachtung der Merkmale der Zieltextsorte<br>• Struktur des Textes<br>• keine Wiederholungen oder umständlichen Formulierungen | 9 |
| Ausdrucksvermögen/Verfügbarkeit sprachlicher Mittel<br>• Verwendung eigener Formulierungen<br>• differenzierter und stilistisch angemessener Wortschatz<br>• variabler Satzbau | 9 |
| Sprachrichtigkeit<br>• korrekte Verwendung des Wortschatzes, der Grammatik und der Orthografie | 9 |
| **Summe** | 45 |

## Die Bearbeitung der verschiedenen Teilaufgaben

### *Comprehension* (Anforderungsbereich I)

Gehen Sie die Aufgabenstellung genau durch und prüfen Sie, auf welche inhaltlichen Aspekte des Textes diese sich bezieht. In der Regel wird hier nämlich keine vollständige Zusammenfassung, sondern eine Fokussierung auf einzelne Elemente erwartet. Lesen Sie dann den Text gründlich und klären Sie ggf. lexikalische Verständnisprobleme mithilfe Ihres Wörterbuches. Schlagen Sie nur die Wörter nach, die für die

Aufgabenstellung oder für ein allgemeines Textverständnis relevant sind, und ignorieren Sie andere Ihnen unbekannte Wörter, um Ihre Zeit effizient zu nutzen. Nehmen Sie anschließend einen Textmarker zur Hand und markieren Sie relevante Textstellen. In der Lösung können Sie manchmal der Chronologie des Textes folgen, es kann für eine logische Darstellung aber auch sinnvoll sein, die Informationen für die Lösung umzustellen. Nummerieren Sie in diesem Fall die einzelnen Textstellen in der Reihenfolge, in der Sie sie anführen wollen. Erstellen Sie sich hierzu ggf. auch ein Konzeptpapier. Abschließend sollten Sie nochmals kontrollieren, ob sich wirklich alle Aspekte, die Sie markiert haben, auf die Aufgabenstellung beziehen.

Leiten Sie Ihren Text **in der Hinführung** mit den Quellenangaben zum Text ein. Diese umfassen Titel, Autor*in, Ort und Jahr der Publikation, sofern diese angegeben sind. Fassen Sie außerdem ganz knapp zusammen, worum es in dem Text – mit Blick auf die Aufgabenstellung – geht.

| | | | |
|---|---|---|---|
| The text<br>The excerpt (from the novel/drama)<br>The novel<br>The short story<br>The drama<br>The poem/The song<br>The (newspaper) article | *(title)* | written by (author's name)<br>and published in (2022)/on (26 May 2022)<br>in (The New York Times/London) | deals with ...<br>is about ...<br>discusses the question if ...<br>provides information on ...<br>presents ... |
| The speech<br>The excerpt from the speech | *(title)* | delivered/given by (speaker's name) on (14 April 2020) in (New York) addresses the public/the members of the UN/the conference/...). | It explores the question whether ...<br>It deals with ...<br>The speaker discusses the question if ... |
| The cartoon | called *(title)* | created by (name of artist) and published in (2021)/on (26 July 2021)<br>in (The New York Times/London)/on the website (www.website.com) | deals with the problem of ...<br>is about ...<br>depicts an attitude towards ...<br>presents a possible view on ... |

Beachten Sie im **Hauptteil**, dass Sie bei der Wiedergabe des Inhalts sprachlich nicht zu nah am Ausgangstext bleiben, sondern soweit möglich eigene Formulierungen verwenden. Zitate und Textverweise sind in diesem Aufgabenteil in aller Regel nicht erwünscht. Versuchen Sie, die Inhalte möglichst prägnant wiederzugeben und vermeiden Sie dabei in jedem Fall wertende Äußerungen. Verwenden Sie das *present tense* und verzichten Sie auf *short forms* (also z. B. „do not" anstatt „don't"). Verwenden Sie verschiedene Einleitungsverben, um die Aussagen des Autors/der Autorin wiederzugeben (z. B. „The author observes that ...").

| to add      | to affirm   | to announce |
| to claim    | to declare  | to demand   |
| to insist   | to maintain | to mention  |
| to observe  | to remark   | to state    |

**Analysis (Anforderungsbereich II)**

Im **ersten Schritt** sollten Sie auch hier die Aufgabenstellung genau prüfen. Der inhaltliche Fokus kann ein anderer sein als in Aufgabe 1. Sie sind auf jeden Fall gefordert, zu untersuchen und darzustellen, wie der vorgegebene inhaltliche Fokus sprachlich und/oder strukturell umgesetzt wird und, besonders wichtig, welche Wirkung bei den Leserinnen und Lesern dadurch erzielt wird.

Je nachdem, welche Textsorte Ihnen vorgelegt wird, können ganz unterschiedliche sprachliche und stilistische Aspekte in den Fokus gerückt werden. Hierzu gehören:

Bei literarischen Texten:
– *atmosphere*
– *characterisation and constellation of characters*
– *dialogue and director's instructions (screenplay only)*
– *dialogue and stage directions (drama only)*
– *lyric speaker and his/her situation (poem and song only)*
– *narrative techniques: narrative perspective and point of view (narrative texts only)*
– *rhetorical/stylistic devices*
– *rhyme, rhythm and metre (poem and song only)*
– *setting (place and time)*
– *structure and plot*
– *themes and conflicts (inner conflicts and conflicts between characters)*
– *interaction between characters*
– *tone*
– *use/means of language, choice of words*

Bei Sach- und Gebrauchstexten:
– *communicative strategies*
– *message (of the text)/intention (of the author)*
– *rhetorical/poetic/stylistic devices*
– *structure*
– *style, register, tone*
– *techniques of argumentation and persuasion/line of argument*
– *use/means of language*

Lesen Sie im nächsten Schritt den Ausgangstext erneut, und zwar nun mit Blick auf die aktuelle Aufgabenstellung. Markieren Sie wiederum relevante Textstellen und notieren Sie Gedanken am Rand. Bringen Sie dann Ihre Ideen auf einem Konzeptpapier in eine Struktur, indem Sie notieren, welche Textstellen eine gleiche bzw. ähnliche Wirkung erzeugen und daher in einem Absatz zusammengefasst werden können. Sehen Sie sich als Beispiel folgende Aufgabenstellung an (vgl. Übungsaufgabe 1):

Analyse how the author tries to convince the readers that they need to *"live within [their] overall environmental thresholds"* (*ll. 56/57*). In doing so, focus on structure, argumentative techniques and the language used.

Verfassen Sie nun in der **Einleitung** eine Arbeitsthese, die einen deutlichen Bezug zur Aufgabenstellung aufweist. Verzichten Sie darauf, die Quellenangaben zum Text zu wiederholen, da sich die Analyse quasi nahtlos an Aufgabe 1 anschließt:

*The author's intention in writing this article is to convince the readers that they need to "live within [their] overall environmental thresholds" (ll. 56/57). He tries to achieve his aim by using a structure that leads to the conclusion quoted above, by employing different argumentative techniques and by making use of words that underline both the difference between Vanuatu and developed nations and the author's interpretation that Vanuatu is suffering instead of these developed countries.*

Im **Hauptteil** belegen Sie Ihre Arbeitsthese dann im Detail, indem Sie die aufgeführten Aspekte jeweils in einem oder mehreren Absätzen vertieft behandeln und Ihre Aussagen am Text belegen.
In dem o. g. Beispiel müssten Sie also zunächst den Aufbau des Textes untersuchen und dann sowohl auf die Argumentation als auch auf die Wortwahl eingehen. Zeigen Sie in jedem Absatz auf, welche Wirkung die verschiedenen Aspekte haben.
Idealerweise beginnen Sie jeden Absatz mit einem sogenannten *topic sentence*, der die These für diesen Absatz enthält. Belegen Sie dann in den folgenden *supporting sentences* diese These und beenden Sie den Absatz, indem Sie die **Wirkung** der gewählten Textstellen erläutern:

*The language employed stresses the view that developed nations are to blame for Vanuatu's misfortune. The differences in lifestyles and their consequences are emphasised.* **(topic sentence)** *Vanuatu's inhabitants are "ecologically successful" (ll. 8/9) and therefore "distinguished" (ll. 7/8). They lead "an exemplary, healthy life" (l. 14/15). All these words have a positive connotation and therefore underline that Vanuatu's people are "innocent" (l. 15). They are contrasted with developed nations, which are accused of causing "a giant climatic steamroller, fuelled by [...] energy-intensive lifestyles" (l. 12).* **(supporting sentences)** *Thus, developed nations are depicted as villains.* **(Wirkung)**

Am **Ende** fassen Sie Ihre Ergebnisse nochmals knapp zusammen und beziehen sich auch hier wieder auf die Arbeitsthese, die Sie eingangs formuliert haben:

*All in all, the journalist makes it clear that people in developed nations need to change their lifestyles if they do not want to live at the expense of somebody else's well-being. He achieves this by using language in a way that clearly contrasts the victim and the perpetrator, by using structure purposefully to make it lead to his final conclusion and by basing his arguments on examples, facts and experts' reports.*

Ihr Text folgt also **drei Schritten**:
1. Stellen Sie eine deutlich auf die Aufgabenstellung bezogene These auf. **(Einleitung)**
2. Zeigen Sie, dass Ihre These begründet ist. **(Hauptteil)**
3. Kommen Sie erneut auf die Eingangsthese zurück, die Sie nun anhand des Hauptteils belegt haben. **(Schluss)**

Eine Herausforderung liegt dabei darin, sich sprachlich nicht zu wiederholen, sondern jeweils andere Formulierungen zu verwenden.

Wie in Aufgabe 1 verwenden Sie auch hier das *present tense* und vermeiden *short forms*. Verzichten Sie auf wertende Äußerungen oder den Gebrauch von informellen Wendungen. Verwenden Sie verschiedene Ausdrücke, um die Intention des Autors zu benennen und die Wirkung zu beschreiben:

## Intention

| | **The author / speaker / writer / journalist / poet / playwright ...** | | |
|---|---|---|---|
| *intends to*<br>*means to*<br>*has the intention to*<br>*aims to*<br>*aspires to*<br>*wants to*<br>*tries to* | *convince*<br>*persuade* | | *that ...*<br>*of his view that ...* |
| | *make* | *the audience /*<br>*readers /*<br>*listeners* | *believe that ...*<br>*feel responsible for ...* |
| | *encourage* | | *to stand up*<br>*against / for ...* |
| | *appeal to* | | *to take action*<br>*against / for ...* |
| | *appeal to the readers' fears / sympathy / emotions.* | | |
| *wants* | *the audience / the*<br>*readers / the listeners* | *to adopt his view(s) on ...*<br>*to understand that ...*<br>*to see that ...* | |

## Wirkung

| | | |
|---|---|---|
| *This particular*<br>*choice of words ...*<br>*This metaphor / anaphora employed ...*<br>*The point of view*<br>*adopted ...* | *emphasises*<br>*underlines*<br>*stresses*<br>*highlights*<br>*puts emphasis on*<br>*accentuates* | *his/her view on/that ...*<br>*his/her opinion about ...*<br>*the difference between ... and ...*<br>*the importance of ...*<br>*the impression that ...*<br>*the fact that ...* |
| | *attracts the readers' attention.* | |
| | *creates*<br>*evokes*<br>*establishes* | *a feeling of (unease / unity).*<br>*a (tense / light) atmosphere.* |
| | *invites the readers* | *to sympathise with ...*<br>*to identify with ...*<br>*to see the action from X's point of view.* |

## Zitieren – aber richtig

In Aufgabe II müssen Sie Ihre Aussagen stets am Text belegen. Hierbei gilt es, die Konventionen des Zitierens zu beachten:
Sie können **indirekt zitieren**, d. h., Sie geben den Inhalt in eigenen Worten wieder und geben dann die Textstelle, auf die Sie sich beziehen, in Klammern an, z. B. (cf. l. 26) oder (cf. ll. 28–30), wenn Sie sich auf mehrere Zeilen beziehen. Die Abkürzung *cf.* steht für *confer* und bedeutet so viel wie „vergleiche". Die Abkürzung *l.* bedeutet *line* (Zeile) und *ll. lines* (Zeilen).

*The author then shows that Vanuatu is not an isolated case but that other countries have been hit by extreme winds, too (cf. ll. 1–6).*

Wenn Sie wörtlich zitieren, wird dieses **direkte Zitat** mit Anführungsstrichen markiert. Beachten Sie, dass im Englischen (anders als im Deutschen) die Anführungsstriche immer oben stehen, also auch am Anfang des Zitats. Beim direkten Zitat gilt es noch zwischen dem eingebundenen und dem eingeleiteten Zitat zu unterscheiden. Insbesondere kürzere Zitate sollten Sie in einen Satz einbauen. Achten Sie dabei darauf, dass Ihre eigenen und die zitierten Worte inhaltlich und grammatikalisch zusammenpassen, also zusammen einen korrekten Satz ergeben.

*He compares Vanuatu to "the individual who leads an exemplary, healthy life only to suffer chronically due to someone else's bad habit – innocent, global victims of passive smoking" (ll. 14–16).*

Alternativ zur Angabe in Klammern können Sie die Angabe der Fundstelle auch in Ihren Fließtext einbauen.

| In lines 10 to 12 it is | said<br>described<br>illustrated<br>shown<br>made clear | that ... | Beachte: kein Komma vor „that" |
|---|---|---|---|
| In line 7 the reader(s) | get(s) to know how/why ...<br>learn(s) that ...<br>is/are informed about ... | | |
| (The character is selfish) | as can be seen in lines 25 to 37 where (the narrator says that ...) | | |

Damit das Zitat richtig in Ihren Satz passt, dürfen Sie dieses auch leicht verändern. Allerdings müssen Sie diese Änderungen genau markieren. Dabei werden Auslassungen, Ergänzungen oder Veränderungen durch eckige Klammern gekennzeichnet:

*He does not consider what implications this operation might have for Tarrin as a human being but only talks about the two of them "being in business together for all [their] lives" (l. 2).*

*Deet and Tarrin lead a very shallow way of life as they move around a lot and live in "bland, anonymous and soulless" (ll. 6/7) motel rooms. From Tarrin's perspective it is an "accommodation equivalent of fast food. [...] It [is] like living in a burger" (ll. 7/8) and worst of all, "Deet [is] a burger too – a burger person" (l. 10).*

Insbesondere längere Zitate werden oft nicht in den Satz eingebaut, sondern eingeleitet. Aus dieser Einleitung müssen der Urheber des Zitats und der Kontext, in dem es verwendet wurde, hervorgehen.

*This contrast is already introduced in the headline, which is an adapted proverb from the Bible: "They that sow wind shall reap whirlwind". The original proverb is applied to people who start trouble that grows larger than planned.*

Gemäß den Bewertungskriterien für die Abiturklausur sollen Sie die verschiedenen genannten Formen des Zitierens verwenden, anstatt sich nur auf eine Zitierweise zu beschränken. Achten Sie außerdem darauf, dass Sie nur exemplarisch zitieren und nicht unbedingt alle Zitate, die Ihre These belegen würden, verwenden.

## Comment (Anforderungsbereich III)

Hier geht es immer darum, dass Sie Ihre Meinung zu einem Sachverhalt zum Ausdruck bringen. Ein besonderes Augenmerk liegt dabei darauf, dass Sie diese stichhaltig begründen. Lediglich der Operator *discuss* fordert dabei explizit ein, dass Sie Pro- und Kontraargumente abwägen, aber auch bei den anderen Operatoren ist es sinnvoll, mögliche Gegenargumente zu benennen und zu entkräften, damit Ihre Darstellungen überzeugend wirken. Selbst wenn Sie in der Aufgabenstellung nicht explizit aufgefordert werden, Hintergrundwissen aus dem Unterricht einzubringen, sind Sie gut beraten, dies dennoch zu tun. Implizit wird immer erwartet, dass Sie auf Ihr sozio-kulturelles Orientierungswissen zurückgreifen, um die Problemstellung zu bearbeiten.

Ähnlich wie in Aufgabe 2 sollten Sie auch hier zuerst ein Konzeptpapier anfertigen, auf dem Sie Ihre Gedanken zunächst sammeln und dann in eine Struktur bringen. Ordnen Sie die Argumente zum Beispiel vom unwichtigsten zum wichtigsten. Stellen Sie zuerst die Argumente dar, die Ihrer Meinung entgegenstehen, und dann die, die Ihre eigene Meinung stützen.

Auch hier besteht Ihr Text aus drei Abschnitten. In der Einleitung benennen Sie das Thema und stellen eine These auf. Versuchen Sie hier, das Interesse des Lesers/der Leserin zu wecken, indem Sie z. B. die Relevanz des Themas hervorheben.

*When discussing climate change, 2 is the magic number. We need to stabilise global temperature within 2 degrees above pre-industrial levels, or else the extra input of greenhouse gases, for example those locked in the arctic ice, will wipe out most of the life on earth. In order to achieve that goal, we need to cut emissions by 80 % by 2050. This goal seems hard to achieve; one might even say it is impossible to achieve. Therefore, the question arises whether it makes any sense at all for individuals to act in a more environmentally friendly way if they are likely to "to suffer chronically due to someone else's bad habit" (l. 15).*

Falls Sie in dieser Aufgabe ein weiteres Material mit einbeziehen müssen, z. B. ein Zitat oder eine Karikatur, dann sollten Sie bereits in der Einleitung kurz auf dieses Material eingehen, indem Sie beispielsweise das Zitat erläutern oder die Kernaussage der Karikatur zusammenfassen. Formulieren Sie auch in diesem Fall eine These, die die Aufgabenstellung aufgreift.

Im Hauptteil stützen Sie dann Ihre These mit Argumenten. Widmen Sie jedem Argument einen eigenen Absatz und gliedern Sie diesen wiederum in einen *topic sentence* und *supporting sentences*. Der *topic sentence* enthält Ihre These oder Behauptung für den Absatz und diese wird in den folgenden Sätzen begründet und mit Beispielen oder Fakten untermauert.

*There are good reasons that support the view that the individual is not powerful enough to stop global warming.* ***(topic sentence)*** *Take Vanuatu as an example: the nation as a whole, and not just the individual inhabitants, led an exemplary life as far as the emission of greenhouse gas is concerned. In spite of that fact, Cyclone Pam destroyed many people's houses. So their excellent behaviour did not save them from suffering the consequences of global warming.* ***(supporting sentences)***

Am Ende wägen Sie die Pro- und Kontraargumente ab und kommen so zu einer begründeten Meinung.

*Altogether, I truly believe that individuals alone are too ineffective to help with climate change. Of course, they can make some effort and set good examples, but if the big spenders do not change their behaviour radically, the 2-degree goal is unattainable. Then it might be wiser to enjoy the remaining years on our planet, without denying ourselves pleasures like weekend trips to Paris or Mallorca, because rough times are certainly ahead.*

**Useful phrases – Anforderungsbereich III**

| Funktion | Sprachliche Wendung |
| --- | --- |
| Aufzählen, hinzufügen, logisch strukturieren | First(ly) ... Second(ly) ... Third(ly) ... Finally/Lastly ... <br> Additionally .../In addition .../Furthermore ... <br> What is more ... |
| Vergleichen, kontrastieren | Both ... and ... <br> Compared to ... <br> On the one hand, ...; on the other hand, ... <br> While the first/former ..., the second/latter ... <br> Whereas ... <br> By contrast, ... |
| Kausalzusammenhänge darstellen | As a consequence, .../Consequently, .../As a result, ... <br> Therefore, .../Thus, ... <br> Since .../As ... |
| Gegenargumente anführen | However, .../On the other hand, ... <br> Still, one must not forget that ... <br> Critics claim that ... |
| Gegenargumente entkräften | Even though ..., it is important to note that ... <br> It may be true that ..., but ... <br> This point of view is not convincing because ... <br> This idea can be countered by the fact that ... |

| Funktion | Sprachliche Wendung |
|---|---|
| Sachverhalte betonen | *As a matter of fact, ...* <br> *At any rate, ...* <br> *Undoubtedly, ...* <br> *It is evident that ... / Evidently, ...* |
| Schlussfolgern | *Taking everything into account / consideration, ... /* <br> *After having balanced the pros and cons, (I come to the conclusion that ...)* <br> *All in all, ... / In conclusion, ... / To sum up, ...* |

### Re-creation of text (Anforderungsbereich III)

Die weitere Teilaufgabe im Anforderungsbereich III ist eine anwendungsorientierte Aufgabe, häufig auch als kreative Aufgabe bezeichnet. Diese Aufgabe kann einen impliziten Rückbezug zum Ausgangstext bedeuten, wenn es z. B. darum geht, aus der Sicht einer Figur des literarischen Textes einen inneren Monolog zu schreiben oder einen Leserbrief als Reaktion auf den zuvor behandelten Zeitungsartikel zu verfassen. Dann können Sie nicht nach Belieben kreativ werden, sondern müssen sich vielmehr genau die Situation im Ausgangstext bewusst machen. Auch der Bezug zu einem weiteren Material (z. B. einem Cartoon oder Poster) ist möglich. Diese Aufgabe kann aber auch ohne Rückbezug zum Ausgangstext gestellt werden, wenn Sie z. B. auf der Grundlage eines Zitats einen Redebeitrag oder einen Artikel verfassen müssen. Dann ist es wichtig, dass Sie Ihr Hintergrundwissen nutzen, um die geforderte Textsorte inhaltlich zu füllen. In der Aufgabenstellung wird stets ein Zieltextformat vorgegeben, dessen Merkmale Sie beachten müssen.

### Formal or personal letter / email

Formale und persönliche Schreiben, egal ob E-Mail oder Brief, unterscheiden sich vor allem im Stil.

|  | **formales Schreiben** | **persönliches Schreiben** |
|---|---|---|
| Adresse | **Brief:** Adresse des Absenders z. B. rechts oben, Adresse des Empfängers links darunter <br> **E-Mail:** Adressen von Absender und Empfänger untereinander, Adressen und Betreff können auch entfallen | kann entfallen |
| Ansprache | *Dear Mr Dean / Mrs / Ms Dean,* (wenn der Name des Adressaten bekannt ist) <br> *Dear Sir or Madam,* (wenn der Name <u>nicht</u> bekannt ist) | *Dear Paul,* <br> *Hi Mary,* |

|  | **formales Schreiben** | **persönliches Schreiben** |
|---|---|---|
| Vokabular/ Satzbau | *formal, polite* | *everyday English* |
|  | *complex* | *informal/colloquial English (e. g. guy, I'm fed up with)* |
|  | *long forms (I am, I will)* | *short forms (I'm, you're, can't)* |
|  |  | *question tags (don't you?)* |
| Grußformel | *Yours sincerely,* (wenn der Name des Adressaten bekannt ist) *Yours faithfully,* (wenn der Name des Adressaten <u>nicht</u> bekannt ist) | *Best wishes, All the best, Love, See you soon,* |
| Unterschrift | *full name* | *first name only* |

**Letter to the editor**
Auch der Leserbrief ist ein formaler Brief, weist aber zusätzlich ein paar Besonderheiten auf.

Datum: rechts oben *(28 April 2023)*
Anrede: *Sir or Madam* (Achtung: ohne *Dear*; der Herausgeber ist in der Regel <u>nicht</u> der Autor des Artikels, sodass Sie den Namen nicht kennen)
Bezug: Im ersten Satz müssen Sie deutlich machen, auf welchen Artikel Sie sich beziehen.
*With reference to your article (title) published on 26 April …*
*I am writing to you with reference to your article (title) published on 26 April.*
Schlussformel: entfällt, stattdessen unterschreiben Sie mit Ihrem vollen Namen und fügen den Wohnort hinzu. (Je nach Aufgabenstellung müssen Sie hier einen fiktiven Namen und Wohnort verwenden.)

Da ein Leserbrief im Grunde auch ein Kommentar ist, verfahren Sie im Hauptteil wie oben beim *comment* beschrieben. Der Leserbrief kann allerdings kürzer ausfallen. Sie brauchen hier nur die Argumente darzustellen, die Ihre Sichtweise unterstützen, achten Sie aber auf den Rückbezug zum Zeitungsartikel.

*After carefully studying the article, I am sorry to say that I do not agree with the author's view that …*
*I read the article with deep interest and therefore would like to take the chance/ opportunity to express my support for the author's view on/that …*
*I definitely agree/disagree with the author's view on/that …*

**Speech script: talk, public/formal speech/debate statement**
All diesen Textsorten ist gemein, dass sie vor einem Publikum, das in der Aufgabenstellung spezifiziert wird, vorgetragen werden. Davon hängt ab, welchen Stil Sie wählen müssen. In aller Regel wird dies aber ein formeller Stil sein. Weiterhin haben alle diese Texte die Absicht, die Zuhörerschaft zu überzeugen. Das heißt, Sie müs-

sen, wie bei einem *comment*, möglichst überzeugende Argumente präsentieren und idealerweise mögliche Gegenargumente antizipieren und entkräften.
Besonderheiten dieser Textsorte sind vor allem die direkte Ansprache der (fiktiven) Zuhörerschaft und ein gewisses Maß an rhetorischen Mitteln. Sie sollten daher bereits bei der Planung Ihrer Rede überlegen, wo sich eventuell eine Metapher, eine Aufzählung, eine Übertreibung o. Ä. anbieten.
In der Einleitung ist es hier besonders wichtig, Aufmerksamkeit zu wecken. Dies kann z. B. passieren, indem Sie nach der Begrüßung eine rhetorische Frage stellen, eine provokante Äußerung machen, eine Anekdote oder einen Witz erzählen oder überraschende Fakten präsentieren.

*Good evening/Good afternoon, ladies and gentlemen, dear fellow speakers ...*
*I feel deeply honoured to have the opportunity to speak to you/to such an impressive audience.*
*It is a great pleasure for me to be here and to talk about such an important issue.*
*As Kennedy said, don't ask what your country can do for you. Ask instead what you can do for your country.*
*Just like Martin Luther King I have a dream. I dream that ...*

Für den Hauptteil gelten die gleichen Anmerkungen wie bei einem *comment*.
Am Ende sollten Sie auch hier Ihre wesentlichen Argumente knapp zusammenfassen und dann z. B. mit einem Appell, einer rhetorischen Frage, einem Zitat, einer Vorhersage oder einem Versprechen enden.

*All my evidence points into one direction: ...*
*Looking at all the facts and figures, I have to draw the conclusion that ...*
*What it all boils down to is the following: ...*
*Let me conclude with the words of ... who said that ...*
*If we don't act now, we'll .../the world will .../future generations will ...*
*I put my trust in you to ...*
*That's why I ask/urge you to ...*

**Newspaper/internet article**
Es gibt natürlich verschiedene Zeitungsartikel, aber in der Regel wird in der Abiturprüfung ein **Zeitungsbericht** *(report)* von Ihnen erwartet. In diesem werden die Sachverhalte möglichst objektiv dargestellt. Ihre eigene Meinung ist in diesem Fall also nicht gefragt, denn hier ist das Ziel nicht, die Leserschaft zu überzeugen, sondern zu informieren. Die wichtigsten Informationen stehen am Anfang, dann folgen weitere Einzelheiten. Weniger Wichtiges steht am Ende, damit die Leser und Leserinnen jederzeit aufhören können zu lesen, wenn sich gut informiert fühlen.
Der Bericht beginnt daher mit einer auffälligen und aussagekräftigen, aber knappen Überschrift und ggf. einem etwas längeren Untertitel. Im ersten Absatz werden dann die wesentlichen Fakten vermittelt. Dabei orientieren Sie sich an den W-Fragen (wer, was, wann, wo, warum). Die folgenden Absätze beinhalten zusätzliche Informationen und ggf. Zitate, Beispiele oder Fakten.

*It is believed that ...*
*The police/public prosecutor confirmed that ...*
*Eye-witnesses report/claim that ...*

*Sources revealed that ...*
*People are concerned/worried about/that ...*

In der Regel werden Sie aufgefordert werden, einen Bericht für ein *quality paper* zu schreiben. Dies bedingt dann *formal English* und komplexere Satzbaumuster. Bei einem Artikel für ein *tabloid* dürfen Sie auch stärker emotionale Sprache und einfachere Sätze verwenden. Auf jeden Fall sollten Sie aber das Abc des Journalismus beachten: *accurate, brief, clear*. Beim **internet article** handelt es sich im Grunde ebenfalls um einen Zeitungsartikel, der aber online veröffentlicht wird.

Bei einem **Zeitungskommentar** können Sie den Schritten, die beim *comment* beschrieben wurden, folgen. Hinzu kommt lediglich noch eine prägnante Überschrift. Vergleichbar mit einem Kommentar ist auch die Textsorte *blog entry*.

**Written interview**

In einem Interview geht es darum, dass der *interviewer* dem *interviewee* möglichst geschickt Fragen stellt, um interessante und relevante Informationen zu erhalten. Im Rahmen der Klausur müssen Sie sich vor allem nochmals mit den Informationen auseinandersetzen, die Sie im Ausgangstext über den *interviewee* erhalten haben, denn sie sind Grundlage für Ihr Interview. Sie dürfen auch weitere Informationen erfinden, diese sollten allerdings realistisch sein und zu dem passen, was Sie bisher über die Person wissen. Evtl. erhalten Sie in der Aufgabenstellung auch Informationen zum *interviewer*, die Sie bei den Fragen, die Sie entwickeln, beachten müssen. Prüfen Sie die Aufgabenstellung auch dahingehend, in welchem Kontext Sie das Interview führen sollen, etwa im Rahmen einer Radioshow. Machen Sie sich bewusst, dass Sie gesprochene Sprache transkribieren, was sich natürlich im Stil bemerkbar macht. Sie dürfen also Kurzformen sowie *question tags* verwenden. Die Sätze müssen nicht immer vollständig beendet werden, Füllwörter wie *ehm, well* etc. können den Eindruck gesprochener Sprache verstärken. Das Register des Wortschatzes wird stark von den Interviewpartnern abhängen, denn mit einer Politikerin spricht man anders als mit Jugendlichen.

Beginnen Sie damit, die teilnehmenden Personen sowie das Thema vorzustellen.

| Interviewer | Interviewee |
| --- | --- |
| *Hello, (Tom). Nice to meet you. Thank you for coming.* | *Nice to meet you, too.* |
| *Good evening. Tonight, we have (Brian McLeod) on our show. Hello (Brian). Thank you for coming.* | *Thank you for inviting me tonight. I'm glad to be here.* |
| *We are working on a series about (immigrants to the US). Our topic tonight is ...* | |

Im Hauptteil stellen Sie viele interessante Fragen. Vermeiden Sie dabei Entscheidungsfragen und verwenden Sie stattdessen Ergänzungsfragen *(wh-questions)*. Haken Sie auch nach und erfragen Sie Details oder Begründungen.

| Interviewer | Interviewee |
|---|---|
| *To start off, would you like to say something about ... / could you tell our listeners/readers something about ...?* | *I'm not sure I've understood your question correctly.*<br>*Sorry, could you rephrase that?* |
| *You just said ... How does that fit your previous statement that ...?*<br>*What do you mean by (saying) ...?* | *I'm glad you brought that up because ...*<br>*I'm happy you asked that question because ...* |
| *Could you elaborate on ...?*<br>*Could you give us some more details on ...?* | *Let me explain that in some more detail.* |
| *If you believe that ..., why did you ...?* | *That's a good question. Let me try to explain why ...* |
| *Let's get back to my original question ...* | |

Beenden Sie das Interview, indem Sie es kurz bewertend kommentieren und Ihrem Gast für das Gespräch danken.

| Interviewer | Interviewee |
|---|---|
| *I'm sorry to say that our time is up.* | |
| *Thank you, (Tom). It was a pleasure to talk to you/to discuss this matter with you.* | *The pleasure was all mine. I'm glad I had the chance to present my views.* |
| *You've given us some great insight into your life/view on ...*<br>*You've presented some thought-provoking views/made some mind-provoking comments.* | *Thank you for the chance to speak to you.* |

## Kreative Ausgestaltung, Fortführung oder Ergänzung eines fiktionalen Ausgangstextes (Erzähltext, Theaterstück, Drehbuch)

Um diese Aufgabe gut zu bewältigen, müssen Sie sich genau mit den Figuren und den Eigenheiten des Ausgangstextes auseinandersetzen. Bei allen drei Textsorten müssen Sie vorab genau untersuchen, wie die fiktiven Charaktere sprechen, denken, fühlen und handeln, und diese Eigenschaften entsprechend in Ihrer kreativen Fortführung weiterführen bzw. bei der kreativen Ausgestaltung zugrunde legen.

Bei einem Erzähltext müssen Sie sich darüber hinaus über die Erzählsituation klar werden. Wenn Sie den Ausgangstext fortsetzen sollen, müssen Sie den gleichen Erzähler und die gleiche Erzählperspektive wählen. Dies hat Einfluss darauf, wie Sie den Text schreiben und was Sie erzählen. Es kann aber auch sein, dass Sie den Ausgangstext aus einer anderen Erzählperspektive schreiben sollen oder dass Sie in der Rolle einer Figur einen Brief, einen Tagebucheintrag o. Ä. verfassen müssen. Immer geht es darum, die Eigenschaften und die Sprache der Figur zu imitieren.

Bei einem Drama oder Drehbuch müssen Sie zusätzlich zu den Charakteren die Eigenheiten der Regieanweisungen beachten. Sind diese ausführlich oder knapp gehalten? Müssen Sie beim Drehbuch auch die Kameraeinstellungen angeben? Sind für Ihre Ausgestaltung bzw. Fortführung Licht und Ton relevant?

Starten Sie mit einem Brainstorming und halten Sie Ihre Gedanken auf einem Konzeptpapier fest. Folgende Fragestellungen können Ihnen dabei helfen:
- Welche Hinweise beinhaltet der Ausgangstext im Hinblick auf die Aufgabenstellung. Gibt es Hinweise darauf, was als Nächstes passieren wird?
- Wie sprechen die Figuren mit- und übereinander? Wie hoch sind die Sprechanteile verschiedener Figuren? Enthält der Erzähltext viele oder wenige Dialoge? Gibt es Formen der Introspektion (innerer Monolog etc.)?
- Wie verhalten sich die Figuren?
- Welche Atmosphäre herrscht in dem Text vor? Und welche Stimmung wollen Sie kreieren? Wie kann das gelingen?

Ordnen Sie dann Ihre Gedanken und beginnen Sie zu schreiben. Prüfen Sie dabei immer wieder, ob Ihr kreatives Produkt noch im Einklang mit den Informationen des Ausgangstextes steht.

| Tipp | |
|---|---|
| Nutzen Sie die Web-App „**MindCards**" zum Lernen und Wiederholen **hilfreicher Wendungen** für verschiedene Aufgabenstellungen im Bereich **Schreiben**. Diese interaktiven Karteikarten können Sie bequem am Smartphone nutzen. |  |

**Die Sprachmittlungsaufgabe**

Unter Sprachmittlung versteht man die sinngemäße (nicht wörtliche!) Übertragung von einer Sprache in die andere. Diese Übertragung wird nötig, weil die Adressaten den Text in der Ausgangssprache nicht verstehen. In der Abiturprüfung wird Ihnen ein deutscher Text vorgelegt, den Sie entsprechend dem vorgegebenen Kontext ins Englische übertragen müssen. Die verwendeten Operatoren entstammen dem Anforderungsbereich I. Sie sollen explizit keine Wertung vornehmen, sondern lediglich die Inhalte übertragen.

Die Aufgabenstellung hat hier eine besondere Relevanz, da sie den Kontext klärt. Sie sollten sich daher ein paar Minuten Zeit nehmen, um die Aufgabe genau zu analysieren. Diese Zeit ist gut investiert. Folgende Fragen können Ihnen dabei helfen:

| Frage | Kommentar |
|---|---|
| Wer ist Ihr*e Adressat*in? | Die Beantwortung dieser Fragen beeinflusst Ihren Stil. Es macht einen großen Unterschied, ob Sie eine E-Mail an einen Freund oder einen Artikel für eine Homepage schreiben sollen. |
| Welche Textsorte sollen Sie verfassen? | |
| Welche Informationen sollen Sie weitergeben? | In aller Regel müssen Sie hier eine Auswahl treffen. |
| Welche Zusatzinformationen braucht Ihr*e Adressat*in eventuell, um z. B. kulturelle Aspekte zu verstehen? | Achten Sie hier vor allem auf kulturell geprägte Begriffe wie z. B. „freiwilliges soziales Jahr" oder „Mottowoche". |

XX

| Frage | Kommentar |
|---|---|
| Welche Informationen sollten Sie weglassen, weil sie entweder irrelevant für die Aufgabe sind oder für den Adressaten verwirrend oder nichtssagend sein könnten? | Namen kleinerer Orte oder Flüsse würden dem Adressaten/der Adressatin vermutlich wenig sagen. Hier können Sie dann besser auf *German cities/rivers* verweisen. |
| Welche Ausdrücke sind schwer zu übertragen, weil es kein englisches Äquivalent gibt? | Greifen Sie z. B. auf eine Umschreibung zurück: *It is a year in which ...* Geben Sie ggf. Beispiele oder fügen Sie erklärende Informationen hinzu. |

Ähnlich wie bei *re-creation of text* wird Ihnen bei der Sprachmittlung ein Zieltextformat vorgegeben. Es wird vorausgesetzt, dass Sie mit den Textsorten *letter, email* und *article* vertraut sind.

Sie dürfen am Prüfungstag ein- und zweisprachige **Wörterbücher** verwenden, die Ihnen eine große Hilfe sein können, deren Verwendung aber auch Zeit braucht. Denken Sie daher daran, dass es nicht um eine genaue Übersetzung, sondern um eine inhaltliche Übertragung geht. Verwenden Sie z. B. Synonyme und Antonyme sowie Verbalphrasen anstelle von Nomen und greifen Sie auf Vereinfachungen (z. B. für Fachtermini) zurück. Redewendungen sollten Sie entweder umschreiben oder nachschlagen, meist gibt es eine englische Entsprechung. Mit einer wörtlichen Übersetzung liegen Sie hingegen in aller Regel falsch. Achten Sie schließlich auch noch auf die sogenannten *false friends*, also auf Wörter, die ähnlich klingen, aber eine andere Bedeutung haben, z. B. dt. „mobben" *(to bully sb)*, dt. „Handy" *(mobile)*.

**Praktische Tipps zur Vorbereitung**

Wie Sie im Abschnitt „Bewertung" gesehen haben, wird die Sprachmittlungsaufgabe stärker gewichtet als die einzelnen Teile der Textaufgabe. Die sprachliche Leistung wiegt schwerer als die inhaltliche. Dies sollten Sie auch in der Vorbereitung der Prüfung berücksichtigen. Jeder und jede von Ihnen hat in den letzten Jahren seine/ihre eigenen Stärken entwickelt und Schwächen kennengelernt und somit jetzt auch jeweils individuelle Entwicklungsschwerpunkte. Falls Ihnen diese noch nicht deutlich sein sollten, nehmen Sie sich die Klausuren aus der Qualifikationsphase vor und prüfen Sie, bei welchen Kriterien Sie wiederholt Punkte gewonnen oder verloren haben. Überlegen Sie, wo es folglich besonders viel Sinn ergibt, mit der Vorbereitung anzusetzen. Zu vielen Kriterien haben Sie auf den vorangehenden Seiten bereits wertvolle Tipps erhalten, was zum Beispiel die Belegtechnik, den Textaufbau oder die Textformate angeht.

**Sprachliche Vorbereitung**

Erfahrungsgemäß sind die Kriterien Wortschatz und Satzbau sowie sprachliche Korrektheit Bereiche, in denen Schülerinnen und Schüler viele Punkte verlieren. Auch hier kann dieses Buch Sie unterstützen. Sie finden hier zahlreiche Übungsaufgaben mit Lösungsvorschlägen. Nachdem Sie die Aufgaben selbst bearbeitet haben, sollten

Sie die Lösungsvorschläge aufmerksam lesen und sich dabei die Ausdrücke notieren, die Ihnen hilfreich für die Erstellung Ihrer eigenen Texte erscheinen. Achten Sie dabei darauf, nie nur isolierte Wörter zu notieren, sondern immer Kollokationen. Das heißt, Sie schreiben ganze *phrases* auf, z. B. *to draw a conclusion* anstatt *conclusion*, damit Sie wissen, wie man die Wörter in einen Satz einbettet. Einige besonders hilfreiche Wendungen finden Sie bereits hier im Hinweiskapitel bei den entsprechenden Aufgaben. Ebenso sollten Sie auch mit den Texten verfahren, die Sie im Unterricht besprechen. So können Sie vor allem Ihren thematischen Wortschatz erweitern.

Auch „MindCards" und „interaktives Training" (Zugangscode vgl. Umschlaginnenseite) bieten Ihnen Möglichkeiten, grundlegende sprachliche Fertigkeiten zu üben, insbesondere das Kapitel *English in use* des „interaktiven Trainings". Für ein gezieltes Üben oberstufenrelevanten Wortschatzes empfiehlt sich zudem die Vorbereitung mit dem Band „Abitur-Training Englisch Themenwortschatz" (Best.-Nr. 82451D).

Prüfen Sie beim Satzbau, welche komplexen Satzbaumuster Sie verwenden. Denkbar sind:
- Relativsätze (eingeleitet durch *who, which, where, that*)
- Konditionalsätze *(if-clauses)*
- Adverbialsätze (mit Konjunktionen wie z. B. *when, although, so that*)
- Partizipialkonstruktionen *(Having considered the pros and cons, I come to the conclusion that …)*
- Gerundialkonstruktionen *(The author tries to persuade the reader by providing biased information.)*
- Infinitivkonstruktionen *(She uses an enumeration to underline her point.)*

Sollten Sie hier noch Entwicklungsbedarf feststellen, so empfiehlt sich die Arbeit mit einem grammatischen Übungsbuch, z. B. „Abitur-Training Englisch Grammatikübungen" (Best.-Nr. 82452D).

In puncto sprachlicher Korrektheit sollten Sie prüfen, ob es gewisse Regeln gibt, gegen die Sie immer wieder verstoßen, und ob dies daran liegt, dass Sie die entsprechende Regel nicht kennen oder verstehen, oder ob es sich um sogenannte Flüchtigkeitsfehler handelt. Im ersten Fall sollten Sie sich die entsprechenden Kapitel in einer englischen Grammatik durchlesen. Im zweiten Fall ist eine genaue Selbstkorrektur zu empfehlen, und zwar speziell mit Blick auf die Strukturen, bei denen Ihnen immer wieder Fehler unterlaufen. Klassische Fehlerquellen sind z. B.
- die Bildung des *simple present* in der 3. Person Singular *(he wants, she does)*
- der Genitiv (z. B. *the author's view*)
- Konditionalsätze (kein *will/would* im *if-clause*)
- Adjektive versus Adverbien (Adjektive beziehen sich auf Nomen, Adverbien beschreiben Adjektive, Verben oder andere Adverbien näher)
- falsche Wahl der Präposition (diese sollten Sie beim Wortschatz mitlernen oder im Wörterbuch nachschlagen)
- Groß- und Kleinschreibung (z. B. *American values*)

**Inhaltliche Vorbereitung**

Im Zentralabitur NRW werden keine bestimmten Texte für die Behandlung im Unterricht vorgeschrieben, sondern lediglich Textsorten, z. B. ein modernes amerikanisches Drama, ein Roman und ein Spielfilm, vorgegeben. Dadurch kann in der Abiturprüfung auch keine inhaltliche Kenntnis der von Ihnen gelesenen Werke überprüft werden, sodass Sie sich in der Vorbereitung nicht mit einer langwierigen Wiederholung dieser Inhalte aufhalten müssen. Relevanter sind die Merkmale dieser Textsorten, also z. B. die typischen Merkmale eines utopischen oder dystopischen Romans. Wichtig sind vor allem die Inhalte der Themenfelder, die zu Beginn dieses Hinweiskapitels aufgeführt sind. Stellen Sie also sicher, dass Sie wissen, was sich hinter dem jeweiligen Thema verbirgt, und dass Sie die wesentlichen Schlagwörter dazu kennen und mit Hintergrundwissen verknüpfen können. Welche Werte stehen z. B. hinter dem Begriff des *American Dream*? Was ist in diesem Kontext mit *independence, individualism* und *Manifest Destiny* gemeint?

In diesem Rahmen ergibt es auch Sinn, die fiktionalen und die nicht-fiktionalen Texte, die Sie im Unterricht behandelt haben, nochmals durchzugehen und Querverbindungen zu den Themen herzustellen. Fragen Sie sich z. B., welche literarische Figur oder auch welcher reale Mensch den *American Dream* verkörpert und warum.

Weitere Hilfe bei der inhaltlichen Vorbereitung bietet das „Abitur-Skript Englisch" (Best.-Nr. 10546S1), in dem Sie knapp zusammengefasstes Basiswissen zu zentralen Prüfungsthemen sowie Listen möglicher Argumente zu wichtigen Diskussionsthemen finden.

**Das Anfertigen der Prüfungsarbeit**

Am Prüfungstag selbst haben Sie für die Bearbeitung der Klausur im Leistungskurs 285 Minuten (= 4 Std. und 45 Min.) **Zeit**. Hierin ist die Auswahlzeit, die Sie benötigen, um sich für einen der Teile A zu entscheiden, bereits enthalten. Es gibt keine zusätzliche Einlese- oder Auswahlzeit. Oftmals entscheiden sich Schüler*innen sehr schnell, sodass Sie einen Teil der Auswahlzeit bereits für die Bearbeitung nutzen können. Überstürzen Sie hier aber nichts, sondern schauen Sie sich in Ruhe alle Texte und alle Aufgabenstellungen an. Sie sollten es unbedingt vermeiden, die Entscheidung nochmals zu ändern, wenn Sie bereits mit der Bearbeitung begonnen haben.

Da Sie die Textaufgabe und die Sprachmittlungsaufgabe zeitgleich erhalten, können Sie selbst entscheiden, mit welcher Aufgabe Sie beginnen wollen.

Wie Sie bei der Bearbeitung der einzelnen Teilaufgaben vorgehen sollten, ist im Abschnitt „Die Bearbeitung der verschiedenen Teilaufgaben" genau beschrieben.

Am Prüfungstag ist die richtige **Zeiteinteilung** elementar. Schauen Sie daher bei der Bearbeitung der Übungsklausuren in diesem Band auf die Uhr. Wie lange brauchen Sie für welche Teilaufgaben? Erstellen Sie sich auf der Grundlage dieser Erfahrungswerte einen Zeitplan für die Anfertigung der Prüfungsarbeit. Ein möglicher Richtwert kann sein:

|  | **Leistungskurs** |
|---|---|
| Aufgabe 1 (inkl. Text lesen und verstehen) | 55 Minuten |
| Aufgabe 2 | 75 Minuten |
| Aufgabe 3 | 55 Minuten |
| Sprachmittlungsaufgabe | 55 Minuten |
| Korrekturlesen | 30 Minuten |

In diesem Vorschlag sind 15 Min. für die Textauswahl eingeplant. Sollten Sie schneller sein, so lassen Sie diese Zeit am besten in die Korrektur einfließen. Nehmen Sie sich hier Zeit, nochmals genau die Inhalte zu prüfen und sprachliche Fehler zu korrigieren. Wenn es die Zeit erlaubt, machen Sie vor dem Beginn der Korrekturphase eine kurze Pause, um Abstand zum eigenen Text zu gewinnen (siehe dazu auch den vorangegangenen Abschnitt zur sprachlichen Vorbereitung).

**Die Arbeit mit diesem Buch**

Dieses Buch enthält neben den Hinweisen und Tipps unter anderem Übungsaufgaben zu verschiedenen Themenbereichen mit Lösungsvorschlägen. Diese Übungsaufgaben entsprechen genau den Anforderungen, die Sie auch in Ihrer Abiturprüfung erwarten. Beachten Sie, dass die Textgrundlagen der Original-Prüfungen bis zum Jahr 2020 etwas kürzer sind. Dennoch eignen sich auch diese Aufgaben sehr gut, um die nötigen Fertigkeiten für die Abiturprüfung zu trainieren.
Wie Sie mit diesem Buch arbeiten, ist Ihnen überlassen und hängt ganz von Ihren individuellen Zielen und Arbeitsweisen ab. Die folgenden Möglichkeiten können Ihnen aber Anregungen für die Arbeit geben.

**Möglichkeit 1**

Wählen Sie die Klausuren, die Sie thematisch am meisten interessieren, und bearbeiten Sie diese zunächst selbstständig – wenn es die Zeit erlaubt, sogar unter Abiturbedingungen, d. h. in der vorgesehenen Zeit. Lesen Sie vorab ruhig nochmals die entsprechenden Seiten zu der jeweiligen Teilaufgabe im Kapitel „Hinweise und Tipps" nach. Vergleichen Sie Ihre Lösung anschließend mit dem abgedruckten Lösungsvorschlag. Bedenken Sie dabei bitte, dass dies nur ein subjektiver Vorschlag sein kann und dass Sie eventuell bei den Teilaufgaben 2 und 3 der Textaufgabe noch andere interessante Aspekte gefunden haben. Achten Sie daher vor allem darauf, dass Ihr Text ähnlich strukturiert ist und vielleicht auch auf ähnliche Textstellen zurückgreift und ähnlich viele Argumente beinhaltet wie die Beispiellösung. Die Inhalte in Teilaufgabe 1 sowie bei der Sprachmittlung sind durch die Aufgabenstellung hingegen ziemlich klar limitiert, sodass hier die inhaltliche Übereinstimmung groß sein sollte.
Sollten Sie bei der Arbeit ins Stocken geraten, können Sie die Musterlösung auch während des Schreibens zu Hilfe nehmen. Nutzen Sie diese dann aber in drei Stufen. Lesen Sie zunächst nur die kurze Einleitung zu der jeweiligen Teilaufgabe. Vielleicht kommen Sie mit diesen Denkanstößen schon weiter. Lesen Sie im Bedarfsfall die

Stichworte, die die Lösung grob skizzieren oder sehen Sie sich nur die Struktur an, die in der Randspalte neben der Musterlösung angegeben ist. Nutzen Sie den anschließenden Fließtext vorzugsweise zunächst nur zum Abgleich mit Ihrer fertigen Lösung. Abschließend sollten Sie den Fließtext auch zur Wortschatzarbeit nutzen, indem Sie sich hilfreiche Formulierungen markieren, herausschreiben und versuchen, diese selbst in zukünftigen Texten anzuwenden.

**Möglichkeit 2**

Vielleicht haben Sie bei der Analyse Ihrer eigenen Klausuren festgestellt, dass Sie bei speziellen Teilaufgaben besondere Schwierigkeiten haben. Oftmals trifft dies auf die Aufgaben im Anforderungsbereich II (Analyse) zu. Dann nehmen Sie sich gezielt diese Teilaufgaben vor und verzichten Sie auf die Bearbeitung der anderen Teilaufgaben dieser Klausur.

**Möglichkeit 3**

Vermutlich werden Sie keine Zeit haben, alle Klausuren im Detail zu bearbeiten und Ihre Gedanken zu verschriftlichen. In dem Fall können Sie einzelne Klausuren auch bloß stichwortartig bearbeiten, indem Sie ein Konzeptpapier erstellen. Dieses können Sie dann mit den Stichworten, die die Lösung grob skizzieren, vergleichen. Zusätzlich können Sie auch noch den Fließtext lesen, um ein wenig Spracharbeit zu betreiben, wie unter Möglichkeit 1 beschrieben.

**Möglichkeit 4**

Wenn es zeitlich ganz eng wird, können Sie das Buch auch einfach aufmerksam lesen. Damit dabei etwas hängen bleibt, ist es aber sinnvoll, sich nach jeder Teilaufgabe nochmals zu vergegenwärtigen, worauf es bei der Bearbeitung zu achten galt und was Sie von der Musterlösung sprachlich und/oder inhaltlich mitnehmen können. Markieren Sie die entsprechenden Stellen – gerne mit zwei verschiedenen Farben für Sprache und Inhalt, sodass Sie sich diese Passagen später nochmals zu Gemüte führen oder auch aufschreiben können.

# Mündliche Abiturprüfung

Für die mündliche Prüfung gelten dieselben curricularen Grundlagen wie für die schriftliche Prüfung, d. h., auch hier werden die Kompetenzen des Kernlehrplans überprüft, wobei der Schwerpunkt naturgemäß auf der Sprechkompetenz liegt. Inhaltlich wird ebenfalls Bezug genommen auf die Themenfelder der Qualifikationsphase.

**Der Aufbau**

Die Prüfung besteht aus zwei Teilen, die beide gleich lang sind und jeweils 10–15 Minuten dauern. Für den ersten Teil haben Sie eine Vorbereitungszeit von 30 Minuten. Hier können Sie verschiedene Ausgangstexte erwarten, die es zu bearbeiten gilt, wobei die unter Punkt 1 genannte Variante erfahrungsgemäß die häufigste ist.
❶ Ein oder mehrere Texte mit einer Gesamtlänge von 200 – 300 Wörtern. Bei Gedichten oder Textimpulsen, z. B. einem bedeutungsreichen Zitat, kann diese Wortzahl auch unterschritten werden.
❷ Ein oder mehrere Bildimpulse, z. B. Cartoon, Grafik und ggf. einen zusätzlichen Text.
❸ Ein Hörtext oder ein audiovisueller Text (z. B. Filmausschnitt) von maximal 3 Minuten und ggf. ergänzende Bildimpulse.

Die begleitenden Aufgaben greifen, ebenso wie in der schriftlichen Prüfung, auf die bekannten Operatoren (vgl. S. III–V) zurück und decken die drei Anforderungsbereiche *comprehension, analysis, comment / (re-)creation of text* ab.
In der Vorbereitungszeit dürfen Sie auch auf ein- und zweisprachige Wörterbücher zurückgreifen und ggf. erhalten Sie auch weiteres Material zur Vorbereitung Ihrer mündlichen Präsentation.
Ihre Aufgabe ist es, auf der Grundlage der bereitgestellten Materialien, einen zusammenhängenden Vortrag zu erarbeiten. Ihre Prüferinnen und Prüfer sind gehalten, Sie nicht zu unterbrechen, Ihnen aber auch keine helfenden Fragen zu stellen, was bedeutet, dass Sie die Texte selbständig und tiefgehend verstehen, analysieren und bewerten müssen.

Der zweite Aufgabenteil ist im Gegenteil dazu ein Prüfungsgespräch, für das Sie keine Vorbereitungszeit haben, da Sie auch keine weiteren Materialien erhalten. Hier geht es primär darum, Ihre Sprechkompetenz im Bereich „an Gespräch teilnehmen" zu überprüfen. Sie sollen zeigen, dass Sie auf Fragen und Äußerungen Ihrer Prüferin oder Ihres Prüfers eingehen können und auch selbst den Gesprächsverlauf mitgestalten können, indem Sie eigene Schwerpunkte setzen. Sie sollen aber natürlich auch Ihre fachlichen Kenntnisse darstellen und Ihre eigene Meinung argumentativ vertreten. Kurz gesagt, geht es auch hier wiederum um die o. g. drei Anforderungsbereiche. Inhaltlich wird Ihr Prüfer oder Ihre Prüferin auf weitere Themenschwerpunkte der Qualifikationsphase eingehen.

**Die Bewertung**

Wie in der schriftlichen Prüfung werden auch in der mündlichen Prüfung die inhaltliche Leistung und die sprachliche Leistung bewertet.

Kriterien für die inhaltliche Leistung (ca. 20 % je Prüfungsteil)
Die Beiträge (sind):
- aufgabenbezogen und sachlich richtig
- umfassend und relevant
- logisch und klar begründet
- interkulturell angemessen
- nehmen Bezug auf im Unterricht erworbene Kenntnisse

Kriterien für die sprachliche Leistung (ca. 30 % je Prüfungsteil)
- Die Beiträge sind:
  - kohärent (das heißt, es werden Konnektoren – z. B. *therefore, as a consequence* – verwendet um logische Zusammenhänge zu verdeutlichen)
  - strukturiert (das heißt, z. B. Einleitung, Hauptteil und Schluss sind erkennbar)
  - flüssig und frei vorgetragen (in 1. Teil auch notizengestützt)
  - situationsangemessen und adressatengerecht (also keine Umgangssprache, sondern eher formelle Sprache)
  - effektiv und ökonomisch (keine Ausschweifungen, Aussagen kurz und präzise)
  - in der Interaktion flexibel (das heißt, insbesondere im 2. Teil sind Sie in der Lage, auf Fragen und Impulse spontan zu reagieren)
- Aussprache und Intonation (Klarheit, Korrektheit)
- Wortschatz (Präzision, Differenziertheit, Idiomatik, Angemessenheit)
- grammatische Strukturen (Korrektheit, Komplexität, Angemessenheit)

**Tipps**

- Nutzen Sie die Vorbereitungszeit, um das Material mehrfach gründlich zu lesen und wichtige Textstellen zu markieren. Schlagen Sie nur relevante Wörter nach und versuchen Sie möglichst viele Worterschließungsstrategien (Wortfamilie, internationale Wörter, Kontext, etc.) anzuwenden.
- Teilen Sie sich die Zeit so ein, dass Sie sich zu allen drei Anforderungsbereichen Notizen anfertigen können. Achten Sie auch darauf, dass Sie zu allen drei Bereichen ähnlich viel zu sagen haben.
- Verwenden Sie die nützlichen Redewendungen für die jeweiligen Anforderungsbereiche (vgl. S. VIII, XI/XII, XIV–XIX) und achten Sie auf die Verwendung von Textbelegen (vgl. S. XII/XIII).
- Wie Sie bei den Kriterien sehen, ist es wichtig, dass Sie in der Prüfung nicht lesen, sondern möglichst frei sprechen. Fertigen Sie daher während der Vorbereitungszeit nur Stichworte an und keinesfalls ganze Sätze oder gar einen mehr oder weniger vollständigen Text. Schauen Sie in der Prüfungssituation ruhig immer wieder kurz auf Ihre Notizen, suchen Sie dann aber wieder den Blickkontakt zu der Prüferin oder dem Prüfer. (Technik *Read and Look Up*)

- Ordnen Sie insbesondere im zweiten Prüfungsteil Ihre Beiträge immer wieder in größere Zusammenhänge ein. Bei Fragen zu einem Roman können Sie z. B. auf das Oberthema der Unterrichtsreihe (*Dystopia, American Dream,* etc.) eingehen und diesen entsprechend einordnen. So können Sie eigene Schwerpunkte setzen.
- Bedenken Sie auch, dass Ihre Prüferin oder Ihr Prüfer auf die Ganzschriften, die Sie gemeinsam im Unterricht behandelt haben, eingehen wird. Es ist also sinnvoll, sich deren Inhalte, Figuren und Themen im Vorfeld nochmals zu vergegenwärtigen.
- Versuchen Sie das Gespräch selbst zu steuern, indem Sie Querverweise zu Themen schaffen, die Ihnen liegen, z. B. können Sie bei Fragen zu Nigeria auf Globalisierung zu sprechen kommen oder Vergleiche zu anderen Kulturen herstellen.
- Sollten Sie ins Stocken geraten, überbrücken Sie Denkpausen mit sprachlichen Floskeln wie z. B. *let me think for a second; just a second, the word is on the tip of my tongue; could you repeat that question, please?*
- Beachten Sie, dass Sie sich in einer formellen Gesprächssituation befinden und verwenden Sie entsprechendes Vokabular.
- Zu guter Letzt: Der erste Eindruck zählt auch. Kleiden Sie sich also angemessen, begrüßen Sie die Prüferinnen und Prüfer höflich und mit einem Lächeln und versuchen Sie selbstbewusst aufzutreten ohne arrogant zu wirken.

**Tipps**
Nutzen Sie auch die Web-App „**MindCards**" zum Lernen und Wiederholen **hilfreicher Wendungen** für den Bereich **Sprechen**. Diese interaktiven Karteikarten können Sie bequem am Smartphone nutzen.
Auf der Plattform MyStark finden Sie außerdem ein **Video** mit fachunabhängigen **praktischen Tipps** zur mündlichen Abiturprüfung.

## Die Arbeit mit diesem Buch

Sie finden in diesem Buch ein konkretes Beispiel für eine mögliche mündliche Prüfung mit Aufgaben für den ersten Prüfungsteil und möglichen weiteren Impulsen für den zweiten Prüfungsteil. Bearbeiten Sie den ersten Prüfungsteil in 30 Minuten und versuchen Sie dann 10–15 Minuten flüssig dazu zu sprechen. Vielleicht finden Sie auch einen Zuhörer oder eine Zuhörerin. Er oder sie könnte Ihnen dann auch die Impulse für den zweiten Prüfungsteil vorlesen, sodass Sie spontan reagieren können. Alternativ können Sie auch alleine vor dem Spiegel üben.

Da die mündliche Prüfung von den Anforderungen her der schriftlichen Prüfung sehr ähnlich ist, können Sie auch mit den anderen Aufgaben dieses Buches sinnvoll arbeiten. Nehmen Sie sich dann aber etwas mehr Zeit für die Vorbereitung, da die Texte auch länger sind. Beachten Sie dazu insbesondere die Möglichkeiten 2–4 zur Arbeit mit diesen Aufgaben (S. XXV). Für die Vorbereitung auf das mündliche Abitur empfehle ich besonders die 3. Möglichkeit, denn die Arbeit mit Notizen auf einem Konzeptpapier hält Sie davon ab, Sätze auszuformulieren, die Sie dann in der Prüfung ablesen anstatt frei zu sprechen.

## Schriftliche Abiturprüfung NRW – Englisch LK
## Leseverstehen und Schreiben – Übungsaufgabe 1

**Aufgabenstellung**                                                                                  Punkte

1. Summarise what happened in Vanuatu and why. Also summarise the
   conclusions the author draws from the event. *(Comprehension)*                                       12

2. Analyse how the author tries to convince the readers that they need to
   "live within [their] overall environmental thresholds" (ll. 56/57). In doing
   so, focus on structure, argumentative techniques and the language used.
   *(Analysis)*                                                                                         16

3. Choose **one** of the following tasks.                                                               14

3.1 Discuss if it makes sense for individuals to act in a more environmentally
    friendly way if they are likely "to suffer chronically due to someone
    else's bad habit" (l. 15) anyway. *(Evaluation: comment)*

3.2 As an inhabitant of a small Pacific Island, you have been invited to attend
    an international youth conference. There you take part in a debate on the
    consequences of climate change. Write an opening statement in which
    you demand developed countries adopt a less energy-intensive lifestyle.
    *(Evaluation: re-creation of text)*

**Text:**
**Andrew Simms: Developed nations have sown the wind, Vanuatu has reaped the whirlwind**

When the president of Vanuatu said that years of progress had been wiped out by a single extreme weather event, it was both a warning and an echo. Hurricane Mitch did the same to Nicaragua and Honduras in 1998; and in 2005 political failure combined with the collapse of sea defences under the onslaught of Hurricane Katrina to wreck
5  the rich, vibrant culture of New Orleans. Climatic extremes in a warming world stand to reverse human progress and expose broken social contracts.
   But in the case of Vanuatu there seems to be a crueller twist. Vanuatu is distinguished by having come top of a global index that measures how ecologically successful (low in impact) nations are at producing good lives for their people – so-called
10 "happy life years". Vanuatu beat all other nations through treading lightest on the Earth for the quality and length of life its people enjoyed. Now it sits in the pathway of a giant climatic steamroller, fuelled by the energy-intensive lifestyles of nations much further down that index.
   Its people are the national equivalent of the individual who leads an exemplary,
15 healthy life only to suffer chronically due to someone else's bad habit – innocent, global victims of passive smoking. Vanuatu's president, Baldwin Lonsdale, was quick to

point the finger of blame at manmade climate change for the severity of Cyclone Pam, saying that "the cyclone seasons, the warm, the rain, all this is affected".

Many may think it's too soon to jump to such conclusions. For years cautious scientists have balked at attributing the effect of warming to individual events. Attribution can sometimes be hard to prove, either for methodological reasons of complexity or due to lack of data. While trepidation remains, things have changed rapidly. Instead of simple claims of cause and effect, climate scientists now readily discuss how the probability of any particular event has been raised by the existence of warming.

Hence joint work in 2011 by the National Oceanic and Atmospheric Administration in the US and the UK's Met Office concluded that a Texas heatwave was 20 times more likely to be caused by climate change than by natural weather variation. A winter warm spell in Britain the same year was 62 times more likely than in the 1960s. The Met Office's Hadley Centre now confidently states that it "can identify any changed risk of such events".

In time, more analysis will be done on Cyclone Pam, but Lonsdale's personal experience and gut reaction fits a pattern of expectations described in the most recent and most comprehensive collation of science on extreme events in the IPCC's Fifth Assessment Report. It concluded that: "The frequency of the most intense storms will more likely than not increase in some basins. More extreme precipitation near the centres of tropical cyclones making landfall is projected in North and Central America, east Africa, west, east, south and southeast Asia as well as in Australia and many Pacific islands."

So, while the present is pretty bad for Vanuatu, in a warming world the future looks set to worsen. For this island nation, that is bitterly ironic. Vanuatu is an archipelago in the western Pacific, famous for having no regular military. When it topped the index in 2006 its ecological footprint per person was no higher than those in non-industrialised countries like Mali and Swaziland, life expectancy matched that in Turkey, and life satisfaction levels were considered as high as New Zealand's. It is democratic, rich in natural wealth but, being remote, exports little, avoiding the scramble of competing in global markets. It is also hugely culturally diverse with more than 100 languages spoken across its islands.

Small island states tend to do very well in the index topped by Vanuatu. Over countless generations and in the face of geographical isolation, many Pacific islands developed more cooperative economies and highly resilient farming methods. In a warming world they are bellwethers, and carry lessons for us all. If climate change renders small island states unliveable, the international community will sooner or later have to learn to accept and support environmental refugees. Though this would be tragic, remote island populations can, at least, relocate. However, blue island-planet populations cannot.

We will seal our own fate if we fail to learn to share and live within our overall environmental thresholds. […] *(717 words)*

*Simms, Andrew: "Developed nations have sown the wind, Vanuatu has reaped the whirlwind".*
*In:* The Guardian.

**Annotations**
l. 1   *Vanuatu:* archipelago in the South Pacific consisting of about 82 islands.
l. 17  *Pam:* Cyclone Pam hit Vanuatu and damaged large parts of the archipelago in March 2015.
l. 33  *IPCC*: Intergovernmental Panel of Climate Change
l. 51  *bellwether:* something that is used as an indicator of what will happen in the future

## Lösungsvorschläge

1. You should briefly name the events in Vanuatu and the reasons that are given for them. Furthermore, you need to mention the conclusions the author draws as presented in the text.
   - What happened:
     - Vanuatu was hit by a cyclone in March 2015.
     - The country was devastated.
   - Reasons:
     - Vanuatu is not to blame for the event because the nation itself lives in a very environmentally friendly way. → They pay for the energy-intensive lifestyles of other nations.
     - The president of Vanuatu blames global warming.
     - While this conclusion is not accepted by everyone, the author quotes a report which supports the president's view.
   - Conclusions:
     - The number of environmental refugees will increase.
     - One day the earth might become uninhabitable.
     - We all need to be more conscious of the effect we are having on our climate and need to live in a more environmentally friendly way.

In his article "Developed nations have sown the wind, Vanuatu has reaped the whirlwind" published in *The Guardian*, the journalist Andrew Simms briefly describes what happened in Vanuatu. He then gives reasons for the event and draws conclusions from it.   **introduction:** reference to source, topic

In March 2015, Vanuatu was hit by Cyclone Pam and its islands were completely devastated. The president of Vanuatu blames global warming for what happened and although Simms admits that not everybody agrees with the president's analysis, he also quotes a report that supports it. Furthermore, the author mentions that Vanuatu itself is not to blame because this nation lives in a very environmentally friendly way. According to him, developed nations who have more energy-intensive lifestyles are to blame but Vanuatu has to pay the price.   **main part:** events, reasons

Simms predicts that the number of environmental refugees will increase and that one day the earth might be uninhabitable. He concludes that we all need to be more conscious of the effect we are having on our planet and its climate and that we need to live in a more environmentally friendly way.   **conclusions**

*(179 words)*

2. *This task demands that you analyse how the author tries to convince the readers of his view. You are meant to focus on structure, argumentative techniques and language.*
   – Structure:
   - Headline: sets the tone → Vanuatu has to pay for the behaviour of developed nations.
   - Shows that Vanuatu is not an isolated case (cf. ll. 1–6)
   - Takes up headline → developed nations and their lifestyles to blame for global warming (cf. ll. 7–18)
   - Reactions to the analysis that global warming is responsible for the cyclone that hit Vanuatu (cf. ll. 19–38)
   - Dire predictions for the future of islands like Vanuatu, our planet and its inhabitants (cf. ll. 34–40)
   - Conclusion that lifestyle must become less energy-intensive (cf. ll. 56/57)
   – Argumentative techniques:
   - Examples (cf. ll. 1–5)
   - Facts (cf. ll. 7–11, 41/42)
   - Numbers (cf. ll. 26, 28)
   - Experts' views and a quotation from a study (cf. ll. 19–38)
   – Language:
   - Biblical proverb which is slightly adapted to emphasise that others caused the damage which Vanuatu has to suffer (cf. headline)
   - Words with a positive connotation to describe Vanuatu and its inhabitants, e. g. "distinguished" (ll. 7/8), "ecologically successful" (ll. 8/9), "exemplary, healthy" (ll. 14/15), "innocent" (l. 15)
   - Contrasted by words with a negative connotation to describe developed nations and climate change, e. g. "giant climatic steamroller" (l. 12), "energy-intensive lifestyles" (l. 12)
   - Figurative language to stress that Vanuatu is a victim (cf. ll. 10–16)
   - Enumeration to stress Vanuatu's achievements (cf. ll. 41–44)

The author's intention in writing this article is to convince the readers that they need to "live within [their] overall environmental thresholds" (ll. 56/57). He tries to achieve his aim by using a structure that leads to the conclusion quoted above, by employing different argumentative techniques and by making use of words that underline both the difference between Vanuatu and developed nations and the author's interpretation that Vanuatu is suffering instead of these developed countries. <sub>introduction:</sub> thesis / reference to assignment

This interpretation is introduced right in the headline. The author then shows that Vanuatu is not an isolated case but that other countries have been hit by extreme winds, too (cf. ll. 1–6). In the second and third paragraph, the journalist takes up the headline again and describes in more detail that developed nations are to blame for global warming and, therefore, climate   main part: structure change (cf. ll. 7–18). In the following three paragraphs he presents reactions to the analysis of Vanuatu's president, who claims that global warming is responsible for the cyclone that hit his country. The author briefly mentions doubts (ll. 19–22) but then dwells on experts, organisations and numbers that support the president's view (cf. ll. 22–38). This indicates that he favours this interpretation of the events himself. In the seventh and eighth paragraph he makes dire predictions about the future of islands like Vanuatu, our planet and its inhabitants to emphasise that we need to take action (cf. ll. 39–55), which leads him to his final conclusion that we have to have less energy-intensive lifestyles (cf. ll. 56/57). Thus, the article's structure leads very logically to the final conclusion that appears to be convincing.

The language employed stresses the view that developed nations are to blame for Vanuatu's misfortune. The differences in lifestyles and their consequences are emphasised. Vanuatu's inhabitants are "ecologically successful" (ll. 8/9) and therefore "distinguished" (ll. 7/8). They lead "an exemplary, healthy life" (ll. 14/15). All these words have a positive connotation and therefore underline that Vanuatu's people are "innocent" (l. 15). They are contrasted with developed nations, which are accused of causing "a giant climatic steamroller, fuelled by [...] energy-intensive lifestyles" (ll. 11/12). Thus, developed nations are depicted as villains.

**language**

→ choice of words
Vanuatu: positive connotation

developed nations: negative connotation

This contrast is already introduced in the headline, which is an adapted proverb from the Bible. The original proverb "they that sow wind shall reap whirlwind" is applied to people who start trouble that grows larger than planned. In this case, however, someone else, namely the developed countries, started the trouble that another party, namely Vanuatu, has to suffer from. This stresses the injustice of the situation.

→ proverb

Additionally, the author uses figurative speech to stress this idea. He compares Vanuatu to "the individual who leads an exemplary, healthy life only to suffer chronically due to someone else's bad habit – innocent, global victims of passive smoking" (ll. 14–16). Furthermore, developed nations, as mentioned above, are blamed for having set free a "steamroller" (l. 12), which ruthlessly destroys other nations. The intended effect of the language used is that people in developed countries should have a guilty conscience and realise that their lifestyle needs to be changed.

→ figurative speech

The argumentative techniques employed support that view. The journalist argues that now extreme weather events happen regularly as Cyclone Pam is an "echo" (l. 2) of preceding hurricanes. To prove this assertion Simms gives several examples (cf. ll. 2–5). The claim that Vanuatu's people lead an exemplary life is backed up by a global index in which Vanuatu excelled (cf. ll. 7–11, 41/42). Thus, the journalist bases his argument on facts, which makes him more trustworthy.

**argumentative techniques**

→ examples, facts

When Simms supports the analysis of Vanuatu's president that Cyclone Pam was caused by global warming, he refers to unnamed climate scientists who "now readily discuss how the probability of any particular event has been raised by the existence of warming" (ll. 23/24). Furthermore, he quotes from the IPCC's Fifth Assessment Report (ll. 34–38), refers to organisations that share his view (cf. ll. 25–30) and uses their numbers (cf. ll. 26, 28) and thus bases his argument on experts' views, which adds authority to his reasoning.

→ reference to experts, numbers

All in all, Simms makes it clear that people in developed nations need to change their lifestyles if they do not want to live at the expense of somebody else's well-being. He achieves this by using language in a way that clearly contrasts the victim and the perpetrator, by using structure purposefully to make it lead to his final conclusion and by basing his arguments on examples, facts and experts' reports.

**conclusion:** reference to task

*(773 words)*

3.1 *Here you need to come up with convincing arguments for and against the individual living in an environmentally friendly way even though they alone may not be able to effect real change like a prevention of global warming. After carefully weighing the pros and cons, you need to come to a conclusion.*
– *Introduction: Present the topic and point out the dilemma for the individual.*
– *Pros:*
   • *It does not help to bury one's head in the sand.*
   • *Every day that is lost, it becomes harder to reach the 2-degree goal, so we cannot wait for others to start.*
   • *A good example may encourage others to follow, e. g. initiative 10:10, which brings together people who want to make a cleaner, cleverer, low-carbon world.*
– *Cons:*
   • *Cite the example of the people in Vanuatu.*
   • *The influence of the individual is too insignificant compared to energy-intensive companies.*
   • *The USA and China are responsible for 40 % of the global greenhouse gas emissions. They finally signed the climate change agreement in 2016 in Paris. However, the reductions they are planning are not sufficient to reach*

> the 2-degree goal. US president Donald Trump even pulled the US out of the agreement.
> - Global warming is not an immediate threat, which makes it hard to persuade people to change their behaviour.
- Conclusion: Balance the pros and cons and state your own opinion.

When discussing climate change, two is the magic number. We need to stabilise global temperature within two degrees above pre-industrial levels, or else the extra input of greenhouse gases, for example those locked in the arctic ice, will wipe out most of the life on earth. In order to achieve that goal, we need to cut emissions by 80 % by 2050. This goal seems hard to achieve; one might even say it is impossible to achieve. Therefore, the question arises whether it makes any sense at all for individuals to act in a more environmentally friendly way if they are likely "to suffer chronically due to someone else's bad habit" (l. 15). *introduction*

People who think it does make sense may point out that no one, at least no doctor, would recommend a non-smoker who contracts lung cancer to start smoking because he will die anyway. Only deeply pessimistic and sarcastic people would do so. The same could be said to be true for global warming because we cannot bury our heads in the sand and do nothing just because the big players, for instance energy-intensive companies like Trimet, emit too much greenhouse gas. *main part: pros*

On the contrary, the individual needs to set a good example to encourage others to follow. Take an initiative such as 10:10. This initiative offers a website on which they bring together individual people and groups who want to make this world a cleaner, cleverer, low-carbon place. On the website one can find hundreds of examples of what individuals have already achieved to cut down emissions and thus get ideas for one's own projects.

On the other hand, there are good reasons that support the view that the individual is not powerful enough to stop global warming. Take Vanuatu as an example: the nation as a whole, and not just the individual inhabitants, led an exemplary life as far as the emission of greenhouse gas is concerned. In spite of that fact, Cyclone Pam destroyed many people's houses. So their excellent behaviour did not save them from suffering the consequences of global warming. *transition – cons*

The USA and China, who together are responsible for 40 % of our global greenhouse gas emissions, finally signed the climate change agreement in 2016. Whereas China seems to be quite serious about tackling climate change, the USA under Donald Trump even pulled out of the agreement again. In any case it will be almost impossible to stay within the 2-degree limit because efforts started too late and too half-heartedly.

The basic problem is that we are evolutionarily equipped to deal with immediate threats. Global warming, however, is not an immediate threat so we do not feel the need to react. Once people start to feel that threat, it will be too late.

Altogether, I truly believe that individuals alone are too ineffective to help with climate change. Of course, they can make some effort and set good examples, but if the big spenders do not change their behaviour radically, the 2-degree goal is unattainable. Then it might be wiser to enjoy the remaining years on our planet, without denying ourselves pleasures like weekend trips to Paris or Mallorca, because rough times are certainly ahead. **conclusion**

*(533 words)*

3.2 *In this assignment you have to prepare an opening statement for a debate at an international youth conference. Your topic is climate change and its consequences; your aim is to convince developed nations to change their lifestyle to a less energy-intensive one. As it is an opening statement, you need to greet the audience and thank them for the invitation before you briefly state your topic and its importance and make your point of view clear. Here you should try to catch the listeners' attention by making a provocative statement or telling an anecdote. In the main part you need to develop your ideas convincingly, supporting your arguments by facts and evidence. Finally, round off your speech by appealing to the audience or depicting a vision of the future.*

*As your audience consists of international youth, your language does not need to be too formal but still, you are giving a debate statement, so informal language is not appropriate either. Very importantly, use language that appeals to your listeners' emotions and, if possible, also try to use some rhetorical devices.*

- *Greet the audience ("Hello everybody/Dear listeners").*
- *Express your thanks for the invitation ("Thank you for inviting me to this important conference").*
- *Announce your topic (climate change and its consequences).*
- *State your opinion ("I demand developed nations abandon their energy-intensive lifestyles").*
- *Support your view:*
  - *Refer to the events in Vanuatu.*
  - *Depict the differences in lifestyle and their consequences.*
  - *Refer to experts who believe that climate change causes extreme weather events.*
  - *Give examples of an energy-intensive lifestyle and show how it can be changed.*
  - *Point out that people in Vanuatu live happily even though they live environmentally friendly lifestyles.*

- *Round off your statement by doing one of the following:*
  - *Summarise your statement.*
  - *Depict a vision of the future (either positive if your aim is reached or negative to show the consequences if not).*
  - *Call for action.*
  - *Appeal to the listeners.*
  - *Ask a rhetorical question.*

Dear fellow youth,     greeting

Thank you for inviting me to this important conference. I am glad to be here because there is something I would like to bring to your attention: On 13 March 2015 I was having a wonderful meal with my family. We were all gathered in our kitchen, talking, laughing and eating food my mum had prepared from what she had harvested from our garden. One day later, on 14 March 2015 there was no more laughing, and there was no more kitchen, no more garden and most importantly, no mother. Cyclone Pam had taken them all. I am standing here today because I do not want other people to suffer that same fate. I am standing here today because I firmly believe that man is to blame for extreme weather events and I am standing here today because I want to ask developed nations to give up their energy-intensive lifestyles.

**introduction:** express thanks, introduce topic

express demand

For years, scientists were hesitant when asked if extreme weather events were caused by climate change. These days it is different. Scientists more readily accept the connection between climate change and disastrous weather events like Hurricane Katrina or Cyclone Pam.

**main part:** support view, present reasons

The catastrophe that hit my country was terrible and I can assure you that none of you would want to experience it. We in Vanuatu were deeply frustrated, not only because we lost most of what was dear to us, but because we felt and still feel today that we paid the price for developed nations that simply do not live within their environmental thresholds. In our country, we have developed cooperative economies and highly resilient farming methods. Altogether we leave only very light carbon footprints and, therefore, excelled in the global index that measures how ecologically successful nations are at producing good lives for their people. Still, our country was hit and destroyed by that cyclone. As a result, we feel like an innocent global victim of passive smoking.

personal experience

The smokers, as we see it, are developed nations. They use and abuse nature and its resources as if there were no hole in the ozone layer, no global warming, no threat to our planet. The problem is, of course, that living in a more environmentally friendly way means you have to do without some of the things you enjoy, like going on a weekend trip by plane, or eating strawberries in December. It means you have to do without some of these things now to prevent horrible living conditions in the future. Unfortunately, the impact of global warming is not felt unless your country is hit by extreme weather and so far, developed nations have mostly been spared these catastrophes. Consequently, they do not feel the need to change anything.   *examples*

However, in the long run, people in developed countries will profit from living in a more environmentally friendly way, too. Firstly, you do not need to have a guilty conscience if you hear about the next ecological catastrophe. Secondly, if we do not have any environmental refugees, they will not overrun your country. Thirdly, you yourself will not become an environmental refugee if you help to keep our planet liveable.   *arguments*

For the sake of us all, I ask you, as of today, to change your lifestyle and to tread more lightly on our beautiful but threatened planet, which is the only home we have.   *(558 words)*   *appeal to audience*

## Schriftliche Abiturprüfung NRW – Englisch LK
## Leseverstehen und Schreiben – Übungsaufgabe 2

Aufgabenstellung                                                                       Punkte

1. State why the author claims that Shakespeare does not belong in the
   classroom. *(Comprehension)*                                                           12

2. Analyse the way the author uses argumentative techniques and language
   to persuade the readers of his view. *(Analysis)*                                      16

3. Choose **one** of the following tasks.                                                 14

   3.1 Evaluate the author's view that "most of the kids have no concept of the
   vitality of [Shakespeare's] youth" (ll. 8/9). Refer to your background
   knowledge as well as film adaptations that you know.
   *(Evaluation: comment)*

   3.2 Write a letter to the editor of *The Guardian* in which you comment on the
   author's view that Shakespeare must be taken "out of the classroom"
   (headline). As a German student of English, take into account your own
   experience with Shakespeare. *(Evaluation: re-creation of text)*

**Text:**
**Mark Powell: Kill Bill: why we must take Shakespeare out of the classroom**

1   Shakespeare wrote to put money in his pocket, food on the table and fire in the bellies
    of his audiences, not strike modern teenagers with fear. Most of Shakespeare's audi-
    ences were illiterate. His words were chosen to be spoken or heard, not to be read and
    deadened behind a desk – they wither when performance is removed.
5       Our schools are full of Shakespeare, but often in completely the wrong places. Old
    uncle Bill has become the relative that we invite to family gatherings out of habit, not
    because we actually want to. He sits there in the corner sharing his stories with anyone
    who'll listen; the adults lend a patient ear out of a sense of duty and most of the kids
    have no concept of the vitality of his youth.
10      Even before, and most definitely since, the recent plummet in drama's status as a
    specialist subject in schools, many young people's first experience of Shakespeare is
    in an English classroom taught by enthusiastic purveyors of imagination, but primarily
    non-theatre practitioners. It's an English teacher's remit to analyse language, but pick
    apart every word of Shakespeare and you've dissected the butterfly – pretty in parts
15  but a nonsensical whole and certainly unable to fly.
        A well-meaning English teacher can take a student through the meaning of every
    word in a sentence and it soon becomes a drawn out and confusing process.
    Shakespeare's audience didn't know the meaning of every word uttered (uncle Bill was
    busily making new ones up) but the sounds and pictures they created kept viewers
20  enthralled for hours.

English teachers agree that Shakespeare's language isn't intended to be desk-bound; it's crafted for stage. Simple. Well, not so simple these days. Recent governments have decreed that Shakespeare is so key to our national identity and intelligence that he should be studied by all the children in a specific year group. Great, you might say, but
25 it's not.

Over the past few years I've welcomed fewer and fewer school groups to our theatre. The planning and paperwork involved is prohibitive. Consider as well the amount of staff needed to accompany such a group and the knock-on cost of cover needed back at school. Don't forget the travel time to get to a theatre for what is often a three hour
30 show, plus travel time back. Trips can rarely happen in a school day because of other "core" subjects missed, and teachers can't be relied upon to give up their evenings to deliver what has become a luxury.

If a teacher does manage to get kids to a theatre for a rare visit, it's not always useful. Students who are inexperienced theatregoers think that a particular director's
35 version is how Shakespeare intended his play to be done, when actually the personal interpretations can be brave, boring or bad enough to put a child off theatre for life. So, a teacher keeps the class in school and tries hard to explain the play.

Teachers are supposed to have all the answers, but dramatic literature is a playground of opinions: why does Juliet say this? Why would Macbeth do that? The real
40 answer is that we don't know, but teachers are not encouraged to say just that: "I don't know." Their own suppositions are often reported back in essays as facts. Plays aren't meant to be taught like this. They are meant to be explored on their feet. Actors and audiences are supposed to argue over meaning, finding multiple ways of delivering word and deed.

45 Our BTEC acting course has just started work on *The Tempest*. These are engaged, talented young people from a range of secondary schools who auditioned to be on the course, but the majority expressed disdain, dislike and hatred for poor uncle Bill. They had all experienced him separately in schools, behind desks. Shakespeare had made them feel stupid rather than empowered.

50 Let's give English teachers a break, give drama teachers a boost and give young people an important sense of equality. You don't need an expensive education to understand the words, but you do need the luxury of time, space and specialism to put his words on their feet and try them out. *(694 words)*

*Powell, Mark: "Kill Bill: why we must take Shakespeare out of the classroom." In: The Guardian, Copyright Guardian News & Media Ltd 2018*

**Annotations**
l. 10 *plummet:* Since 2012 various decisions in educational policy have severely decreased the status of drama as school subject.
l. 45 *BTEC (Business and Technology Education Council):* it provides secondary school leaving qualifications and further education qualifications

## Lösungsvorschläge

1. *Here you are meant to report the reasons the author gives for not dealing with Shakespeare in the usual school context.*
   - *Shakespeare's plays are to be seen and heard but not to be read.*
   - *It has become more difficult to take school groups to the theatre for organisational reasons.*
   - *Decisions in educational policy have decreased the importance of drama as a school subject.*
   - *It is more of a duty than a real desire to study and teach Shakespeare.*
   - *Teachers analyse Shakespeare's words, which deprives the plays of their entertainment and may even lead to confusion.*
   - *Teachers are believed to know how to interpret Shakespeare's plays but that is not true because there is no one truth about them, their meaning needs to be discussed.*
   - *Dealing with Shakespeare in class makes students feel ignorant.*

In his article "Kill Bill: why we must take Shakespeare out of the classroom" published in *The Guardian*, Mark Powell argues that Shakespeare's plays should no longer be taught in school.     **introduction:** reference to source, topic

The most important reason he gives is that these plays are not to be read but to be seen and heard in a theatre. This, however, is becoming more and more difficult as the regulations for taking school groups to the theatre are getting stricter and stricter according to the author. Moreover, he complains that decisions in educational policy have decreased the importance of drama as a school subject in its own right.     **main part:** reasons

Furthermore, Powell holds the view that Shakespeare is taught more out of a sense of duty than a real desire to deal with the playwright. He adds that English teachers tend to analyse Shakespeare's words and thus deprive his plays of their entertainment. Actually he claims that this approach to Shakespeare makes it more difficult for students to understand the text and thus leads to even more confusion.

Finally, teachers are believed to know how to interpret Shakespeare's plays. As a result, the plays' meaning or, even better, meanings are not discussed but students just convey their teachers' understanding of the plays in their papers. As a result, Powell's experience shows that students hate Shakespeare because he makes them feel ignorant.

So, Powell argues that plays should not be taught by English teachers but by drama teachers, who teach their students how to stage Shakespeare's plays.

*(250 words)*

2. In this task you need to analyse how the author tries to persuade the readers of his view that Shakespeare should be removed from the classroom. You are meant to focus on argumentative techniques such as stating facts and displaying authoritative knowledge as well as on language, for example figurative speech, allegory, imperatives and contrasts. Make sure to not just describe what you find in the text but also to interpret how it affects the readers.
   – Argumentative techniques:
     - Powell bases arguments on ...
       * historical facts (cf. ll. 1–4) → stresses differences between Elizabethan age and the present
       * references to recent decisions in educational policy (cf. ll. 10/11, 22 – 25) → displays his authoritative knowledge
       * authoritative knowledge (ll. 26–32) → explains why fewer and fewer classes go to the theatre
       * personal experience (ll. 45–49) → students want to put Shakespeare on stage even though most of them learned to hate him at school
     - Powell anticipates readers' reaction and contradicts (cf. ll. 24/25) → refutes counterarguments
   – Language (examples):
     Powell uses ...
     - numerous contrasts to underline the difference between Shakespeare's plays as they were intended and received in the Elizabethan age and today (cf. e. g. ll. 1–4, 21/22)
     - figurative speech:
       * His plays "wither" (l. 4) like flowers without water if they are not performed. → stresses importance of seeing the plays in a theatre
       * Analysing Shakespeare is like "dissect[ing] the butterfly" (l. 14). → easier for the reader to imagine the detailed approach that is taken to deal with Shakespeare; also implies that the butterfly is dead; imagination cannot fly
       * Students have to explore Shakespeare "on their feet" (ll. 42, 53). → stresses importance of drama teachers
       * Allegory (ll. 5–9) → the reader can easily imagine the situation described
     - imperatives/parallelism/enumeration in ll. 50–53 to underline the demand to have drama teachers teach Shakespeare and not English teachers
     - lists numerous reasons why less and less school groups come to the theatre cf. ll. 27–32) → it is virtually impossible to take students to the theatre
     - alliteration, enumeration (l. 36) → if one manages to take students to a play, it might even be a poor performance
     - enumeration ("disdain, dislike and hatred", l. 47) → studying Shakespeare in school makes students hate the bard
     - contrast ("stupid rather than empowered", l. 49) Shakespeare makes them feel ignorant

| | |
|---|---|
| The author stresses his view that Shakespeare should be removed from the classroom by employing different argumentative techniques which are supported by stylistic devices such as contrasts, figurative speech, allegory and imperatives. | **introduction:** thesis / reference to assignment |
| Throughout the whole text Powell emphasises that Shakespeare cannot be taught without acting his plays out, or at least seeing them in a theatre. To prove this assertion, he describes what Shakespeare intended to achieve with his plays when he wrote them 450 years ago, namely to "put [...] fire in the bellies of his audiences, not strike modern teenagers with fear" (ll. 1/2). The contrast underlines the counter-productive effect Shakespeare's plays have when taught inside today's classrooms. Further contrasts which stress that the plays belong on stage can be found for example in lines 3/4 and 21/22. | **main part: argumentative technique** → reference to historical facts  **language** → contrasts |
| The author also claims that Shakespeare's plays are dead if their language is analysed and they are not put "on their feet" (l. 42). When he makes this point, he uses figurative speech. For instance, he employs the verb "wither" (l. 4) to describe what happens to the words "when performance is removed" (l. 4) and compares the analysis of the plays' language to "dissect[ing] the butterfly – pretty in parts but a nonsensical whole and certainly unable to fly" (ll. 14/15). The comparison to the butterfly allows the readers to vividly imagine the detailed approach that is taken when dealing with Shakespeare in the English classroom. Furthermore, most people probably would not want to dissect a butterfly as the beauty of the creature is slowly destroyed leaving but parts of a dead body. So it can be deduced that they would not want to analyse Shakespeare word by word either. | **language** → figurative speech |
| Powell uses different stylistic devices to stress the effect this approach has on the students. He employs an enumeration to show that students are left feeling "disdain, dislike and hatred" (l. 47) for the poet. Using a contrast he points out that dealing with Shakespeare's plays makes students "feel stupid rather than empowered" (l. 49). Thus, it seems entirely counterproductive to teach Shakespeare at school. | → enumeration, contrast |
| Additionally, the author argues that Shakespeare is only dealt with out of traditions and not out of enthusiasm. To stress this argument Powell employs an allegory in which he calls Shakespeare "[o]ld uncle Bill" (ll. 5/6) and compares him to a relative who we invite "out of habit, not because we actually want to" (ll. 6/7). The reader can easily relate to this situation as it is a typical experience many families share. | → allegory |

Powell argues that the situation gets worse due to recent decisions in educational policy. Dealing with Shakespeare has become obligatory for students "in a specific year group" (l. 24). Powell assumes that many readers might agree with that decision and therefore he anticipates what readers might think and contradicts. "Great, you might say, but it's not" (ll. 24/25). Thus, he can refute possible counterarguments. The problem he perceives is that the status of drama as a subject in its own right has decreased. The word "plummet" (l. 10) emphasises the seriousness of the situation. To make things worse it also becomes harder and harder for teachers to take their students to a theatre because of the "planning and paperwork involved", which he calls "prohibitive" (l. 27). The adjective stresses the hopelessness of the situation. Furthermore, Powell lists numerous other reasons why less and less students come to the theatre (cf. ll. 26–32). On the rare occasion that a group attends a performance, they even risk seeing a poor one. Here Powell uses an enumeration and alliteration to make his point ("brave, boring or bad" (l. 27). The readers readily believe the author as he has first-hand experience (cf. ll. 20–23) and therefore radiates authority. Increasing the importance of Shakespeare for the national curriculum while at the same time weakening drama as a subject in its own right, does not seem to make much sense.

**argumentative technique**

anticipates readers' reaction, refutes counter-arguments

**language**
→ choice of words

lists reasons

→ enumeration, alliteration

**argumentative technique**
→ radiates authority

Finally, the author uses imperatives (cf. l. 50) and an enumeration (cf. l. 52) to summarise his demands in a nutshell. As he does so in the last paragraph of his comment, the readers can easily keep his demands in mind.

**language**
→ imperatives, enumeration

To sum it up, Powell uses the historical perspective, a humorous allegory and his personal experience to support his most important argument for taking Shakespeare out of the classroom: the fact that a play without performance is pointless. *(746 words)*

**conclusion**

3.1 *Start your evaluation by explaining the meaning of the given quotation. Afterwards you need to balance the pros and cons to finally form your own opinion.*
 – *Explanation: Young people do not understand that Shakespeare's plays are still up-to-date.*
 – *Pros:*
   • *Their language is outdated.*
   • *Shakespeare made up new words, which may be difficult to understand.*
   • *Characters and their values are old-fashioned (e. g. role of women)*
 – *Cons:*
   • *Shakespeare's topics are still important, e. g. love, power, jealousy.*
   • *His themes can easily be transferred into our time, e. g.* Romeo and Juliet.

– Conclusion: It depends on how the plays are put on stage, turned into films or discussed in class.

In his article, Mark Powell claims that young people today fail to see that Shakespeare's plays are still up-to-date. According to him, they are bored by the plays because they do not grasp the energy and enthusiasm that are inherent in them. Whereas it is certainly true that it is difficult to fill young people with enthusiasm for Shakespeare, it is not impossible.    **introduction:** reference to article

The major reason why it is hard for young people to accept that Shakespeare's plays are still up-to-date is probably their language. These plays were written about 450 years ago in Elizabethan English and many of their words are outdated like "thee" and "thou". Also, Shakespeare made up many words, some of which have become part of everyday language but sometimes their meaning is difficult to grasp. Therefore, this language is hard to understand for British teenagers and all the more so for students who learn English as a second language. They need to decode the meaning of Shakespeare's words, which often means hard work, before they can grasp the ideas he wants to convey. Some of his characters and their values also seem old-fashioned. Especially the role of women has changed considerably. These days they usually are not dominated by their father or husband.    **main part:** pros

On the other hand, modern theatre productions and films can demonstrate Shakespeare's vitality. As teenagers are more likely to go to the cinema than to the theatre, films are an adequate medium to bring Shakespeare closer to young people. Baz Luhrmann's film adaptation of *Romeo and Juliet*, for example, is set in the present but still uses Shakespeare's words. As these are supported by very powerful pictures, they become understandable.    cons

Moreover, the action of the film is convincing for a young audience. Romeo and Juliet are madly in love with each other and cannot imagine their lives apart. Even though today most young people hopefully would not commit suicide out of lovesickness, they still dream of passionate and overwhelming love. Other plays deal, for instance, with jealousy, hatred or ambition, which are also feelings young people today may easily share.

All in all, to my mind, it is a question of how Shakespeare's plays are put on stage or adapted to film. If these productions manage to convey the impression that the action and the message are still important in today's world, many young people will readily accept Shakespeare's vitality.    *(398 words)*    **conclusion**

3.2 In a letter to the editor you need to refer to the article and express your view on whether Shakespeare should still be taught in school or not. Make sure to state your opinion precisely but briefly. The assignment also requires you to take into account your own experience as a German student. Therefore, you should explain whether you enjoyed dealing with Shakespeare's plays or not and why.
– Name the article you are referring to.
– Express your agreement or disagreement and give reasons for your view. The following example is one advocating the view that Shakespeare's plays should not be taught in English classrooms.
- Agreement:
  - Shakespeare is too difficult; his language and the content of his plays are outdated (give examples of plays you have dealt with).
  - Society has changed since Shakespeare's time (e. g. multiculturalism).
  - Modern authors are more appropriate in a modern world (give examples of novels or plays you have read).
  - In Germany, students who do not choose an advanced English course do not have to read his plays any longer but just deal with film adaptations.

(- Disagreement:
  - Shakespeare is of enormous cultural importance.
  - Characters, conflicts and values are timeless (give examples of plays you have dealt with).
  - Dealing with the poet's works may stir discussion on today's values.
  - You just have to leave room for different interpretations.
  - Film adaptations make the plays interesting and understandable even for German students.)

Selina Mayer — sender's name and address
Schillerstr. 24
50968 Köln
Germany

The Guardian — addressee's name and address
Kings Place
90 York Way
London
N19GU

17 March, 2016 — date

Sir or Madam, — greeting

In his article "Kill Bill: why we must take Shakespeare out of the classroom", the author Mark Powell demands Shakespeare be removed from British classrooms. I as a German student of English share his view whole-heartedly. — **introduction:** reference to article

The language Shakespeare uses is in large parts incomprehensible for young students today, even more so if they learn English as a foreign language. Even though our teacher really tried hard to make us understand Shakespeare's language and to see — **main part:** first argument

19

his wit, I must admit that she failed with me. Despite managing to understand some witty remarks by a character like Beatrice or Benedick in *Much Ado About Nothing*, I did not feel like laughing after all the hard work it took me to understand them.

I think it is also important to acknowledge that society has changed a lot since Shakespeare's time. These days we are much more concerned with multiculturalism and the effect of modern technology and there are contemporary writers who deal with these topics, e. g. Amanda Craig in her novel *Hearts and Minds* or Dave Eggers in his novel *The Circle*. So why should we not rather spend more time on literature that actually concerns us? — second argument

In North Rhine-Westphalia, where I live, the Ministry of Education has taken a step in the right direction. Students who do not choose an advanced English course do not read Shakespeare's plays any longer; they watch film adaptations and discuss these. That way we get some insight into Shakespeare's work but the pictures help a great deal in understanding the message. Maybe the British should also try this approach. — closing paragraph: suggestion

Yours faithfully, — closing
Selina Mayer — name
Cologne, Germany — location

*(294 words)*

**Schriftliche Abiturprüfung NRW – Englisch LK
Leseverstehen und Schreiben – Übungsaufgabe 3**

Aufgabenstellung    criticises    Punkte

1. Point out what Peter Kellner reproaches different parties with in his article (Material A).    12

2. Analyse the campaign poster (Material B) and how it fits Kellner's article.    16

3. Choose one of the following tasks:    14

3.1 Comment on the consequences of Brexit on young people of both sides of the Channel. *(Evaluation: comment)*

3.2 *Refugee Action* is a UK charity which aims at helping refugees and asylum seekers to build new lives in the UK. Write an article as a contribution to its website assessing the importance of learning English to establish a productive life in the UK. Use the campaign poster (Material B) and Zarlasht Halaimzai's example (Material A) as a starting point. *(Evaluation: re-creation of text)*

**Text (Material A):
Peter Kellner, The Other Britain Waiting to Surface**

Dear Europe, don't give up on us. The best of Britain can be found not around Boris Johnson's cabinet table in London but in the hills of Greece; not snarling at France but helping traumatized Afghan families who have reached the European Union to rebuild their lives.

The Refugee Trauma Initiative (RTI), founded six years ago, is one of many British charities making a difference beyond our borders. Quietly, away from the headlines, they demonstrate daily that the cause of deep, committed cooperation with the rest of Europe lives on.

The news agenda is different. It reports battles with the EU on various fronts. The most notable of these just now are with Brussels over the Northern Ireland Protocol – part of the Brexit deal that Johnson signed two years ago but now wants to ditch – and with France over deadly trade in people paying traffickers to make the hazardous journey across the English Channel to Britain in dinghies.

On November 24, 2021, twenty-seven migrants drowned when their dinghy capsized. This should have been a moment when Britain and France came together to solve a political problem that has now become a human tragedy. However, Johnson defied the accepted norms of what to do in situations that call for delicacy and quiet diplomacy. Seeking to make President Emmanuel Macron a scapegoat, he wrote a provocative letter to France's leader and released it in time for the next day's papers. Macron responded by disinviting Priti Patel, Britain's home secretary, to a meeting that had been planned to tackle the crisis.

Across the board, friction is growing between the UK and the continent. There is a reason for this. Five years ago, the UK voted by 52–48 percent to leave the EU. The campaign that achieved this narrow victory was straightforwardly nationalist: "take back control." The message was that Britain was being held back by rules and regulations that stymied the country's economy and prevented it from controlling its borders to keep out immigrants.

The trouble is that the promise of better times has not been kept. Trade with the EU is sharply down. Manufacturers whose exports have to meet EU standards don't want separate UK rules that will complicate what they do and increase their costs. The government's own Office for Budget Responsibility has predicted that Brexit will cost Britain's economy more than COVID-19 and reduce Britain's potential gross domestic product in the long term by 4 percent.

To this catalogue of failure must now be added the disaster of events in the Channel. Brexit was supposed to increase Britain's ability to keep out immigrants. Had the UK remained within the EU, it could have employed systems that were being developed to return people who did not qualify for asylum. This had some chance of deterring people from risking their lives to cross the Channel in the first place. Outside the EU, Britain must negotiate afresh. As we have seen, this is not going well.

Following the tragedy on November 24, 2021, one of the normally loyal and fiercely pro-Brexit Conservative members of parliament, Sir John Hayes, addressed the home secretary: "People who voted to take back control have every right to ask the question: 'If you cannot protect the integrity of the borders, what can you control?'" The minister had no answer.

The Brexit chickens, then, are coming home to roost. There is a fundamental reason for this – indeed, a fundamental reason why the politics of nationalist populism in all countries at all times seldom turn out well. It is that voters are swayed by grievance and the demonization of scapegoats – unwelcome immigrants, greedy bankers, dishonest politicians, interfering foreigners, arrogant elites.

Such campaigns never map out a plausible road to the future once these ne'er-do-wells have been shoved aside. The Leave campaigners conformed to type in the Brexit referendum. They steered well clear of saying what Brexit Britain would be like. It would be a debate they knew they would lose. Events have shown how wise they were.

[…] Johnson's default mode, especially with the EU, is to seek scapegoats rather than solutions. He ignores the old truth that blaming scapegoats is one way to run a campaign, but no way to run a country. While this lasts, the flame of rational, outward-looking patriotism must be kept alight by civil society. Which brings us back to the Refugee Trauma Initiative.

Three years ago I encountered its founder at an event organized by UpRising, a mentoring charity that helps talented youngsters to achieve their potential. Some years earlier, she had served on UpRising's first program. She went on to start RTI in 2016 after working with refugees in Turkey near the Syrian border. In 2018, we celebrated her selection as one of the first group of twenty community rising stars from around the world to be awarded the Obama Foundation Fellowship, established by Michelle and Barack Obama.

Her name is Zarlasht Halaimzai. She is a refugee from Afghanistan. In the mid-1990s, at the age of eleven, she escaped with her family from the Taliban. After four years without a permanent home, she arrived in the UK, speaking no English. She had to race to catch up, and did.

Zarlasht is just one example of the best of today's Britain. Dear Europe, don't give up on us. *(886 words)*

Peter Kellner, *"The Other Britain Waiting to Surface"*.
https://carnegieeurope.eu/strategiceurope/85879, 30. 11. 2021

**Poster (Material B):**

**TURNING WORDS INTO ACTION:**
**WHY THE GOVERNMENT MUST INVEST NOW TO LET REFUGEES LEARN**
**REFUGEE ACTION**

**Our report: Turning Words into Action**

1 The Government does recognise the importance of learning English to refugees, but the resources made available are in stark contrast to ministers' stated ambition that "everyone living in England
5 should be able to speak and understand English."

This report presents the results of a survey of 128 refugees across England. Almost two thirds of respondents told us that they did not think they had received enough ESOL teaching hours.
10 More than three quarters of parents requiring childcare told us that lack of childcare had been a barrier to their ability to attend English lessons.

Two out of every three respondents told us that they are not confident that their current level of
15 English makes them ready to work in the UK.

**Read the report**

https://www.refugee-action.org.uk/let-refugees-learn/

## Lösungsvorschläge

1. *In this task you first need to identify which parties Kellner addresses and then say what he reproaches them with. Note that a party can be a single person or a group of people.*
   - *Boris Johnson ...*
     - *does not stick to a deal made (Northern Ireland Protocol)*
     - *does not adhere to behavioural norms*
     - *makes Macron a scapegoat instead of using diplomacy*
     - *does not offer solutions*
     - *is not capable of running a country (implicit reproach)*
   - *Leave campaigners ...*
     - *resort to a nationalist campaign*
     - *demonize scapegoats*
     - *do not offer visions for the future*

| | |
|---|---|
| In his article "The Other Britain Waiting to Surface" published online on 30 November 2021, Peter Kellner presents the negative consequences of the UK withdrawing from the EU. He reproaches Leave campaigners in general and Boris Johnson in particular with several mistakes made in the process. | introduction |
| According to Kellner, Johnson does not honour a deal made, namely the Northern Ireland Protocol. He blames the Prime Minister for not adhering to behavioural norms when twenty-seven migrants drowned on their way across the Channel. Instead of resorting to quiet diplomacy, Boris Johnson tried to publicly put the blame on French President Macron. In general, he is convinced that Johnson is not capable of running the country because he does not offer any solutions but only looks for scapegoats. | reproaches Johnson |
| Kellner reproaches Leave campaigners with the same tactic. He claims that their campaign was very nationalist as they only demonized scapegoats but did not offer any visions for the future. Thus, they are at least partly to blame for the problems resulting from Brexit. *(170 words)* | reproaches Leave campaigners |

2. *This task is twofold and refers to both materials. First you have to analyse the campaign poster. This includes the analysis of both the visual and the textual elements and their effect on their audience. Once you have shown what the topic and the message are and how they are got across you can relate them to the given article. Show what similarities and differences regarding content there are. Don't forget to prove your point using quotes.*
   *Intention of the poster:*
   - *Raise interest in the report: eye-catching words in bold print*

- *"Turning words into action"* → refers to the saying that actions speak louder than words
- *"words"* are part of a language, which helps refugees to make themselves be heard in a society
- *"Why the government must invest now to let refugees learn"* → demand that government invests in teaching English and promises reasons why this investment is important → draws attention to the report by giving its gist
- *"Refugee Action"* → name of organization publishing the campaign; *"action"* is used again → suggests that this organization really acts and does not only talk

- Convey a positive impression of refugees and migrants
  - Dark hair and eyes, darker skin → supposedly a refugee, person with migrant background
  - Wearing glasses, carrying a backpack (straps are visible) and a notepad → appears to be a student, someone eager to learn
  - Smiling, looking at the viewer → seems to be nice, friendly and open
- Stress importance of mastering English
  - Quote of ministers (Material B, cf. ll. 3–5)
  - Relation between being proficient at English and being able to work established (ibid, cf. ll. 14/15)
- Reproach the government with being all words
  - Headline
  - *"stark contrast"* (ibid, l. 3) between recognising *"the importance of learning English to refugees"* (ibid, ll. 1/2) and spending an appropriate amount of money on that aim
  - Numbers and facts underline the claim (ibid, ll. 6–15).

Relation to the article:
- Similarities:
  - Charity helping refugees; comparable to RTI (Material A, l. 5) → example of *"the other Britain waiting to surface"* (ibid, headline)
  - Kellner uses Zarlasht Halaimzai as an *"example of the best of today's Britain"* (ibid, l. 70) → refugee from Afghanistan
  - Man in the campaign poster could also become such an example
  - Zarlasht Halaimzai didn't speak English (cf. ibid, l. 68) but managed to *"catch up"* (ibid, l. 69) → importance of language proficiency
  - Reproaches towards the government
- Differences:
  - Campaign is about helping refugees across England
  - Article focuses on the negative effects of the UK withdrawing from the EU, e. g. human tragedy of migrants drowning in the Channel

| | |
|---|---|
| The poster published on the website www.refugee-action.org.uk aims at raising interest in the work of the organization Refugee Action, more specifically in their report on the importance of refugees learning English. To do so, it relies on visual and textual elements. Its message can easily be put in relation to the article by Peter Kellner. | **introduction**<br><br><br><br>thesis |
| The campaign poster is divided into two sections. On the left there is a picture with a couple of words written on it. The text accompanying the poster is printed on the right-hand side of the poster. | **main part:**<br>poster, layout |
| The words on the left-hand side are eye-catching because they are printed in big, bold and capitalized letters. On the top it says "TURNING WORDS INTO ACTION", which refers to the saying that actions speak louder than words. But as the entire campaign is about funding language classes for refugees, "words" may here also stand for the language, which allows a person to act more capably in a society. | eye-catching words |
| In the lower left corner, it says, "WHY THE GOVERNMENT MUST INVEST NOW TO LET REFUGEES LEARN", which is a clear demand that the government should invest in teaching refugees English. The phrase also promises reasons why this investment is so important and thus motivates the viewer to read the report, which can be accessed by following a link. | |
| In the lower right-hand corner, the name of the organization behind the campaign is printed. It is "REFUGEE ACTION". Here the word "action" is used again, which suggests that this organization really acts and does not only talk. | |
| Also on the left-hand side, there is the picture of a man in a medium shot. We can see a man with dark hair, beard and eyes, who has dark skin. Thus, it can be assumed that he is one of the refugees the campaign is about. He is wearing glasses and carrying a notepad. One can also see straps, which indicate a backpack. Accordingly, the man seems to be a student, eager to learn. He is smiling and is looking straight at the viewer. As a result, he seems to be nice, friendly and open. All in all, the image conveys a positive impression of refugee seekers. | visual elements |
| The text on the right-hand side stresses the importance of mastering English. First, there is the quote of "ministers" (Material B, l. 3), who are not named but can nevertheless be considered authorities and who demand that "everyone living in England should be able to speak and understand English" (ibid, ll. 4/5). Second, the text establishes a relation between being proficient in English and being able to work in the country (cf. ibid, cf. ll. 14/15). | textual elements<br>quotation of authority |

The organization reproaches the government with being all words (cf. ibid, headlines) as there is "a stark contrast" (ibid, l. 3) between recognising "the importance of learning English to refugees" (ibid, ll. 1/2) and spending an appropriate amount of money on that aim. Numbers and facts given from the report (cf. ibid, cf. ll. 6–15) support that claim by showing what experience refugees have.    numbers, facts

As the campaign is about an organization which helps refugees, it fits Peter Kellner's article. Like the organization RTI (Material A, cf. l. 5), Refugee Action can be seen as an example of "the other Britain waiting to surface" (ibid, headline).    relation article – poster

While Kellner uses Zarlasht Halaimzai, a refugee from Afghanistan who founded RTI, as an "example of the best of today's Britain" (ibid, l. 70), the campaign poster relies on a male refugee, who could probably become such an example as well, if he gets the chance and support. Also, Zarlasht Halaimzai did not speak English when she came to England (cf. ibid, l. 68) but managed to "catch up" (ibid, l. 69). Thus, the importance of language proficiency is another common aspect in both texts as well as reproaches towards the government.    similarities

However, there are also differences. The campaign is about helping refugees across England. The article focuses mainly on the negative effects of the UK withdrawing from the EU. The consequence this withdrawal has for refugees is one important example. The author mentions the "human tragedy" (ibid, l. 16) of migrants drowning in the Channel in an effort to reach the UK.    differences

On the whole, the campaign poster fits the article well because it is another example illustrating Kellner's headline and also reproaches the government with not dealing appropriately with refugees.    conclusion

*(735 words)*

3.1 *This task is only loosely connected to the text. The topic is still the same, but you do not need to refer to the texts at hand. Since you are asked to "comment on" the effects of Brexit you do not necessarily need to weigh the pros and cons. You can also decide to only give arguments regarding the negative (or positive) consequences of Brexit on young people in Britain and on the continent.*
- *Introduction*
  - *Outcome of the vote very narrow: 52% voted to leave, 48% to remain*
  - *Among 18- to 24-year-olds 70% voted to stay*
  - *However, only 64% cast their vote at all*
  - *Thesis: for young people the disadvantages prevail*

- British people lose opportunities and rights associated with EU membership
  - Students can no longer participate in exchange programmes like Erasmus Plus
  - However, Britain has established new one-way programmes, which only British students profit from
  - Lose freedom of movement across Europe
  - Employment rights elsewhere decline → more difficult to gain work experience, e. g. during an internship
- Young people from the EU only lose these rights in Britain, although this still affects them:
  - Youth and educational exchanges are more difficult
  - School groups that include students who are not from the EU now require expensive visas, EU students need full passports, not just identity cards → fewer school groups travel to Britain
  - People from the EU can only stay in Britain for six months without a visa → negative effect on studying and working in Britain as well as on relationships
- Collaboration across the Channel is deteriorating: e. g. regarding business, science or global issues such as climate change
- Conclusion:
  - Summarise your findings; disadvantages prevail
  - Give an outlook for the future: global issues that affect the future of those still young today are better tackled together, e. g. climate change

  or
  - Appeal to readers: young people should vote

In 2016, 52% of the people who cast their vote in the Brexit referendum voted to leave the EU. It was therefore a very narrow result. However, if one looks at the votes by age, the decision was much clearer. Of those aged 18 to 24, 70% voted to stay. Unfortunately, only 64% of that age group cast their vote at all. Despite this, young people now have to live with a result that often has a negative effect on their lives.

**introduction:** background information on Brexit and young people

After the transition period ended in 2021, British people lost all rights of EU membership. This affects young people's studies, their employment opportunities and their freedom of movement, for example. Students can no longer participate in exchange programmes like Erasmus Plus. To soften the blow, however, Britain has established new one-way programmes, which only British students profit from. Nevertheless, the British have lost their freedom of movement across Europe, which makes travelling more complicated. Furthermore, the employment rights for British people in the EU are declining. It has therefore become more difficult to gain work experience, by doing an internship abroad,

negative consequences for British citizens

for instance. International work experience is expected on today's employment market, however.

Whereas British young people have lost those rights in all EU countries, young people from the EU have only lost these rights in Britain. This still affects them to a certain extent, however. Youth and educational exchanges are more difficult, for example. Groups including students who do not have EU citizenship now require expensive visas and EU students need full passports, not just identity cards. As a result, there are now fewer school groups travelling to Britain. In addition, EU citizens can only stay in Britain for six months without a visa. This makes it harder to study and work in Britain, let alone to enter long-term relationships across the Channel. *negative consequences for EU citizens*

In general, it has become more difficult to work together, no matter whether we are talking about business, science or involvement in joint projects. For start-ups in Britain, it has become more difficult to draw on the expertise of people from EU countries, for example. EU grants for research projects are no longer available for British universities, which makes it less attractive for young scientists to work in Britain. Apart from that, the exchange between academics in Britain and the EU is deteriorating. However, there are also global issues like climate change which we need to tackle together. Again, young people are affected for longer and therefore more intensely than older generations, so, they will suffer more as a result of Brexit and its direct and indirect consequences. *negative impact on collaboration*

As one can see, Brexit comes with multiple disadvantages for young people on both sides of the Channel. If there is one lesson to be learned from the referendum leading to Brexit, it is that everyone should exercise their right to vote. Everyone has to live with the decision taken by the majority, so everyone should vote. *conclusion: appeal to young people to vote*

*(495 words)*

3.2 *In this task you need to assess the importance for immigrants to learn English in order to integrate and be able to live a productive life in the UK. The article is to be published on the website of Refugee Action. Therefore, its content needs to fit their aim, which is to promote English classes for refugees. Consider what aspects of daily life can be dealt with more easily if one speaks the language of the host country. Think about work, education, social life, for instance. You are also required to refer to the campaign poster (Material B) and to the example of Zarlasht Halaimzai (Material A). Therefore, you should read the relevant passages again and consider how to use them in your article. Remember to find an appropriate headline for the article.*

- *Material A*
  - *Halaimzai did not speak English when she came to the UK (cf. l. 68)*
  - *Caught up quickly (cf. l. 69)*
  - *Took part in a programme by UpRising, moved on to found a charity herself: RTI (cf. ll. 59–61) → in return helps others to lead a more productive life*
- *Material B*
  - *Promotes the importance of learning English*
  - *Two thirds of the people questioned in the survey "are not confident that their current level of English makes them ready to work in the UK" (ll. 14/15). → most probably will not apply for higher skilled work*
- *Jobs*
  - *Immigrants limited to working in immigrant community or take on lower paid jobs, if they do not speak English well enough*
- *Housing market*
  - *Adverts for houses in English*
  - *Landlords tend to prefer people who speak English.*
  - *Necessity to read and sign contracts*
- *Social life*
  - *Harder to make friends, to join clubs, to integrate and feel at home*
- *Getting things done depends on language skills*
  - *Filling in forms*
  - *Travelling in the country*
- *Conclusion: Both the immigrant and the host community profit, if immigrants learn English*

**Language is the key to a productive life**  | headline

Everybody who has travelled to a country where people speak no or little English has first-hand experience what it means not to be able to communicate with people of the host community. While being on holiday this may be a minor problem or even seem an exciting challenge. However, if one wants to stay in the country, it soon becomes a major problem. Refugees coming to the UK can tell you a thing or two about it. | **opening paragraph:** raise the problem

Without speaking English, it is very difficult to get things done. On arriving in the UK, refugees have a lot of contact with public authorities. They need to fill in innumerable forms. All this is difficult if one does not speak English. Daily life is also difficult, as it is harder to buy tickets for public transport or do the shopping, for example. That's why refugees tend to stay in immigrant communities with others who speak the same language and can help one another. This is something we tend to mistake as proof that immigrants do not want to integrate. | first problem: getting things done

The housing market is another challenge. Obviously, adverts are published in English. Often, landlords prefer people who speak English and then there is the rental contract, of course, which is | second problem: housing hard to read and risky to sign, if one does not understand its content. Again, under these circumstances it makes sense for refugees to stay within their own community.

Finding a job is an important part of leading a productive life. A survey we conducted among 128 refugees shows that two thirds of the participants "are not confident that their current level of English makes them ready to work in the UK." (Material B, ll. 14/15) As a consequence, these people will only take on jobs which do not involve a lot of talking and rely more on using one's hands. However, these are often low-paid jobs and many refugees are learned workers or academics, whose skills could be put to better use in the UK. — third problem: jobs / reference to article

Zarlasht Halaimzai, who came to the UK at the age of 15, did not speak a word of English upon her arrival. However, she worked hard to catch up and has helped other refugees ever since. Her example shows that speaking English helps refugees not only to lead a productive life themselves but to support others to do so as well. Thus, they become successful members of our community. — reference to Zarlasht Halaimzai

Offering language classes to refugees is a major precondition for enabling them to integrate into our society. It is to the advantage of both the refugees and of the host community. There- — **conclusion**

fore, our government must be true to its word and invest in English classes for refugees. *(457 words)* — demand

## Schriftliche Abiturprüfung NRW – Englisch LK
## Leseverstehen und Schreiben – Übungsaufgabe 4

Aufgabenstellung                                                                    Punkte

1. Describe the cartoon and the political issues and views concerning
   democracy presented in both cartoon and speech. *(Comprehension)*               12
2. Examine how these issues and views are presented. Consider the textual
   and visual features of the cartoon and the rhetorical devices of the speech
   as well as the effects created. *(Analysis)*                                    16
3. Choose **one** of the following tasks.                                          14
3.1 Comment on the cartoon. Refer to work done in class on global challenges. *(Evaluation: comment)*
3.2 After you have read Sanders' speech, you write a post to submit to an American quality blog in which you comment on Sanders' view on the threats to democracy in the USA and also refer to the situation in Germany. *(Evaluation: re-creation of text)*

Text:
**Bernie Sanders: 58th Green Foundation Lecture**

*Bernie Sanders is the Senator of the US State of Vermont. In 2015/2016 he initially campaigned to become the Democratic presidential nominee before he withdrew and supported Hillary Clinton against Republican Donald Trump.*

*Bernie Sanders, Westminster College, Missouri, 21 September 2017*

Foreign policy is about whether we continue to champion the values of freedom, democracy and justice, values which have been a beacon of hope for people throughout the world, or whether we support undemocratic, repressive regimes, which torture, jail and deny basic rights to their citizens.

What foreign policy also means is that if we are going to expound the virtues of democracy and justice abroad, and be taken seriously, we need to practice those values here at home. That means continuing the struggle to end racism, sexism, xenophobia and homophobia here in the United States and making it clear that when people in America march on our streets as neo-Nazis or white supremacists, we have no ambiguity in condemning everything they stand for.

There are no two sides on that issue. […]

A great concern that I have today is that many in our country are losing faith in our common future and in our democratic values.

For far too many of our people, here in the United States and people all over the world, the promises of self-government – of government by the people, for the people, and of the people – have not been kept. And people are losing faith.

In the United States and other countries, a majority of people are working longer hours for lower wages than they used to. They see big money buying elections, and they see a political and economic elite growing wealthier, even as their own children's future grows dimmer.

So when we talk about foreign policy, and our belief in democracy, at the very top of our list of concerns is the need to revitalize American democracy to ensure that governmental decisions reflect the interests of a majority of our people, and not just the few – whether that few is Wall Street, the military industrial complex or the fossil fuel industry. We cannot convincingly promote democracy abroad if we do not live it vigorously here at home.

Maybe it's because I come from the small state of Vermont, a state that prides itself on town meetings and grassroots democracy, that I strongly agree with Winston Churchill when he stated his belief that "democracy is the worst form of government, except for all those other forms."

In both Europe and the United States, the international order which the United States helped establish over the past 70 years, one which put great emphasis on democracy and human rights, and promoted greater trade and economic development, is under great strain. Many Europeans are questioning the value of the European Union. Many Americans are questioning the value of the United Nations, of the transatlantic alliance, and other multilateral organizations.

We also see a rise in authoritarianism and right-wing extremism – both domestic and foreign – which further weakens this order by exploiting and amplifying resentments, stoking intolerance and fanning ethnic and racial hatreds among those in our societies who are struggling.

We saw this anti-democratic effort take place in the 2016 election right here in the United States, where we now know that the Russian government was engaged in a massive effort to undermine one of our greatest strengths: The integrity of our elections, and our faith in our own democracy.

[…] Today I say to Mr. Putin: we will not allow you to undermine American democracy or democracies around the world. In fact, our goal is to not only strengthen American democracy, but to work in solidarity with supporters of democracy around the globe, including in Russia. In the struggle of democracy versus authoritarianism, we intend to win. […]

*(594 words)*

*Bernie Sanders: Green Foundation Lecture, 21 Sept 2017 – Westminster College, Fulton, Missouri*

**Annotation**
l. 11 Here Sanders is referring to a protest in Charlottesville in 2017 during which a woman was killed by white supremacists. Trump explained that both sides (left and right) were to blame for the violence.

**Cartoon:**

*Stephen Bolton /cartoonstock.com*

## Lösungsvorschläge

1. *The task involves several steps: Firstly, you need to describe the cartoon in detail and then you need to summarise the message with regard to the issues addressed and the view expressed. Finally, you must point out what issues and views Bernie Sanders presents in his speech given at Westminster College, Missouri.*
   − Description of the cartoon:
     - Title: democracy wear − this northern hemisphere summer
     - In the foreground, a person in protective wear, covered from head to toe
     - Carrying a baton and a gun
     - Textual elements describe the protective wear and its function: baton to encourage democracy, armour to defend it, helmet to protect it, visor to shield against undemocratic things, gun to guarantee democracy
     - In the background, a whole unit of people dressed exactly like the person in the foreground
     - Very dark image
   − The cartoon's message:
     - Democracy is threatened in the entire northern hemisphere
     - It will not be easily protected
   − Issues and views presented in Sanders' speech:
     - Topic: the importance of democracy, freedom and justice
     - Foreign policy implies that the USA promotes freedom, democracy and justice
     - To do so convincingly the USA has to set an example at home → live and act according to these values
     - Democracy is threatened in the USA and in Europe
       ◆ People are disappointed by democratic values
       ◆ Gap between political and economical elite and the people becomes bigger
       ◆ More and more people rely on authoritarian rulers and share view of the extreme right
       ◆ Russian government manipulated the 2016 election
       ◆ Multilateral organizations which value democracy receive less support
     - Sanders promises to work to strengthen democracy around the world

The cartoon, published in 2017, and the speech delivered on 21 September 2017 by Bernie Sanders at Westminster College in Missouri, deal with the question of how democracy can be protected.   *reference to sources / topic*

In the foreground, the cartoon shows a huge person, who is covered from head to toe in protective wear and is carrying a baton in his or her right hand and a gun in the left hand. The protective   *description of cartoon* wear and the weapons, as well as their respective function are described in the textual elements. According to these, the baton is meant to encourage democracy. The armour is used to defend democracy, the helmet to protect it, the visor to shield against undemocratic things and finally the gun to guarantee democracy. The caption above the person describes this protective wear as "democracy wear" in the northern hemisphere that summer. In the background, a whole unit of people dressed exactly like the person in the foreground can be seen. The colours of the cartoon seem to be rather dark and gloomy.

The message of the cartoon seems to be that democracy is under threat in the entire northern half of the Earth and needs to be rigorously protected. <!-- message of cartoon -->

In his speech, Bernie Sanders also addresses the threat under which democracy supposedly finds itself. He, as well, perceives that this threat is present not only in the USA but also in Europe and around the world. According to him, the USA has to promote values like democracy, freedom and justice through its foreign policy. In order to be able to do so convincingly, US Americans have to live up to these values in their own country. However, he criticizes the fact that this is currently not the case because President Trump is ambiguous when it comes to condemning white supremacy and the government as a whole only takes into account the interests of a minority. <!-- issues addressed in the speech -->

Sanders observes that people are disappointed by democratic values because they realize that the gap between the political and economical elite and the people is becoming bigger and bigger. According to him there is an increasing support of authoritarianism and of right wing extremism, not only in the USA but also in other countries. At the same time the support of multilateral organisations is decreasing. Sanders calls the 2016 election anti-democratic because of the influence the Russian government had on the outcome. He believes that all these developments pose a threat to democracy and therefore he promises to work to strengthen democracy in the USA and around the world.

Thus, both materials deal with the threat that democracy is facing and the question of how it can be protected. *(443 words)* <!-- similarities -->

2. *Both the speech and the cartoon deal with the threat that democracy is facing and make suggestions how democracy can be safeguarded. You need to analyse how the cartoonist conveys this threat and what his suggestion is. Therefore, you need to take into account both the textual and visual elements described above. Though Sanders also sees the threat that democracy is facing, his solutions are different.*

*Focus on the rhetorical devices he uses to convey his view. Finally, analyse the effect both the cartoon and the speech have on the audience.*
- The **cartoon** depicts democracy as being threatened.
  - Protection wear becomes democracy wear; to defend democracy one needs to be heavily protected → heavy and maybe even violent struggle
  - Huge soldier and army; dehumanized, like machines → intimidating
  - a whole unit is standing ready behind the huge soldier/policeman → it needs many people to protect democracy
  - Choice of words: to defend, to protect, to shield against → stress the protection that democracy needs
  - Choice of words: guarantee, encourage = positive → convey hope that task can be fulfilled
  - Dark image → threatening atmosphere
- The solution offered is a violent one.
  - Soldiers/police not citizens protect democracy
  - Baton and gun are used instead of words and arguments
  - Solution is paradoxical
- Bernie Sanders stresses the importance of democracy.
  - Enumeration (ll. 1/2) → important values to be promoted
  - Image ("beacon of hope" (l. 2) → importance of these values all over the world
  - Parallel sentence structure (ll. 1–4) → stresses behaviour of undemocratic regimes
  - Quotes Abraham Lincoln (cf. ll. 15/16) → reference to basic and approved value
  - Quotes authority (ll. 29/30) → there is no alternative to democracy
- The US American government needs to set an example at home.
  - Enumeration of attitudes that are undemocratic and need to be fought (ll. 7/8) → shows what needs to be improved in the US
  - Allusion (l. 11) → criticizes President Trump
  - Enumeration (ll. 24/25) → names minority whose influence on domestic policies must be reduced
- Democracy is threatened.
  - Parallelisms (ll. 17/18, 19/20) → difference between the elite and the people
  - Enumeration (ll. 35/36) and parallelism (ll. 34–36) → decreasing support of multilateral organizations apparent in US and Europe, threat to democracy
  - Enumeration (ll. 38/39) → adds further threats to democracy

Both the cartoon and the speech deal with the threat that democracy is facing and both present suggestions how to strengthen and to defend democracy. However, the solutions offered differ strongly. To convey their views the cartoonist relies on visual and textual elements whereas the speaker uses rhetorical devices, mainly enumeration.

**introduction:** reference to task, thesis

The visual and textual elements of the cartoon indicate that democracy is severely threatened. The image, which is dark and gloomy, creates a threatening atmosphere. The huge person dressed in protective wear, supposedly a soldier or a member of a special unit, is intimidating due to its sheer size. This is further supported by the dehumanized appearance of the creatures. What is usually protective wear, and which is used in combat, is called democracy wear in the cartoon. And according to the caption it is employed "in the northern hemisphere [that] summer". This indicates that one needs to be heavily protected to defend democracy, which in itself seems to convey the view that it may be a fierce and even violent struggle to do so. This impression is further stressed by the fact that there is a whole unit standing ready behind the huge soldier. Obviously, a lot of manpower is needed for the task at hand, especially as the threat spreads over the entire northern hemisphere. The viewer appears to be facing this army, which further increases the threatening atmosphere.

*main part: textual and visual features of cartoon, effects*

The choice of words stresses the soldiers' task ("armour to defend", "helmet to protect", "visor to shield against"). All these verbs indicate that democracy needs support. The other two verbs employed are more positive ("baton to encourage", "gun to guarantee democracy"). The last verb in particular expresses some hope that the task can be fulfilled. As a consequence, the size of the soldier can then also be seen as rather reassuring because he should be able to guarantee safety.

*choice of words, effects*

Still, it appears rather paradoxical that soldiers should defend democracy and not citizens who peacefully march in its support. The same is true for the weapons. Words and arguments are usually used to defend democracy, as opposed to soldiers. The cartoonist, however, seems to suggest the need for a violent solution or at least indicates that one should be ready to go to extremes to safeguard democracy. This emphasizes even more how very much endangered it must be.

*message of the cartoon*

Bernie Sanders' focus is slightly different. He stresses more the importance of democracy and shows non-violent ways to protect it because he, too, accepts that democracy is threatened and needs protection.

*transition: message of the speech*

To underline its importance, he employs the word democracy in an enumeration with other indisputably important values, namely "freedom, democracy and justice" (ll. 1/2). Furthermore, the speaker uses a well-known image to stress the far-reaching influence of democracy when he calls the aforementioned values "a beacon of hope" (l. 2).

*rhetorical devices in the speech and their effects*
→ *enumeration*
→ *image*

The parallel sentence structure in this first paragraph and another enumeration also point at the inacceptable behaviour of undemocratic states as they "torture, jail and deny basic rights" (ll. 3/4). Later on, Sanders quotes Abraham Lincoln (cf. ll. 15/16) and Winston Churchill (cf. ll. 29/30) to show that democracy is an approved value to which there is no alternative to democracy. These quotes support Sanders' view and also disarm those who might oppose democracy. → parallelism, enumeration

→ quotes authority

In order to defend democracy, Sanders relies on foreign policy and on positive examples. He demands the USA to "practice those values [...] at home" (ll. 6/7). To prove that there is indeed work to be done, he enumerates attitudes which are undemocratic and need to be fought (cf. ll. 7/8). He also criticizes President Trump when he alludes to the fact that he did not take a clear stand against white supremacists in 2017 (cf. l. 11). He also accuses the Trump administration of not working for the majority of the American people but for the select few, namely for "Wall Street, the military industrial complex or the fossil fuel industry" (ll. 24/25). Thus, at least implicitly, Trump and his administration are presented as enemies to democracy.

→ enumeration

→ allusion

Sanders believes that the people "are losing faith" (l. 12) in democracy. To underline the reasons why that is, he uses two parallelisms emphasizing the difference between the selected few and the majority of the people. The majority "are working longer hours for lower wages" (ll. 17/18) and "see a political and economic elite growing wealthier, even as their own children's future grows dimmer" (ll. 19/20).

→ parallelism

Another threat to democracy, according to Sanders, is the decreasing support of multilateral organizations. The use of parallelism (cf. ll. 34–36) stresses that this tendency can be found in the USA and in Europe which makes it even more dangerous as it is widely spread. Finally, the politician identifies "a rise in authoritarianism and right-wing extremism" (l. 37) as a further threat to democracy and enumerates its consequences (cf. ll. 38/39). Thus, he depicts a negative image of a society which does not defend democracy.

→ parallelism

→ enumeration

All in all, it can be said that both texts point out the danger democracy is facing but in different ways. The cartoonist seems to suggest a violent struggle. Sanders, by contrast, favours a peaceful way and demands the USA to set a positive example. Due to the different genres, the cartoonist relies more on visual elements to convey his message whereas Sanders makes use of rhetorical devices. *(902 words)*

**conclusion**

3.1 *It is your task to express your opinion on the cartoon's message and give arguments to support it. As you are asked to write a comment, you do not have to present the pros and cons but may argue for your view only. However, it is always a good idea to disarm possible counterarguments to be more convincing. The arguments you use need to be based on background knowledge acquired in class on global challenges, here especially on the threat democracy is facing and on possible consequences.*
- *Briefly refer to the cartoon's message as explained above.*
- *Possible arguments*
  - Democracy is under threat
    - Number of people casting their votes is declining
    - Social media, especially bots influence elections
    - Trump is often said to be a threat to democracy
      - He does not reject violence unambiguously
      - He deepens the social divide in the USA
      - He attacks the press
  - Many people inside and outside the USA stand up for their rights.
    - Women's March
    - Arabellion
    - Occupy Camps
- *Conclusion: Partially approve of the cartoon's message.*

The cartoon creates the impression that democracy is heavily under threat in the entire northern hemisphere and that we need to be ready to go to extremes, implying violent measures, to protect democracy. Both aspects need to be considered carefully before coming to a conclusion.

**introduction:** reference to cartoon

The cartoon remains rather vague when it comes to the threats against democracy. It only mentions the need "to shield against undemocratic things". There certainly are numerous reasons why democracy can be considered endangered. For one, the number of people casting their vote in elections is decreasing, especially among young people. Secondly, voters are influenced by social media, especially through social bots, which purposefully spread news, sometimes even fake news, to discredit politicians. These bots are also used from abroad to influence elections in another country. The most prominent example is the presidential election in the USA in 2016. Thirdly, there are politicians in different countries in the northern hemisphere who jeopardize democracy. Trump, for example, does not reject violence unambiguously and does not distance himself unequivocally from right-wing extremists, as could be seen after the tragic incident in Charlottesville in 2017. Furthermore, he attacks the press, which is a vital force in a democratic country. Finally, in some countries, e. g. in Turkey or Poland, leading politicians

**main part:** arguments to support that democracy is in danger

have a strong influence on the legislative or judicial power, which contradicts the separation of powers.

On the other hand, there are people who stand up against this tendency. Shortly after Trump's election, there were women's marches spreading around the globe to promote not only women's rights but also civil rights in general. People marched against nationalism and injustice as well. Also, Occupy Camps can be found in many countries around the globe. Their main aim is to fight economic injustice. These two examples go to show that people are still willing to fight for their rights and thus form a vital part of democracy. They mostly do so peacefully without turning to violent measures. *arguments against the cartoon's call for a violent solution*

I firmly believe that non-violent measures to protect democracy are, in the long run, more efficient than violent measures because violence discredits the fight for democracy. I certainly hope that it will not become necessary to put on combat wear to defend democracy because it would be a contradiction in itself. Thus, I certainly share the cartoonist's view when it comes to the state of democracy in the northern hemisphere but I do not approve of the measures he seems to suggest. *(410 words)* **conclusion**

3.2 *Writing a blog post implies that you make your opinion clear and support it with arguments. In this case you need to comment on the state of democracy in the USA and in Germany. You also need to catch your reader's attention, for example by coming up with a catchy title. A blog is a rather informal text genre. However, here you are writing it for an American quality blog so you should stick to everyday English rather than using colloquial expressions.*
- *Find a title that catches the reader's eye and refers to the content of your blog entry.*
- *Make your main point right at the start.*
  - *Say if you share Sanders' views or not*
  - *Briefly state your view on the situation in Germany*
- *Use the following paragraphs to go into detail, to add background information and to present your arguments.*
  - *Set examples at home*
  - *Both countries face an increase in authoritarianism and right-wing extremism: USA: Charlottesville, Germany: AfD, Pegida*
  - *In both countries the government does not always work for its people: increasing social divide, lobbyism*
  - *In both countries many people are becoming more doubtful of multilateral organizations: USA: NATO, UN; Germany: EU*

- *Foreign policy certainly could help to promote democracy: both countries support undemocratic countries or at least deal with them economically, e. g. China, Saudi Arabia (particularly controversial: selling weapons to undemocratic countries)*
- *Add your name or nickname.*

**Hope for democracy?!**     heading

In his widely received speech on foreign policy, Bernie Sanders draws a bleak picture of democracy. Unfortunately, his view is all too right and not limited to the situation in his home country. Germany is facing a similar situation.     reference to speech, your view on the speech and the situation in Germany

Both the USA and Germany claim that they are trying to promote democracy outside their own territory. It was one of the official reasons for the USA to start a war on Iraq and for German politicians to try to talk some sense into leaders of undemocratic states. However, both countries do not hesitate to deal economically with countries like China or Saudi Arabia. Financial profit seems to be more important than human rights and democracy.     **main part:** first argument

Furthermore, in both countries more and more people are becoming increasingly doubtful of multilateral organizations in which different countries work together democratically. In Germany the government is still mostly very much in favour of the EU. However, smaller parties and especially many people wish to turn their back on the EU and rather follow Britain's example of a Brexit of their own. In the USA, President Trump has repeatedly claimed that the UN and the NATO are useless. He only seems willing to work with them if it is to the USA's advantage, following his slogan "America first."     second argument

Sanders also rightly points out that we need to set an example at home if we truly want to promote democracy. Else we lose credibility. However, both countries face an increase in authoritarianism and right-wing extremism. In Germany the AfD, a right-wing party, has become a member of parliament even though quite a number of its politicians incite violence and even play down the atrocities committed during the Third Reich. In the USA even the president does not distance himself unequivocally from white supremacists. In his speech, Sanders alludes to President Trump's reaction to the incidents in Charlottesville in 2017 when white supremacists killed a demonstrator, but Trump said that both sides were to blame.     third argument

Also, in both countries one can no longer really be sure that the government sees itself as a government for the people. The social divide is getting bigger and bigger and lobbyists seem to     fourth argument have a more important influence on politicians than the people. Thus, firms profit from Trump's tax reform whereas the people will have to pay the bill. While the richest 1 % of German households hold 33 % of the capital, the poorest 50 % only own 2.5 % and most politicians don't seem to be willing to do anything about it.

The only glimmer of hope are manifestations like the Women's March or Pulse of Europe, which prove that there are still some people who are willing to stand up for democracy. If we pin our hopes on them, we should support them – out there in the streets.
*Your (nick)name* *(475 words)*

closing paragraph

nickname

**Schriftliche Abiturprüfung NRW – Englisch LK
Leseverstehen und Schreiben – Übungsaufgabe 5**

Aufgabenstellung                                                                                         Punkte

1. Present the situation of children, especially of Tarrin, as conveyed in the
   excerpt. *(Comprehension)*                                                                                12

2. Illustrate how this excerpt serves to criticise the fictional society depicted.
   *(Analysis)*                                                                                               16

3. Choose **one** of the following tasks.                                                                     14

3.1 Judging from the excerpt, assess whether *The Hunted* might be called a
    dystopian novel. *(Evaluation: comment)*

3.2 As Deet talks about the PP more and more often (cf. l. 59), Tarrin feels it
    is important to make a stand against it. Write the dialogue between Tarrin
    and Deet in which they discuss the advantages and disadvantages of
    having the PP. *(Evaluation: re-creation of text)*

Text:
**Alex Shearer, *The Hunted* (excerpt)**

The Hunted *tells the story of Tarrin, a young boy, who travels with Deet, a grown-up who claims to have won Tarrin in a card game. Deet uses Tarrin to earn money by renting him to people who want to have a child for some hours. As most people in that society are not able to conceive children any longer due to medical measures which allow them to stay young, Tarrin is much in demand.*

1   [...] "Well, I'm away now, kid. You think over what I said to you about the PP implant and you and me being in business together for all our lives. You think about that while I'm out. I'm serious. It's a serious economic proposition. And remember to lock that door." [...]

5   Tarrin looked around the room. It was like every other motel room he had stayed in, and there must have been hundreds of those over the years. It was bland, anonymous and soulless. It was the accommodation equivalent of fast food. It was a burger, that was what it was. It was like living in a burger. He had lived on them and lived in them for years – burger meals, burger rooms. It was a burger room with fries and cola and a
10  spot of salad. Deet was a burger too – a burger person. He was fast food, ready to go.
    A house would have been nice. A real room in a real home. A slow, home-cooked room in a home-cooked home. A fresh-fruit room, a home-baked room. That would have been nice, that would have been wonderful. But all the days of his childhood had gone like this – acting the part, acting the child, one or two hours at a time, a child for
15  the morning, a child for the afternoon, bringing a taste of what it was to have a family to those who had none themselves.

Yet neither did he. That was the irony. Neither did he. He was as lonely as they were. He had nobody either. Just Deet. And sometimes that was worse than nobody. Nobody would have been a much better option.

20   Tarrin sat and opened the geography pack and started to read through it. He was good at geography. He should be. He'd been to enough places. He went over to the keyboard next to the screen and went online. He tested himself on what he had just learned and a "Congratulations! 100 %" message came up, along with some dancing cartoon rabbits, leaping for joy at his success.

25   Then he typed his name in and did a search. But there was nothing. Just as there was always nothing. But what did he really expect? A message saying, "Tarrin – you are our long-lost son. Please contact us at this address so that we can take you home."?

Fat chance. No chance at all.

He thought again of the DNA library. If he could just find the pattern of his own
30 DNA, the fingerprint of his genetic being, and match that against all those in the national register, he might find a near and significant match. And a near and significant match might mean somebody close to him, a blood relative, a member of his own family, a brother, a sister, a father, a mother – anyone.

But he didn't have the pattern of his own DNA, nor the likelihood of finding it. Deet
35 preferred him not to know. All it needed was a blood or a saliva sample and a visit to the lab, but he had neither the money to pay for it nor the means of getting there. Deet watched him like a hawk, and the only times he didn't watch him were like now, when it was dark, and too dangerous to go out – when the Kiddernappers were about. At this time of night most of the DNA labs would be closed anyway, except the late-nite phar-
40 macy place in the centre. [...]

At times he longed for the company of other children more than he even longed to discover some clue to the past. He saw them occasionally, but rarely got near. They mostly passed by in securely locked cars, with a minder sitting next to them or a security guard staring out from the back window.

45   Poor parents, who couldn't afford that kind of protection, instantly fled the city at the first sign of pregnancy, to take up residence in some remote cottage, in a farmhouse or a smallholding, where they could sleep at nights without a gun by the bed and a ferocious watchdog prowling the yard, worrying about an unannounced nocturnal visit from the Kiddernappers.

50   The early months and years of childhood were the worst in terms of risk and vulnerability, for they were also when the child was most valuable. Then the commercial worth of a child steadily diminished with age – just as Tarrin's own value was gradually diminishing – until one day you were grown up.

And then you weren't worth a damn thing to anybody. Unless they were mad
55 enough to love you, of course. Once you had reached the age when you were not a child any more, the Kiddernappers weren't interested.

Tarrin gave up on his Net search and picked up the geography Edu-Pack again, but try as he did to read it, his concentration wavered.

It was the PP. Deet talked about it more and more now, about getting the PP implant.
60   "A few more years, kid, that's maybe all we've got, then nobody's going to want you. You're going to be just one more nobody in a world of nobodies. The world's full

of nobodies, kid, all with faces on them like stopped clocks. Just look around you and see it for yourself. People get to forty and they start to take the Anti-Ageing and then they all look the same – waxworks, kid, frozen smiles, plastic complexions. It's the
65 world's revenge, kid, if you ask me." *(915 words)*

*Excerpt from: Alex Shearer.* The Hunted. *London: Macmillan Children's Books, 2005.*

**Annotations**
l. 1   *PP:* an operation that keeps children from growing up, short for Peter Pan, the boy who always remained a child
l. 38  *Kiddernappers:* They kidnap children to sell them to people who are willing to pay for the child they could never have themselves.
l. 63  *Anti-Ageing:* Anti-Ageing pills suppress all signs of ageing. The people who take the pills will always look the way they did when they started to swallow them.
l. 65  *world's revenge:* Deet refers to the fact that the people in that society grow very old but hardly anyone can conceive children any longer.

## Lösungsvorschläge

1. In this task you have to find and present all the information you get in the extract about the situation of children in general and about Tarrin in particular.
   – Situation of children in general:
     - They are rarely seen.
     - They are valuable and sometimes treated like commercial goods.
     - As such they are worth more the younger they are.
     - Kiddernappers steal children from their families.
     - Only some are really loved (probably by their parents).
     - Parents protect their offspring. → hire minders and security guards or move to remote areas
   – Tarrin's situation:
     - He lives with Deet, whom he does not really like and who does not really care for him.
     - He is hired by people who do not have any children of their own.
     - He lives in motels, moves around a lot and mostly eats fast food.
     - He is ignorant about his past and his family, never meets other children, studies online and is very lonely.
     - Deet wants to persuade him to have an operation that would prevent him from growing up.

In the excerpt from the novel *The Hunted* by Alex Shearer published in 2005, the readers learn about the situation of children in a fictional society. They find out both about the life of a boy called Tarrin and the situation of children in general. **introduction:** reference to source, topic

Children seem to be scarce in that society because they are rarely seen. As most people are unable to conceive children, those who exist are very valuable and are treated like commercial goods by some people. So-called Kiddernappers try to steal them from their families to sell them to rich people who do not have a child of their own. The younger the children, the more valuable they are. **main part:** situation of children in general

Children are only really loved by their parents, who have to protect their offspring from the Kiddernappers. Rich parents hire minders or security guards, other parents move to remote areas where they feel safer.

Tarrin is a child that has apparently been taken from his family so that he does not know anything about his family. He lives with Deet, who rents him by the hour to people who do not have a child of their own. There Tarrin has to act like a child to please those people, but in reality, he is very unhappy with his situation. He and Deet sleep in motels but are often on the move. Tarrin's situation

Tarrin feels lonely because he longs for a real home but is ignorant about his own past, does not get to meet other children, studies online and feels that he would be better off without Deet. Deet also wants to persuade him to have a PP, an operation that would prevent him from growing up, an idea which preoccupies Tarrin.

*(285 words)*

2. *To carry out this assignment you need to analyse what aspects of the future society are criticised in this excerpt. In a second step you need to find and present examples to prove your point.*
   - *Relationships between people:*
     - *Relationships are dehumanised.*
     - *Deet is only interested in Tarrin as a vital part of his business (cf. ll. 1–3).*
     - *He is not interested in his well-being, e. g. he only fulfils his physical needs (food and accommodation), not his emotional needs (cf. ll. 5–19).*
     - *Tarrin is treated like a commercial good but is not allowed to really be a child (cf. ll. 13–16).*
     - *Deet always calls him "kid" (cf. l. 1, 60–65).*
     - *Tarrin is extremely unhappy (cf. ll. 17–19).*
     - *Tarrin does not have any roots, would like to find his real family (cf. ll. 25–33)*
     - *Children are only valuable while they are young, once they grow old, they are worthless because they are not really loved by the people who hire them (cf. ll. 50–55).*
     - *People are lonely (cf. ll. 17/18).*
   - *The way of life:*
     - *Deet and Tarrin live in "soulless" (l. 7) motels.*
     - *Those are in sharp contrast to what Tarrin is longing for. → "a real home" (l. 11)*
     - *They seem to live in a world where illusion is more important than reality. → Deet brings people "a taste" (l. 15) of what it is like to have a child and Tarrin "act[s] the child" (l. 14).*
     - *People who have children of their own need to protect them from Kiddernappers (cf. ll. 42–44).*
   - *People's desire not to grow old/abuse of medical progress:*
     - *Deet tries to convince Tarrin of having the PP but obviously, Tarrin is reluctant (cf. ll. 1–3, 59).*
     - *When people turn 40, they start taking the Anti-Ageing pills but they seem to lose their human features (cf. ll. 63/64). → Deet calls it "the world's revenge" (ll. 64/65). → seen as punishment for their desire to remain young*
     - *They have paid for their eternal youth with their inability to bear children.*

| | |
|---|---|
| The excerpt serves to criticise the fictional society depicted in the novel. This society is above all criticised for the dehumanised relationships between people but also for the life these people lead and for their desire to remain youthful. Tarrin and Deet serve as examples to illustrate the negative traits of the society of the future. Furthermore, Tarrin's thoughts and Deet's observations give additional insight into that society. | **introduction:** thesis, reference to assignment |
| The relationships between people seem to be based on financial benefit rather than personal interest. This becomes evident in the way Deet talks to Tarrin when he tries to persuade him to have the PP implant. He does not consider what implications this operation might have for Tarrin as a human being but only talks about the two of them "being in business together for all [their] lives" (l. 2). This PP is so important to Deet because children are not "worth a damn thing to anybody" (l. 54) once they are grown up. That Deet is not interested in Tarrin as a person is further underlined by the fact that he always calls him "kid" (e. g. ll. 1, 60–65) and never by his proper name. Tarrin is the "kid" that can be rented out for money to earn a living but not someone who is really loved (cf. ll. 54/55). He does not know his real family (cf. ll. 20–28), which leaves him without loving parents and without roots. Unlike loving parents, Deet does not really care for Tarrin, which is further supported by the fact that he does not answer his emotional needs (cf. ll. 17–19) because Tarrin feels lonely even though, or even because of Deet. | **main part:** criticism of the relationships between people → dehumanized → utilitarian |
| Deet and Tarrin lead a very shallow way of life as they move around a lot and live in "bland, anonymous and soulless" (ll. 6/7) motel rooms. From Tarrin's perspective it is an "accommodation equivalent of fast food. [...] It [is] like living in a burger" (ll. 7/8) and worst of all, "Deet [is] a burger too – a burger person" (l. 10). These living conditions are in sharp contrast to what Tarrin dreams of, namely "[a] real room in a real home. A slow, home-cooked room in a home-cooked home" (ll. 11/12). This contrast demonstrates the meaninglessness and hollowness of Tarrin and Deet's life. | criticism of the way of life → shallow, meaningless |
| The society in the novel is also criticised for the life its people in general lead. To them illusion seems to be more important than reality because they hire children like Tarrin to bring them "a taste" (l. 15) of what it would be like to have a child and Tarrin has to "[act] the child" (l. 14) although he knows perfectly well that it is only business. Ironically, childhood is precious but cannot be savoured by the children themselves because they are either hired out (cf. ll. 13–16) or massively protected by their families from Kiddernappers (cf. ll. 42–44) so that they | → illusion instead of reality |

49

can never simply meet at a playground, or do what children normally do. As a consequence, both children and grown-ups are lonely (cf. ll. 17/18).

Finally, the people in the novel are criticised for their desire not to grow old which is closely linked to a thoughtless use of medical progress. Deet's attempt to convince Tarrin to have the PP implant without considering the implications this has for Tarrin has been mentioned above. While this procedure seems to be adopted less often, the Anti-Ageing pills are obviously widely used despite their negative side effects. Deet observes that "[p]eople get to forty and they start to take the Anti-Ageing and then they all look the same – waxworks, [...] frozen smiles, plastic complexions" (ll. 63/64). As a consequence, this future society is "full of nobodies, [...] all with faces on them like stopped clocks" (ll. 61/62). Thus, people are exchangeable and seem to slowly lose their human features.

*criticism of attitude to age, abuse of medical progress*

→ *dehumanized society*

Altogether, the society of the future is depicted as very inhumane as the relationships between people are mostly utilitarian and people's faces are also devoid of human traits. Although they have achieved their dream of eternal youth, people are dissatisfied because they cannot conceive children any longer and are lonely.

*conclusion*

*(703 words)*

3.1 *Here you need to explain what characterises a dystopian novel and present arguments for and against this novel being dystopian. Obviously, you need to back up your arguments by referring to the excerpt. After having weighed the pros and cons, you need to express your opinion on the question under discussion.*
  – Dystopian novels ...
    • *present pessimistic views of the future.*
    • *usually warn against inhumane totalitarian states that oppress their citizens (e. g. Huxley's* Brave New World, *Orwell's* Nineteen Eighty-Four*).*
    • *portray alternative societies which implicitly criticise present societies.*
  – Arguments against the novel The Hunted *being a dystopian one:*
    • *The government is not presented but the excerpt focuses purely on human relationships.*
    • *There is no totalitarian state or dictator trying to manipulate citizens.*
  – *Arguments for the novel being a dystopian one:*
    • *Present trends are exaggerated and turned negative.*
    • *Medical progress makes eternal youth possible, but also leads to infertility.*
    • *Though people grow very old, they are also very unhappy.*
    • *Human relationships are devoid of emotions but based on financial benefit.*
    • *People have a shallow way of life.* → *Illusion is more important than reality.*

Dystopian novels in the sense of Aldous Huxley's *Brave New World* or George Orwell's *Nineteen Eighty-Four* are novels which present very pessimistic views of the future. In particular, the two novels cited are used to warn readers against inhuman totalitarian states that oppress their citizens. To do so, the authors develop contemporary trends, for instance mass media or medical progress, further to show what negative consequences they might have in the future. Thus, present societies are implicitly criticised. Alex Shearer also presents a future society in his novel *The Hunted* which leaves the reader with a very negative impression. Does that mean it is a dystopian novel?

The most important argument against *The Hunted* being a dystopian novel is the absence of a political message. Judging from the given excerpt, the government of the future society does not play an important role. The citizens are not manipulated or oppressed by a totalitarian state or a dictator but have brought their fate upon themselves by pursuing eternal youth.

However, the future society depicted in the excerpt is described as very inhumane. Relationships are superficial and the two main characters Tarrin and Deet are only linked by Deet's business interest in Tarrin. As most people in that future world are infertile, the few children that exist are in high demand. Childless people rent children like Tarrin to spend some hours with them. This shows how superficial and shallow relations have become. While the criticism of the future in the novel is very clear, it is more difficult to see what trends in *our* society the novel is aiming at. At first, one might think of the negative influence of social networks. However, the change in relationships in the novel is a result of medical progress.

The effect medical progress might have in the future is illustrated very well in the excerpt. Man's dream of eternal youth seems to have finally come true. At the age of forty, the people in the novel "start to take the Anti-Ageing" (l. 63) and their complexions do not change any longer. That way they appear to be young even when they have grown old but they also look like "waxworks [with] frozen smiles [and] plastic complexions" (l. 64). Children can get a PP implant, which keeps them from growing up. Here, today's obsession with youth is clearly criticised. People take all kinds of pills and injections to keep their youthful appearance and many people have plastic surgery to live up to beauty ideals.

---

characteristics of dystopian novels

introduction of discussion

main part: cons
→ no political message

pros
→ inhumane society

→ criticism of the future

→ medical progress turned negative

In the novel, the biggest side effect of this medical progress is, however, that people cannot conceive children any longer, which leads to the degradation of children as commercial goods. The author might be critical of the fact that in many Western societies there has been a significant decrease in childbirth. Primarily, this comparison seems flawed because the reason for this decrease is different. People are not infertile but tend to put their career and hobbies before children and, therefore, remain childless willingly, while they have lost the physical ability to have children in the novel. Still one can draw a parallel as children like Tarrin have become a "hobby" in *The Hunted*. People can rent them for a few hours only and the responsibilities that usually come with having a child no longer play a role for them. Still, the novel shows the reader what life would be like if children became a curiosity – their increased worth, as children seem to be of financial value, but also the loss of humanity as a world without children becomes loveless and lonely. → loss of humanity, utilitarian attitude towards children

Although the novel *The Hunted* is not in line with *Brave New World*, *Nineteen Eighty-Four* or more recent dystopian novels like *The Hunger Games*, which bear a political message, it clearly can be called dystopian. Sometimes the readers might have to look twice to see what trends in our present society are criticised, but if they do so, they see the criticism of today's youth mania and the egocentric lives many people lead.   *(672 words)* conclusion: novel can be called dystopian

3.2 *Before you start writing your dialogue, you need to consider the character traits and views of Deet and Tarrin carefully. You should also take into account how they might talk to each other. While the excerpt gives you quite a good idea of Deet and the way he speaks, Tarrin does not say a word. However, you learn a lot about his thoughts and feelings. From these, you can deduce how Tarrin will talk to Deet. You also need to collect arguments for and against the PP. Again, the excerpt gives more information on Deet's view, whereas you must make up the arguments Tarrin might come up with on the basis of the excerpt.*
 – *Deet:*
   • *He talks about the PP more and more often.* → *He will probably start the conversation.*
   • *He calls Tarrin "kid".*
   • *He speaks standard English.*
   • *He needs Tarrin to have the PP, or else he will be out of business.*
   • *He will, therefore, try to calm Tarrin and describe the PP and its effects in a very positive light, e. g. ...*
     ✦ *the procedure will not hurt,*
     ✦ *he will never have to look after himself because Deet will care for him,*
     ✦ *they have a profitable business and do not have to work hard,*

52

- *the people who rent Tarrin treat him very well,*
  - *as long as they are in business, they do not need to worry about money, food, etc.*
- He might be surprised or even angry when he learns that Tarrin is not satisfied with the life they lead.
- He might put his foot down or postpone the decision.

– Tarrin:
- On the one hand, Tarrin seems very shy and withdrawn as he does not talk in the given excerpt, so he will probably remain polite and try not to annoy Deet.
- On the other hand, he does not want the PP and must not back off too easily.
- Judging from the passages that are told from Tarrin's point of view, he seems to be a very thoughtful person. → He will try to convince Deet by reasoning with him.
- He will probably speak standard English.
- As he is not fond of Deet, he will probably call him by his name and not a nickname.
- He might suggest a new way for Deet to earn a living.
- Possible arguments:
  - *He does not want to be a child forever.*
  - *No one will take him seriously although he will have a lot of experience.*
  - *He does not like their business because it is all a pretence.*
  - *He never gets to meet people his own age.*
  - *He wants to be independent.*
  - *He wants to settle down and is fed up with motels and fast food.*
  - *He might worry that his complexion will also look frozen (just like the people who have taken the Anti-Ageing pills).*
- He might either give up and try again later to convince Deet, or become emotional.

DEET: Listen, kid, I've been thinking about that PP and I think it is time to have it done before you get too old. — Deet presents his idea

TARRIN: But, Deet, … — Tarrin: shy

DEET: You know, kid, people want to rent a child not a teenager or grown-up, so we must not wait any longer.

TARRIN: I don't want this PP, Deet.

DEET: What do you mean, you don't want it? We're going to run out of business if you grow any older, and then what? — Deet: business-oriented

TARRIN: I thought, we might find another business. Maybe …

DEET: Another business? Do you know what you're talking about? We've got a great business. You get to spend time each day with nice people who are really fond of you and treat you very kindly. — Deet: dominant

TARRIN: But they don't love me. It is all so superficial. I don't want to lead this fast food life any longer. — reference to excerpt

53

DEET: Fast food life? What on earth are you talking about, kid?
TARRIN: Just look at us. We live in motel rooms and move around so much.
DEET: I thought you liked that.
TARRIN: No, Deet, I don't. I want a real home and home-cooked meals.
DEET: Wake up, kid, you're dreaming. In real life you need to pay for all this.
TARRIN: You could earn the money and I could take care of the house. And when I'm older, I'll also find a job.    *Tarrin tries to argue*
DEET: I can't believe we're even having this discussion. You know, I won you in a card game. You're mine and I want you to have this PP.    *Deet: dominant*
TARRIN: But, Deet, I want to grow up. I don't want to be a child forever. If I don't grow up, no one will take me seriously, not even in thirty years, despite all the experience I'll have gathered by then. Don't you see?
DEET: No, you don't see, kid. You've got what most people want and you're throwing it away because you want a "home-cooked meal". Now listen, we don't have to move around so much. If we go to bigger cities, we'll have more clients and might even rent an apartment and cook our own meals. What about that?    *Deet suggest compromise*
TARRIN: Deet, we don't even know what this PP will do to me. You know how people look when they start taking the Anti-Ageing pill. You said so yourself, they all look the same, waxworks. I don't want a frozen smile and I'm sure our clients don't want a child with a frozen smile either. Why don't we stay in business as long as we can and save some money. Then we could start our own business. Maybe open a small shop or something.    *reference to excerpt*
DEET: Now, don't you start all over again. I'm not discussing this any longer. I'll get an appointment for you and you'll have the PP and that's the end of it.    *Deet ends discussion*
TARRIN: But …
DEET: No more buts. I'm going out. I need a drink. Lock that door when I'm out because if the Kiddernappers get you, they won't be as nice to you as I am.
*(Deet leaves the room, slamming the door.)*    *(499 words)*

## Schriftliche Abiturprüfung NRW – Englisch LK
## Leseverstehen und Schreiben – Übungsaufgabe 6

Aufgabenstellung  Punkte

1. Describe what event led to the increased media attention in north-east Nigeria and how the region is depicted in the media including the effects of this depiction according to Chitra Nagarajan. *(Comprehension)*  12

2. Analyse how the writer brings across her view on the journalists' work and on the way women in north-east Nigeria are depicted in the media. Focus on communicative strategies and the use of language. *(Analysis)*  16

3. Choose **one** of the following tasks.  14

3.1 Comment on the present situation of girls and women in Nigeria. Refer to the text at hand and to work done in class. *(Evaluation: comment)*

3.2 Chitra Nagarajan, who lives in Maiduguri in northeast Nigeria, has been interviewed for the Guardian Newspaper Nigeria on her work on peace-building and human rights. Write the interview.
*(Evaluation: re-creation of text)*

**Text:**
**Focusing on schoolgirl abductions distorts the view of life in Nigeria**
*It is simplistic to imply that all victims are female or that women are not active agents in domestic and community life*

@chitranagarajan
*Fri 2 Mar 2018 08.00 GMT Last modified on Fri 2 Mar 2018 14.18 GMT*

1 Once again, abducted Nigerian schoolgirls are making international headlines. Last Monday, 110 girls were taken from the Government Girls Science and Technical School in the town of Dapchi in Nigeria's north-eastern Yobe state. Fighters belonging to one of the armed opposition groups (commonly known as Boko Haram) operating
5 in the area attacked the town and took the girls who were unable to escape.
   The attack came shortly after the military withdrew troops from the town. Then came a pattern that is familiar to anyone following events in north-east Nigeria, where the abduction of girls from Chibok in April 2014 brought the region to national and global attention. First, there was silence from government officials, followed by dispu-
10 tes in the media about the number of girls missing. Then an announcement that girls had been rescued by the army, which was later retracted.
   The abductions from Chibok were neither the first nor the last in north-east Nigeria (at least 2,000 women and girls were kidnapped between January 2014 to April 2015, and large numbers of men and boys have also been taken). But, the Chibok case cap-
15 tured international imagination. This focus on abductions shows the kinds of stories

that media pick up, but it also means we have a partial picture of what is actually going on.

Yes, this was greatly due to the hard work of women's activists in Maiduguri and the phenomenon that was #BringBackOurGirls. It also made a compelling media story and offered the chance for those involved – from journalists to those who tweeted using the hashtag – to take action and feel good about themselves. Those of us working in north-east Nigeria at the time were at the epicentre of an international media circus. Hordes of journalists descended on Abuja, Maiduguri and Chibok, asking the same questions of the same people, often retraumatising family members of the abducted girls in the process.

That, almost four years later, we see them in one of the first scenes of *Black Panther*, the global cultural phenomenon of 2018 so far is telling; Nakia, an intelligence officer played by Lupita Nyong is seen undercover in north-east Nigeria's Sambisa Forest with dozens of girls being transported by armed fighters. It was the obvious choice for film-makers looking for something topical about the African continent that could symbolise the nascent Wakandan saviour complex – in contrast to the reality of women's activism in north-east Nigeria. All we know or care about when it comes to north-east Nigeria seems to be either abducted schoolgirls or female "suicide bombers".

This level of attention has resulted in differential treatment for those abducted from Chibok compared with everyone else, with high-level negotiations conducted to free them. Every time abducted women and girls are released, the first question asked is whether Chibok girls are among them.

Of course we should care about and campaign for action to be taken when it comes to the girls of Dapchi. However, what happened around the Chibok abductions serves as a salutary warning of how media coverage can inadvertently lead to a hierarchy of humanity – some people being valued above others.

I have been working on peacebuilding and human rights in north-east Nigeria for almost five years. Last year, I spent weeks interviewing women and men for a gender assessment of the region. I found stories of women and girls choosing to join armed opposition groups. They have taken part in attacks on villages and towns, recruited members, made bombs and recruited others. Women and girls have also been part of militias set up to protect communities. They screen women and girls at checkpoints, fight alongside the men, patrol towns and villages and, in some cases, command groups of fighters, including men. Moreover, women have saved men from being killed, in many cases hiding them in their homes, dressing them in women's clothing and smuggling them to safety.

Indeed, men "of fighting age" – roughly 14 to 50 – are often the first to be killed or detained, leaving women to take on new roles and decision-making power. Even if husbands and fathers are present, men are no longer able to provide for families, meaning women have to find ways of earning incomes, including through "survival sex". In some cases, this changed dynamic has caused problems in households where men, fearing a loss to their power, try to prove they are the ones still in charge. In other cases, women say they have more power at home and their husbands have to adjust. After all, if he divorces her to marry another, the dynamics with the new wife will be the same.

Of course, women suffer greatly during conflict. They are displaced, disabled, killed, lose family and friends, and experience higher levels of gender-based violence. But they are not just victims. Conflict is also a time where women have greater agency – whether they want it or not. This focus on women as victims also means we lose sight of what happens to men and boys. We all know about the Chibok girls but how many of us know about the Buni Yadi boys? A few weeks before the abductions from Chibok, an estimated 59 boys were lined up in the Federal Government College in Buni Yadi, had knives drawn across their throat, were gunned down or burned alive. Seeing only women and girls as victims plays into gendered stereotypes that we must move away from. It also presents a highly distorted version of reality. *(907 words)*

*Chitra Nagarajan: Focusing on schoolgirl abductions distorts the view of life in Nigeria, 2. 3. 2018, https://www.theguardian.com/commentisfree/2018/mar/02/nigeria-boko-haram-abductions-chitra-nagarajan, Copyright Guardian News & Media Ltd 2019*

**Annotations**
l. 26 *Black Panther:* An American superhero film released in 2018 and produced by Marvel Studios, starring mostly Black actors and actresses.
l. 28 *Lupita Nyong:* A Kenyan-Mexican actress who stars in the film *Black Panther*.
l. 31 *Wakanda* is a fictional country created by Marvel Comics and located in Africa.
The film *Black Panther* is set in Wakanda.

## Lösungsvorschläge

1. *This task is threefold. First you need to describe what happened in north-east Nigeria to make the media become involved. Then you need to extract what Nagarajan says about the way north-east Nigeria is depicted in the media, which involves both news stories as well as film. Finally, you are required to state what effects this depiction has according to the author. The following aspects should be included:*
   - *Initial event*
     - *Abduction of girls*
     - *April 2014*
     - *Chibok, north-east Nigeria*
     - *Women's activists created Twitter hashtag*
   - *Depiction in the media*
     - *Focus on abduction of girls*
     - *Misleading information, disputable number of victims, false announcements of their rescue*
     - *In a film, girls in the region are shown to be rescued*
   - *Effects*
     - *Region is brought to national and global attention*
     - *Evokes a certain kind of picture, which is incomplete*
     - *Creates a media circus in the area, retraumatising family members of the abducted girls due to repeated interviews*
     - *Focus is on abducted schoolgirls or female suicide bombers*
     - *Higher focus on that particular group of abducted girls → hierarchy of humanity*
     - *Focus on women as victims → reinforces gender stereotypes*

The article "Focusing on schoolgirl abductions distorts the view of life in Nigeria" by Chitra Nagarajan and published on 2 March 2018 is about the abduction of a group of schoolgirls and the resulting media attention as well as the effect of that attention.     **introduction:** reference to source, topic

The initial event happened in April 2014 when a group of girls were abducted from Chibok in north-east Nigeria and a group of women's activists started a Twitter hashtag to save the girls.     **main part:** initial event

As a result, this region caught the increased attention of international media, which focused on the abduction of the girls. The information spread in the media was partly misleading as the number of victims first was not clear and as announcements of their rescue were premature. Four years later the event is used in the Marvel film *Black Panther* showing some girls being rescued, which illustrates the distorted picture of this region.     depiction in the media

As a consequence, the region became known nationwide but also globally. Families of the victims were interviewed several times     effects

by different journalist, which kept them traumatised as they are reminded of the events time and again. Additionally, the image of north-east Nigeria created in the media is incomplete as the focus is solely on one group of abducted girls. This, according to the author, leads to the neglect of other victims, for instance boys who were not only abducted but brutally killed. Moreover, it reinforces gender stereotypes as girls and women are merely seen as victims although they are also active members of society.
*(254 words)*

2. *In this task you need to analyse how the depiction of north-east Nigeria in the media is judged by the author of the article at hand. You are meant to look at the way she perceives the journalists' work and the way women are depicted. Note that here the focus is not on media in general but on journalists only. Take into account communicative strategies, such as relating personal experience, as well as language, for instance choice of words and stylistic devices.*
   – *Journalists act irresponsibly (choice of words)*
     • *Follow a "compelling media story" (l. 19) → cannot resist*
     • *"feel good about themselves" (l. 21) by taking action → implies that it is about themselves not about the victims*
     • *"descend" in "hordes" (l. 23) on towns involved → large numbers, cause harm*
     • *"media circus" (l. 22) → not serious*
     • *"epicentre" (l. 22): usually connected to earthquake → negative impact*
     • *"retraumatising" (l. 24) families → act irresponsibly, cause harm → feel pity for families*
     • *Offer highly distorted view (cf. headline and last line of the text)*
     • *Simplify reality (cf. subheading)*
   – *Everybody is influenced by media and media determine our view on the world*
     • *Use of the pronouns "we" (ll. 64/65) and "us" (l. 66)*
     • *Question (ll. 65/66) to draw attention to information readers probably do not have*
     • *Example of pieces of information readers do not have (cf. ll. 66–68)*
     • *Underlines her first-hand experience → more accurate information and picture*
     • *Use of the first-person singular pronoun "I", (e. g. ll. 42–44)*
     • *Enumerates personal involvement (ll. 42–44)*
     • *Present at the "epicentre" (ll. 21/22)*
   – *Broadens picture of women's situation*
     • *Women are active in the situation (cf. ll. 45–51) (enumerations)*
     • *Women are victimised in several ways (cf. ll. 61–62) (enumerations)*
     • *"but" (l. 62) indicates that there is more to it*
     • *Indicates numbers to show the extent of the problem (cf. ll. 13/14)*

The author of the article has a negative opinion about the journalists' work in north-east Nigeria because the image conveyed of women in that region is incomplete. Nagarajan employs communicative strategies and language both to convey her criticism and to complete the picture according to her view.

**introduction:**
thesis / reference to assignment

The journalists reporting on the abduction of girls in north-east Nigeria seem to be unreliable and to act irresponsibly. Instead of offering a realistic image and relaying correct information there are "disputes in the media about the numbers of girls missing" (ll. 9/10). Right in the headline the author reproaches the journalists with "distort[ing] the view of life in Nigeria" and giving a "simplistic" (subheading) account of a complex reality. The choice of words makes it clear that the journalists do not do their job properly. They cannot resist a "compelling media story" (l. 19) and seem to care more about themselves than about the girls abducted because their reports make them "feel good about themselves" (l. 21). This impression of journalists simply being keen on a good story is further stressed by the use of the expression "media circus" (l. 22).

**main part:**

**communicative strategies**
→ headline, subheading

**language**
→ choice of words

Furthermore, the journalists have a negative impact on the region as they "descen[d]" in "hordes" (l. 23) and "retraumati[se]" (l. 24) the victims' families with their repeated questions. They create an "epicentre" (l. 22), a word usually connected with an earthquake and thereby with a harmful effect. All these words connected with journalists have a negative connotation and thus stress the author's unfavourable view on their work.

→ choice of words, negative connotation

This criticism is all the more significant as Nagarajan claims that everybody is influenced by the media and that the media determine our view on the world and the information we obtain. To stress this point, she uses the pronouns "we" (ll. 64/65) and "us" (l. 66) to show that this concerns everyone. She also raises a question (cf. ll. 65/66) to make the reader realize that they cannot answer that question because the media only offer parts of reality. She then gives an example of pieces of information needed (cf. ll. 66–68) to complete the picture of the situation in north-east Nigeria.

**communicative strategies**

→ pronouns

→ question

→ example

To indicate that she is trustworthy, the journalist stresses that she has got first-hand experience. To do so, she repeatedly uses the first-person singular pronoun "I" (e. g. ll. 42–44) and enumerates the incidents of her personal involvement. She also mentions the amount of time she has spent in the region (cf. ll. 42/43) to further emphasize her thorough knowledge of the

author is trustworthy
→ use of pronoun

situation. She was also at Chibok (cf. ll. 21/22) when the journalists worked there and thus her judgement of their work seems reliable, too.

Furthermore, she mentions numbers (cf. ll. 13/14) to show that her judgement is based on facts. → numbers

Nagarajan uses her insight to broaden the picture of the women's situation in north-east Nigeria. She uses enumerations to show that they are not only victims but active members in the conflict (cf. ll. 45–51). Women "have taken part in attacks on villages and towns, recruited members, made bombs and recruited others" (ll. 45/46). She also enumerates the many ways in which women are victimised. "They are displaced, disabled, killed, lose family and friends, and experience higher levels of gender-based violence" (ll. 61/62). The use of the conjunction "[b]ut" immediately after that enumeration stresses, however, that women "are not just victims" (l. 63). → enumerations

→ conjunction "but"

All in all, it becomes clear that the author has a very negative view on the journalists' work in north-east Nigeria, which is mostly conveyed by her choice of words. Using many enumerations, she presents a different perspective on the situation of women to prove that the journalists' depiction is incomplete and stresses her first-hand knowledge of the situation. *(627 words)* **conclusion**

3.1 *Here you need to express your own view on the situation of girls and women in contemporary Nigeria. Whenever possible, you should support your view by mentioning facts or examples. The text at hand offers some ideas but you should also refer to your background knowledge. Note that the text deals with the situation in northeast Nigeria only. If possible, add some information on other parts of the country.*

– *Aspects mentioned in the excerpt referring to north-east Nigeria*
- *Girls and women become victims of Boko Haram related violence (cf. ll. 1–5)*
- *"at least 2000 women and girls kidnapped between January 2014 to April 2015" (l. 13)*
- *Women's activists use hashtag (#BringBackOurGirls) to help girls abducted from Chibok (cf. ll. 18–21)* → *women use the resources at hand*
- *Women are also used as suicide bombers (cf. l. 33), "[take] part in attacks" (l. 45), protect men (cf. ll. 49–51)* → *take active part in the conflict either forced or willingly*
- *Replace men and take over their role, e. g. "decision-making power" (l. 53), earn income (cf. l. 55)*
- → *Girls and women are not only victims but take action themselves*
- → *Not only women but also boys and men suffer from the conflict*

– *Possible further aspects*

61

- *Situation differs a lot depending on religious and regional factors*
- *According to Islamic norms women in the north are often confined to the house*
- *Situation for women in the south better, especially concerning education*
- *Primary education is free and compulsory but especially in the north girls are kept from school or attend Islamic schools which often do not teach them to read and to calculate*
- *More educated women emerge from the education system*
- *Throughout the whole country child marriage is a problem, almost half of the women are married before they turn 18*
- *Average number of births per woman is five; women suffer health issues related to giving birth, high maternal mortality rate*
- *Female genital mutilation is still taking place, although forbidden by law since 2015*
- *Nigeria scores very low in the global Gender Gap Index*
- *Attention is drawn to the situation, e. g. through literature*
- *Hashtag #BeingFemaleInNigeria makes sexism women face public*
- *Documentary on Aisha, a young woman hunting Boko Haram*

As the situation of girls and women in Nigeria differs a lot depending on regional and religious factors, it is very complex and therefore difficult to assess. However, it can be said that, in general, life in Nigeria is not easy for women and girls. **introduction**

The article at hand focuses on the situation of women in northeast Nigeria, a region dominated by the Boko Haram conflict. To the author it seems very important to point out that girls and women do not only become victims but also take actions themselves. Taking a closer look at the examples she mentions, it becomes obvious, however, that none of the roles women can take in the conflict is desirable. The conflict definitely has a very negative impact on their lives. Often, they become victims of Boko Haram related violence (cf. ll. 1–5) and "at least 2000 women and girls [were] kidnapped between January 2014 to April 2015" (l. 13). Some women also become active parts in the conflict, e. g. as suicide bombers (cf. l. 33), or by protecting men from being killed (cf. ll. 49–51). They also replace men, who increasingly are absent from their homes due to the conflict. Thus, women take over "decision-making power" (l. 53) or provide their family with an income (cf. l. 55), e. g. through "survival sex" (l. 55). This last example points out very forcefully that the choice is one between bad or worse. In class we saw a documentary about a young Boko Haram huntress called Aisha. The documentary portrays her as a very brave, proud and highly regarded woman. Still, she risks her life every day, which is not a desirable way to live one's life. **main part: situation in north-east Nigeria, reference to article**

**first argument**

**women as victims**

**women in active roles**

Another important aspect, which the article does not mention, is education. Education usually is a way to improve one's chances in life and although primary education is supposed to be free and compulsory in Nigeria many girls do not attend school. In the north, which is mostly ruled by Islamic norms, girls attend school less often than in the south. If they attend school, these are often Islamic ones, which usually do not teach them to read, write and do Maths. This shows that the Nigerian state is trying to improve the situation of girls and women but often still fails. **second argument** education

Also, their role as wives, daughters and mothers endangers women in Nigeria. Child marriage is still a problem and almost half of the girls and young women are married before they turn 18. As a result, they bear many children, five on average, but they suffer many health issues surrounding birth with a high maternal mortality rate. The fact that female genital mutilation still occurs far too often adds to female health issues. All these facts point out that women, just for being females, are put under enormous pressure and often do not have a say over their own body. **third argument** child marriage / health issues / female genital mutilation

But of course, Nagarajan is right in stressing that there are also other examples. There are examples showing that the situation of women in Nigeria is improving. There are well-known female authors who draw attention to the situation. For example, there is a hashtag making public the sexism women face in their workplace, public places and at home. Women's rights activists have quite successfully campaigned against female genital mutilation. As a result, it became unlawful in 2015, which unfortunately does not mean that it does not take place any longer. This shows that progress is slow but possible. **transition / fourth argument**

Despite this slow progress, the facts and examples provided show very clearly that it is not easy to be a girl or a woman in Nigeria. Men and women alike face multiple dangers and hardships. But the fact that Nigeria scores very low in the global Gender Gap Index makes it clear that the situation for women is still worse. **conclusion**

*(641 words)*

3.2 *In this task you need to write an interview for the Guardian Newspaper Nigeria with the author of the article at hand. The focus is on her work on peacebuilding and human rights. The article will give you some ideas what questions you could ask and what Nagarajan might answer. Additionally, you can invent some information as long as it is reasonable and fits the impression we have got from the article at hand. Make sure to use your own words. As the interview is for a quality newspaper the language will be rather formal. It also needs a headline and a short introduction.*

*– Headline*
*– Introduction, e. g. where the interview takes place and why, Nagarajan's occupation, etc.*
*– Information from the article*
  *• Works on peacebuilding and human rights in north-east Nigeria (ll. 42/43)*
  *• Spent time interviewing women and men for a gender assessment of the region (cf. ll. 43–60)*
  *• Does not see women solely as victims*
  *• Conflict offers new possibilities for women*
  *• Her view on the way women are presented in the media*
*– Possible additional ideas*
  *• Her aims: more gender equality, better education, peaceful co-existence in north-east Nigeria*
  *• How to reach these aims: draw attention to the situation, support women who try to live more independently, resistance against Boko Haram*
  *• Reasons for not leaving the conflict-ridden area: her home, does not want to give up the country to destructive forces, does her share to build a better future*
  *• Her background: young or middle-aged, well-educated, maybe spent some time abroad, maybe some personal experience set her writing about the situation in north-east Nigeria and triggered her focus on gender equality*

**Promoting human rights in north-east Nigeria**  headline

I am facing a young and resolute Nigerian woman. Chitra Nagarajan lives in Maiduguri in northeast Nigeria and works to promote human rights in an area which is strongly influenced by Boko Haram. We have met in her apartment to talk about her work in Nigeria.  introduction

GUARDIAN: What is the situation like for you personally here in Maiduguri?  first question: personal situation

C.N.: It is not easy. The conflict in our region is always present and I am known to promote women's and human rights, which is not seen favourably by everybody. But that does not mean that I'm constantly threatened. In my hometown I feel mostly safe.

GUARDIAN: So, you're not considering leaving the region?  second question: stay or leave the region

C.N.: No, not at all. I think my work here is important and I strongly believe we must not watch our country take a turn for the worse without trying to change things.

GUARDIAN: What is it exactly you would like to change?  third question: aims

C.N.: Obviously I would love to see people living peacefully together. It is terrible the way the conflict influences everyone, children, grown-ups, men, women, everybody. Everyone has lost at least someone dear to them. Fear and death are omnipresent. But I would also like to see the situation of women change. They need to have an equal say and presence in all walks of life.

GUARDIAN: How do you try to reach these aims? — fourth question: ways to reach aims

C.N.: There are different ways. I talk to people I meet here. I try to enlighten them about their rights, for example that female genital mutilation is forbidden, that primary school is compulsory and free. But I also listen to people's stories. Last year, I spent several weeks interviewing people to assess the way in which gender roles are filled in this region. I came up with some very revealing stories. — reference to text

GUARDIAN: Such as?

C.N.: Well, often women are seen as victims of the conflict, as passive members of society who quietly accept their fate. But that is not true. Of course, women also become victims, far too often really, but there are also others who fight back. There are those who join Boko Haram willingly and there are those who fight against them. There are those who try to protect others and in doing so risk their own lives, e. g. when they hide men in their homes or smuggle them to safety. — reference to text

GUARDIAN: But how do these stories help? — sixth question: relevance of her work

C.N.: In different ways, I hope. For one, I write articles for international newspapers and thus can draw attention to the situation here in north-east Nigeria. But my presentation of the situation is far more accurate and complete because I'm an insider. I do not come for a quick and superficial assessment of the situation but I'm here to stay and I'm much closer to the people than most European or American journalists. Also, I share the stories within my own country, and this encourages people to lead their own lives differently. They see that others do not submit to traditional rules and norms. They realize that it can actually be done. I think that is very important. The people in my stories become some kind of role models.

GUARDIAN: So maybe this interview can also help in a tiny way.

C.N.: I hope so. The more we show what is going on, the more we tell people what is possible, the more people will dare to stand up and fight for their rights. I'm afraid we cannot wait for some external force to help us, we must do it ourselves. — **conclusion**

GUARDIAN: That's what we see in different countries, too. People standing up and fighting for their rights.

C.N.: Exactly, and I believe it can happen here, too.

GUARDIAN: Let's hope you're right. Thank you for the interview.

C.N.: Thank you. *(636 words)* — thank you

## Schriftliche Abiturprüfung NRW – Englisch LK
## Leseverstehen und Schreiben – Übungsaufgabe 7

Aufgabenstellung                                                                 Punkte

1. Describe the measures taken by the oil company to obtain the villagers'
   land. *(Comprehension)*                                                           12

2. Compare how the villagers as well as their situation and the oil company
   are portrayed. Focus on narrative techniques and the use of language.
   *(Analysis)*                                                                      16

3. Choose **one** of the following tasks.                                            14

3.1 "It's true that globalisation, with all its fantastic improvements in the
    world and the technological progress linked to it, has increased inequality
    at country level, especially inside countries. And there are people that
    were left behind – people, sectors, regions – that has created a sense of
    frustration in the rust belts of the world." (Antonio Guterres, Secretary-
    General of the UN since 2017, *1949)
    Assess to what extent Guterres' view reflects the current situation in
    Nigeria. *(Evaluation: comment)*

3.2 The natural science course of your Nigerian friend has been dealing with
    the impact of the oil industry on Nigeria's environment. You friend has
    asked you whether there are similar problems in Germany. Write an
    article for the Nigerian school paper in which you assess to what extent
    the production of energy influences the environment.
    *(Evaluation: re-creation of text)*

**Annotation**
rust belt: a region (within a country) which is characterised by a decline in industrial work, e. g.
    Midwest of the USA

**Text:**
**Helon Habila, *Oil on Water* (excerpt)**
*The novel* Oil on Water *is told by Rufus, a young Nigerian journalist. Together with Zaq, a far more experienced local journalist, he travels to the Niger Delta in search of a British oil engineer's wife, who has been kidnapped. On their journey they spend some days with some villagers. Their chief, Chief Ibiram, tells them about their encounter with an oil company.*

My mind went back to our first night in Chief Ibiram's house. We had finished eating. It was too early to sleep, and the Chief and his brother had withdrawn to one side, speaking softly, listening to the radio. And the Chief had hesitated a long time when

Zaq asked him, Are you happy here? But finally, he lowered the radio volume and cleared his voice. [...]

Once upon a time they lived in paradise, he said, in a small village close to Yellow Island. They lacked for nothing, fishing and hunting and farming and watching their children growing up before them, happy. The village was close-knit, made up of cousins and uncles and aunts and brothers and sisters, and, though they were happily insulated from the rest of the world by their creeks and rivers and forests, they were not totally unaware of the changes going on all around them: the gas flares that lit up neighbouring villages all day and all night, and the cars and TVs and video players in the front rooms of their neighbours who had allowed the flares to be set up. Some of the neighbours were even bragging that the oil companies had offered to send their kids to Europe and America to become engineers, so that one day they could return and work as oil executives in Port Harcourt. For the first time the close, unified community was divided – for how could they not be tempted, with the flare in the next village burning over them every night, its flame long and coiled like a snake, whispering, winking, hissing? Already the oil-company men had started visiting, accompanied by important politicians from Port Harcourt, holding long conferences with Chief Malabo, the head chief, who was also Chief Ibiram's uncle.

One day, early in the morning, Chief Malabo called the whole village to a meeting. Of course he had heard the murmurs from the young people, and the suspicious whispers from the old people, all wondering what it was he had been discussing with the oil men and the politicians. Well, they had made an offer, they had offered to buy the whole village, and with the money – and yes, there was a lot of money, more money than any of them had ever imagined – and with the money they could relocate elsewhere and live a rich life. But Chief Malabo had said no, on behalf of the whole village he had said no. This was their ancestral land, this was where their fathers and their fathers' fathers were buried. They'd been born here, they'd grown up here, they were happy here, and though they may not be rich, the land had been good to them, they never lacked for anything. What kind of custodians of the land would they be if they sold it off? [...]

But the snake, the snake in the garden wouldn't rest, it kept on hissing and the apple only grew larger and more alluring each day. And already far off in the surrounding waters the oil-company boats were patrolling, sometimes openly sending their men to the village to take samples of soil and water. The village decided to keep them away by sending out their own patrols over the surrounding rivers, in canoes, all armed with bows and arrows and clubs and a few guns. [...] The canoe patrol was something of a desperate measure, and this soon became very clear. It turned out to be the excuse the oil companies and the politicians who worked for them needed to make their next move. One day the patrol came upon two oil workers piling soil samples into a speedboat. There was a brief skirmish, nothing too serious – one of the oil workers escaped with a swollen jaw, the other with a broken arm – but the next day the soldiers came. Chief Malabo was arrested, his hands tied behind his back as if he were a petty criminal, on charges of supporting the militants and plotting against the federal government and threatening to kidnap foreign oil workers. The list was long – but, the lawyer said, if the elders would consent to the oil company's demands, sell the land ...

[...] But the villagers remained firm. Chief Malabo, whenever they went to see him, told them not to give in, not to worry about him – but they could see how he was deteriorating every day. And then they went to see him one day and were told he was dead.

Here Chief Ibiram paused in his story, his voice breaking. They were given his body, which was wrapped in a raffia mat and a white cloth, and told to take him away.

Just like that. The following week, even before Chief Malabo had been buried, the oil companies moved in. They came with a whole army, waving guns and looking like they meant business. They had a contract, they said, Chief Malabo had signed it in prison before he died, selling them all of his family land, and that was where they'd start drilling, and whoever wanted to join him and sell his land would be paid handsomely, but the longer the people held out, the more the value of their land would fall.

Zaq shifted. – So what happened?

– They sold. One by one. The rigs went up, and the gas flares, and the workers came and set up camp in our midst, we saw our village change, right before our eyes.

And that was why we decided to leave, ten families. We didn't take their money. The money would be our curse on them, for taking our land, and for killing our chief. We left, we headed northwards, we've lived in five different places now, but always we've had to move. We are looking for a place where we can live in peace. But it is hard. So your question, are we happy here? I say how can we be happy when we are mere wanderers without a home? *(1,000 words)*

*Excerpt from:* Helon Habila, Oil on Water. Hamish Hamilton. 2010, pp. 40–44

**Annotation**
ll. 6/7 Yellow Island: a place on Nigeria's coast

## Lösungsvorschläge

1. *Here you only need to focus on the different steps the oil company has taken to drive the villagers off their land. The following aspects should be included:*
   - Work together with local politicians
   - Meet and discuss with the villagers' chief
   - Offer huge amounts of money;
   - Want to relocate villagers, promise a life in luxury
   - Send boat patrols, first only watch the village from a distance
   - Come closer, take samples of soil and water in the village
   - Two oil company workers get in a minor fight with villagers
   - Accuse chief of several crimes, have him taken away and arrested
   - Arrive at village with guns after the death of Chief Malabo
   - Claim chief had signed a contract to sell his land before he died
   - Start drilling there
   - Offer to buy the other villagers' land
   - The sooner the villagers sell, the more money they get

In the excerpt from the novel *Oil on Water* written by Helon Habila and published in 2010, a Nigerian chief tells two local journalists how an oil company expelled them from their land in the Niger Delta.  
**introduction:** reference to source, topic

The oil company works together with local politicians. Together they meet with the villagers' chief to persuade him to sell the land to the company. To bribe the chief and the villagers they offer huge amounts of money, which is meant to help the villagers relocate to another part of the country. When the chief does not accept the offer, the oil company tries to intimidate the villagers by sending patrols to the area. First, they do not come too close but later they come to the land and take samples of soil and water. By doing so, they get in a minor fight with some of the villagers, who have started to patrol their own land. As a consequence, the oil company has an excuse to accuse the chief of several crimes, which leads to his arrest. When the villagers are still not willing to give up their land, they are told that their chief has died.  
**main part:** oil company's strategy

The following week the oil company men come in great numbers and heavily armed to take over the village and to start drilling. They claim that the chief has sold them his part of the land and offer to pay the other villagers off, too. However, they will pay less the later they decide to sell. That way, they put pressure on the villagers who either sell their land or leave without taking the company's money. *(271 words)*

2. In this task the focus is slightly different from the one in the first task. Here you do not focus on the oil company's action but on the way the company is portrayed. Also, you need to compare the image conveyed to the image conveyed of the villagers and their situation. You are asked to pay special attention to the way the narrative situation influences the way you perceive the villagers and the oil company and to the way language is used to portray both parties. Take into account aspects like choice of words and stylistic devices.
   - Narrative technique:
     - First person narrator
     - Relates story as told by Chief Ibiram → involved in the action
     - Limited point of view
     - Highly subjective → reader is presented the villagers' perspective → reader is influenced
   - Portrayal of villagers
     - "Once upon a time" (l. 6) → fairy tale
     - "happy" (l. 8) before the oil company arrived
       ◆ Enumerations underline image of a self-sufficient community (cf. ll. 7–10)
       ◆ "paradise" (l. 6) → reference to Bible → no worries
     - Villagers have lived on the land for a long time (cf. ll. 30/31)
     - See themselves as "custodians of the land" (l. 32)
     - More or less defenceless against oil company
       ◆ Enumeration (cf. l. 39)
       ◆ "snake" (l. 34) and "apple" (l. 34) → reference to Bible → expulsion from Paradise
       ◆ "desperate measure" (l. 40)
       ◆ Their chief is criminalised ("petty criminal", ll. 45/46), accusations seem far-fetched (cf. ll. 45–48)
     - Remain "firm" (l. 49): Chief Malabo suffers bravely, repetition of "not to" (l. 50) to stress that he does not want his people to give in
     - After their chief's death their fighting spirit is broken
       ◆ Short sentences stress finality (cf. l. 62)
       ◆ Those who left become "wanderers" (l. 69)
       ◆ Not "happy" (l. 68) any longer
   - Portrayal of oil company
     - Evil force
       ◆ Allusion to the expulsion from Paradise (cf. ll. 34/35)
       ◆ Repetition of the word "money" (ll. 26/27) → importance of money → meant to tempt the villagers → sow dissent → materialistic
     - Powerful
       ◆ Adverbs of time emphasize speed with which they proceed (ll. 19, 35, 55)
     - Deceitful
       ◆ Use an "excuse" (l. 40) to arrest Chief Malabo
       ◆ Blackmail villagers (cf. ll. 47/48, l. 60)
       ◆ Kill Chief Malabo (cf. l. 65)

- Claim he sold his land ("they said", l. 57)
- Disrespectful
  - The chief's body is handed over unceremoniously: "[j]ust like that" (l. 55)
  - Disrupt villagers' mourning (cf. ll. 55/56)
- Dehumanized: mostly "the oil companies" (cf. ll. 14, 41, 56), rarely "the oil-company men" (l. 19)

In this excerpt the oil company is portrayed as a disruptive, evil force whereas the villagers are portrayed as their victims. This image is stressed by the use of narrative techniques and language, especially choice of words.     **introduction: thesis / reference to assignment**

The novel is told by a first-person narrator (cf. l. 1), namely Rufus, a young Nigerian journalist. Rufus relates the events involving the villagers and the oil company as told by Chief Ibiram, which makes it seem like a first-hand report although Rufus himself did not witness any of the action. This becomes apparent by the insertion "he said" in line 6. Chief Ibiram, however, is involved in the action. Thus, the actions are presented from a highly subjective, limited point of view. The reader only sees the action through the chief's eyes and not from the perspective of the oil company. As a result, the narration is biased and the reader is invited to feel with the villagers and to take on their standpoint.     **main part: narrative technique**

Before the oil company became interested in their land, the villagers were "happy" (l. 8), they lived as in a fairy tale (cf. l. 6). This image is underlined by two enumerations (cf. ll. 7–9) which show that they were self-sufficient and a closely-knit community. Furthermore, Chief Ibiram says they used to live in "paradise" (l. 6), which is a reference to the Bible and indicates that the villagers did not know any worries and "lacked for nothing" (l. 7).     **language**
→ enumerations
→ reference to Bible

The villagers live in harmony with the land they inhabit. They see themselves as "custodians of the land" (l. 32), a word which indicates that they take responsibility for the land and protect it. Also, the repetition of the word father (cf. ll. 29/30) makes it clear that it is important to them to live on "ancestral land" (l. 29). Additionally, the repetition of "here", as opposed to "there", underlines their attachment to that particular piece of land. (cf. ll. 30/31).     → choice of words, repetition

Their happiness ends when the oil company offers them money in exchange for their land. The word "money" is repeated four times to stress its importance (cf. ll. 26/27) and to characterize the oil company as materialistic. The money is the "apple [which] only [grows] larger and more alluring each day" (l. 34). Together with the word "paradise" (l. 6) and the word "snake" (l. 34), which here represents the oil, the reference to Adam and Eve's expulsion from Paradise becomes obvious. In this extract, the oil company is the driving force behind the villagers' expulsion from their paradise and thus it is undeniably evil.  → repetition
→ reference to Bible

However, the villagers do not accept the offer but remain firm, a word which is later on used to characterize them explicitly (cf. l. 49), although they are more or less defenceless. This is stressed by another enumeration listing their means of defence. They are "armed with bows and arrows and clubs and a few guns" (ll. 38/39). Chief Ibiram uses the word "desperate" (l. 40) to describe their attempt to keep away the oil company's men and to portray the villagers as victims.  → choice of words, enumeration

The oil company, on the other hand, is powerful. They have "important politicians from Port Harcourt" (l. 20) on their side and "a whole army" (l. 56). They use their power to deceive the villagers. They use "a brief skirmish, nothing too serious" (l. 43) as an "excuse" (l. 40) to arrest Chief Malabo. Here, the choice of words portrays the oil company as dishonest. This image is further underlined by their attempt at blackmailing the villagers (cf. ll. 47/48). Though Chief Ibiram does not call it blackmail, his unfinished sentence is clearly meant to lead the listeners to that conclusion. What is worse, the oil company is said to have killed Chief Malabo (cf. l. 65) and to pretend that he sold them his land (cf. ll. 57/58). The insertion "they said" (l. 57) indicates doubt. Thus, the oil company is portrayed not only as dishonest but as an unscrupulous murderer. In this context it is also interesting to note that the narrator rarely speaks of "men" (l. 19) but rather of "the oil companies" (e. g. ll. 14, 41, 56), which serves to dehumanize them.  → choice of words

Their chief's death finally breaks the villagers' fighting spirt. Some sell their land and stay, others leave without taking the money. The use of short sentences (cf. l. 62) underlines the finality of their loss. Those who leave become "wanderers" (l. 69) which is a sharp contrast to their former life, and they are not "happy" (l. 68) any longer because they have lost everything.  → sentence structure

All in all, it can be said that the villagers and the oil company are portrayed as antagonists. Whereas the villagers are the victimised heroes, the oil companies are the evil characters. This image is supported by the choice of words, especially by the allusion to the bible. Due to the narrative technique chosen, the narration is biased, which gives the reader very subjective insight into the action and influences their perception of both parties tremendously. *(842 words)*

**conclusion**

3.1 *In this evaluation task you need to explain Guterres' statement and assess in how far it can be applied to the current situation in Nigeria. You do not have to refer to the extract of the novel, but you should take into account the background knowledge on Nigeria you have acquired in class.*
- *Explain the quote:*
  - *Globalisation seen as ambivalent: improvements due to globalisation on the one hand, inequality on the other; not only between different countries but within them*
  - *Some people are left behind → leads to frustration*
  - *Rust belts of the world → areas left behind due to deindustrialisation*
- *Aspects that do not fit Nigeria*
  - *Not a traditional rust belt country → term is normally applied to regions in the US that suffer from deindustrialisation, especially in the Midwest*
  - *Nigeria's era of industrialisation is not over yet → inequality is not due to a decline in wealth but to its uneven distribution*
- *Aspects that fit Nigeria*
  - *People profit very differently from the country's resources; depending on gender, age, religion, ethnicity, for example*
  - *Oil companies (multinational corporations) import labour, especially skilled jobs; high unemployment rate in Nigeria*
  - *Child labour in cities (e. g. street vendors, car washers, beggars) and rural areas (e. g. domestic servants, farm hands); situation in rural areas is worse, girls drop out of school sooner than boys*
  - *Corruption: people who cannot afford to offer bribes have less chances to get their children admitted to a public school, to get government contracts, etc.*
- *Poverty and inequality in Nigeria are not due to a lack of resources, but to the ill-use of the income generated*
- *Globalisation is only partly to blame*

Antonio Guterres voices an ambivalent view on globalisation. On the one hand, he believes that globalisation has led to technological progress and improvement, but on the other hand it is also said to be responsible for inequality not only between different countries but also within them. According to him, people who are left behind are frustrated, especially in areas which he

**introduction: explanation of quote**

calls the "rust belts of the world". In this essay I am going to explore to what extent Guterres' statement can be applied to the current situation in Nigeria.

Although I believe that inequality is a major issue in Nigeria, I would not apply the term "rust belt" here. This expression was coined to describe areas in the USA, especially in the Midwest, which suffer or used to suffer from the effects of deindustrialisation. After a boom in the steel and automobile industry, these regions declined and were hit by poverty. Nigeria's era of industrialisation, however, is not over yet. The oil and coal industry, for example, are striving there. The poverty of large parts of the population is not caused by a general decline in wealth in some regions but by its uneven distribution.   **main part:** aspects that do not fit Nigeria: no "rust belt"

Whether people profit from Nigeria's natural resources or not depends among other things on gender, age, religion and ethnicity. Huge parts of the profit go to multinational corporations like Exxon and Shell or the political and economic elite of the country. Yet the majority of the population does not profit. Oil companies, for example, import labour, especially for highly skilled jobs, whereas the unemployment rate in the country is high.   aspects that fit Nigeria: distribution of wealth

Children often have to work to help support their families. In the cities they often work as street vendors, car washers or beggars. The situation in rural areas is even worse, where children work as domestic servants or farm hands. In general, girls drop out of school even sooner than boys. Thus, a lack in education robs them of a better future.   child labour, education

Corruption is another tremendous problem in Nigeria. People who cannot afford to offer bribes have less chances to get their children admitted to public schools or to obtain government contracts. The income the state generates from the country's resources often enriches only the political and economic elite, whereas large parts of the population do not benefit at all. Therefore, poverty and inequality in Nigeria are not due to a lack of resources, but to the ill-use of the income. Globalisation is only part of the problem here.   corruption

In conclusion, it can be said that Guterres' statement is partly applicable to Nigeria because parts of the population and some areas of the country are left behind and this certainly leads to frustration among the people concerned. However, neither are the areas that are left behind a "rust belt", nor can Nigeria as a whole be called a rust belt country. Quite the opposite is true, it is a country which is striving due to its resources.   *(489 words)*   **conclusion**

3.2 *This task is only loosely connected to the text you've dealt with so far. The focus shifts from Nigeria to Germany and from oil to energy in general, more precisely to the influence the production of energy has on the environment here in Germany. The text you need to write is an article for the Nigerian school paper. Therefore, you need to consider the structure of an article as well as background information you may need to provide.*
   – *Headline*
   – *Resources in Germany:*
   - *Hard and brown coal*
   - *Oil*
   - *Nuclear energy*
   - *Biomass*
   - *Wind*
   - *Water*
   - *Sun*
   – *Influence on the environment:*
   - *Coal → changes landscape due to open cast mining, emission of $CO_2$*
   - *Oil → changes landscape; less spills than in Nigeria; very little oil in Germany*
   - *Nuclear energy → cleaner but more dangerous; nuclear waste*
   - *Biomass → cultivation of maize damages soil*
   - *Wind, water and sun → more environmentally friendly but offshore wind parks are a problem for fish and mammals; people do not want turbines in their proximity; energy needs to be transported (and stored); people do not want energy lines in their proximity*

**Germany's difficult way to green energy** — headline

Unlike Nigeria, Germany is not rich in oil. The production of oil makes up for a very small part of Germany's energy production. Instead Germany has focused for a very long time on coal. The country is relatively rich in hard and brown coal. However, the extraction and burning of coal is a very dirty job both for the people working in the mines and for the environment. In recent years, more and more people have fought against the clearing of forests to extract coal and in order to reach our goals in the reduction of $CO_2$ Germany has to do without coal in the long run. — **introduction:** comparison to Nigeria; importance of coal

For quite some time nuclear energy seemed to be an alternative to coal. Nuclear energy is often said to be a clean energy but there is always the danger of a nuclear accident, which has disastrous effects on nature and on human beings. Furthermore, there is the problem of the disposing of nuclear waste. After the accident in the nuclear power plant in Fukushima, Japan, German politicians decided to reduce and eventually stop the production of nuclear energy. — **main part:** nuclear energy

Renewable energy is meant to replace both nuclear energy and coal. Energy from wind, water and sun is often called "clean energy" because these sources of energy do not cause $CO_2$ emissions, but they also have disadvantages. — renewable energy

In the North Sea one finds huge wind parks. Marine biologists are discussing the danger these wind parks pose for sea life. Another problem with wind energy is that it needs to be transported from the North of Germany to the rest of the country. These energy routes also destroy the landscape. — wind parks

To use water energy man also must interfere with nature, e. g. the hydrologic balance may change the ecological system in a region considerably. Solar energy has probably the least negative impact on the environment because the panels can be put on roofs of houses which exist already. The problem here is that it is still difficult and expensive to store solar energy for times when the sun does not shine. Another problem might be the disposal of panels which contain toxic material. — water energy / solar energy

The use of biomass to produce biogas is not really an alternative because the maize that is used damages the soil.

As can be seen, Germany is trying to find ways to produce energy in a more environmentally friendly way but there is still quite a way to go because people need to be convinced and efficient technology needs to be developed more quickly. — **conclusion**

*(429 words)*

## Schriftliche Abiturprüfung NRW – Englisch LK
## Sprachmittlung – Übungsaufgabe 1

**Aufgabenstellung**
You are following a Nigerian journalist who focuses on the presentation of girls and women in the media. She asks her followers to tell her about the situation in their countries in an email. You have found two interesting texts. One is an article on the question at hand and the other one some research on how girls present themselves on social media. Use the information to write an email to this journalist on the presentation and self-presentation of girls and women in the media.

**Material 1: Leitwölfe und Powerfrauen**
*Erstaunlich, wie unterschiedlich Frauen und Männer in den Medien immer noch dargestellt werden. Von Gleichberechtigung kann da nicht die Rede sein*

Bei dem Wort „Mutti" denken wohl die meisten nicht unbedingt an eine politisch einflussreiche Frau. Und doch wird die Bundeskanzlerin, die mächtigste Frau Deutschlands, in der Berichterstattung immer wieder „Mutti" genannt. Kann das wirklich nur als positives Markenzeichen zu verstehen sein, wie das Magazin *Cicero* meint?

Für die Wissenschaftlerinnen von der Freien Universität Berlin und der Leuphana-Universität Lüneburg, die sechs Monate lang 23 Medien im Auftrag des Bundesministeriums für Bildung und Forschung analysiert haben, hat die mediale Darstellung von Frauen System: Weibliche Führungskräfte werden in den untersuchten Medien als „Femme fatale" oder „listige Witwe" tituliert – im besten Fall noch als „Powerfrau". Das männliche Pendant dagegen ist ein „Alphatier", ein „Leitwolf" oder ein „Managerdenkmal".

Schon diese Formulierungen machen deutlich, wie anders die Geschlechterbilder in Tageszeitungen, Zeitschriften oder Fernsehsendungen ausfallen. Und das obwohl es sich bei den untersuchten Personen in beiden Fällen um Frauen und Männer in Spitzenpositionen aus Politik, Wirtschaft und Wissenschaft handelte.

Frauen kommen in den Medien zudem viel seltener vor als Männer – nicht einmal jede fünfte Person ist weiblich. Betrachtet man die Berichterstattung im Bereich der Wirtschaft, sind es sogar noch weniger – insgesamt nur fünf Prozent. In der Wissenschaft spielen immerhin zwölf Prozent Frauen eine Rolle.

Nur in der Politik sind es auffällig mehr – nämlich 20 Prozent. Dass der Anteil der Nennung von Spitzenpolitikerinnen sogar 30 Prozent beträgt, ist dem sogenannten Merkel-Faktor zu verdanken. Denn die Kanzlerin ist die meistgewähnte Person in allen ausgewählten Medien – von Tageszeitungen wie *Bild* oder *Süddeutsche Zeitung* bis hin zu Wochenmagazinen wie *Stern* oder *Spiegel*. Durch ihre Omnipräsenz tut Angela Merkel also durchaus etwas für die Gleichberechtigung: Aufgrund ihrer Kanzlerschaft treten Frauen in den Medien verstärkt in Erscheinung und werden dadurch anders wahrgenommen.

*(279 Wörter)*

*Natascha Roshani: Leitwölfe und Powerfrauen, Fluter (2. 1. 2016), https://www.fluter.de/leitwoelfe-und-powerfrauen*

## Material 2: Selbstinszenierung in den neuen Medien

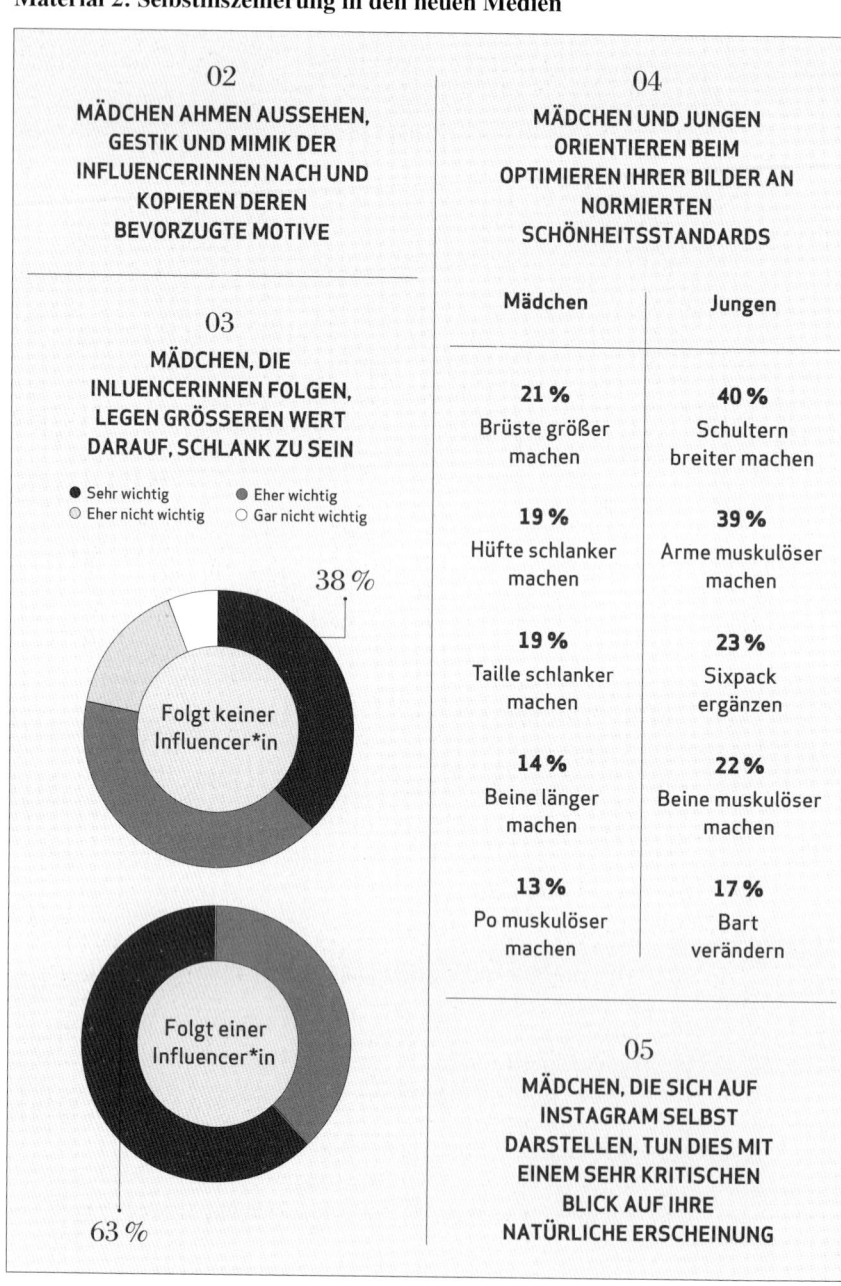

### 02
**MÄDCHEN AHMEN AUSSEHEN, GESTIK UND MIMIK DER INFLUENCERINNEN NACH UND KOPIEREN DEREN BEVORZUGTE MOTIVE**

### 03
**MÄDCHEN, DIE INLUENCERINNEN FOLGEN, LEGEN GRÖSSEREN WERT DARAUF, SCHLANK ZU SEIN**

- Sehr wichtig
- Eher nicht wichtig
- Eher wichtig
- Gar nicht wichtig

Folgt keiner Influencer*in — 38 %

Folgt einer Influencer*in — 63 %

### 04
**MÄDCHEN UND JUNGEN ORIENTIEREN BEIM OPTIMIEREN IHRER BILDER AN NORMIERTEN SCHÖNHEITSSTANDARDS**

| Mädchen | Jungen |
|---|---|
| 21 % Brüste größer machen | 40 % Schultern breiter machen |
| 19 % Hüfte schlanker machen | 39 % Arme muskulöser machen |
| 19 % Taille schlanker machen | 23 % Sixpack ergänzen |
| 14 % Beine länger machen | 22 % Beine muskulöser machen |
| 13 % Po muskulöser machen | 17 % Bart verändern |

### 05
**MÄDCHEN, DIE SICH AUF INSTAGRAM SELBST DARSTELLEN, TUN DIES MIT EINEM SEHR KRITISCHEN BLICK AUF IHRE NATÜRLICHE ERSCHEINUNG**

## 06
### MÄDCHEN, DIE BESTIMMTEN INFLUENCERINNEN FOLGEN, OPTIMIEREN IHRE BILDER NOCH STÄRKER

● hellen Zähne auf   ○ hellen Zähne nicht auf

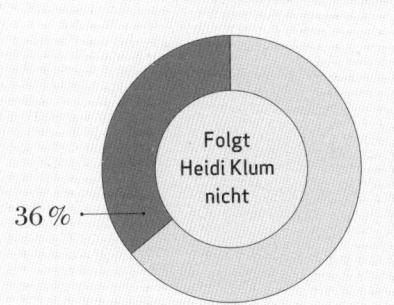

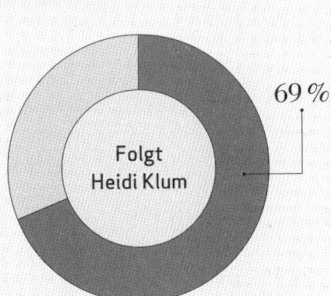

36 %  — Folgt Heidi Klum nicht

69 % — Folgt Heidi Klum

## 07
Wenn die eigene Erscheinung der Mädchen für die Erreichung des Influencerinnen-Standards nicht reicht, wird mit Inszenierungstricks und Filtern zur Optimierung nachgeholfen. Es kommt zu einer Verzerrung des Verständnisses von „natürlich" und „spontan"

**100** Prozent der Mädchen, die Dagi Bee folgen, optimieren ihre Haut

## 08
ES ENTSTEHT EINE NORMIERUNG, IN DER DIE SELBSTINSZENIERUNG DER MÄDCHEN – ABER AUCH DER PROFIS – IMMER GLEICHFÖRMIGER WIRD. VIELFALT GEHT VERLOREN

*MaLisa Stiftung – Weibliche Selbstinszenierung in den Neuen Medien, 2019*

**Anmerkung**
Dagi Bee: sehr erfolgreiche deutsche Influencerin, deren Videos sich vor allem mit den Themen Mode und Kosmetik beschäftigen

## Lösungsvorschläge

*In dieser Aufgabe müssen Sie eine E-Mail an eine nigerianische Journalistin verfassen, die sich mit der Darstellung von Mädchen und Frauen in den Medien beschäftigt und nach Berichten aus verschiedenen Ländern sucht. Da Sie nicht besser bekannt sind, wird der Ton freundlich, der Stil aber eher formell sein. Inhaltlich geht es um die Darstellung von Frauen in den deutschen Medien (Text 1) und um die Selbstdarstellung von Mädchen und jungen Frauen in den sozialen Netzwerken (Text 2). Überlegen Sie hier vor allem auch, wie Sie die diskontinuierlichen Texte umstrukturieren können, um einen Fließtext daraus zu machen.*

- Anrede (Name darf fiktiv sein, da kein Name vorgegeben ist)
- Einleitungssatz
- Aufgreifen des Anlasses für die Mail
- Darstellung der Frauen in den deutschen Medien
  - Artikel basiert auf Studie von 23 Medien über sechs Monate
  - Frauen kommen viel seltener vor als Männer
  - Nicht einmal 20 % der Personen sind weiblich
  - Wirtschaft: nur 5 %
  - Wissenschaft: 12 %
  - Politik: 20 %, bei Spitzenpolitikerinnen 30 %
  - Merkel-Faktor → Omnipräsenz → Frauen treten in den Medien verstärkt in Erscheinung und werden dadurch anders wahrgenommen
  - Auffällige Formulierungen:
    - „femme fatale", „listige Witwe", „Powerfrau"
    - Merkel, obwohl (damals) mächtigste Frau Deutschlands, als „Mutti" bezeichnet
    - Männer hingegen sind „Leitwölfe", „Alphatiere" oder „Managerdenkmäler"
- Selbstdarstellung in sozialen Netzwerken
  - Mädchen, die sich auf Instagram inszenieren, haben ein sehr kritischen Blick auf ihr natürliches Erscheinungsbild
  - Nutzen Inszenierungstricks und Filter zur Optimierung
  - Mädchen unterwerfen sich Normierung, ahmen Influencerinnen nach → Vielfalt geht verloren
  - Verständnis von natürlich und spontan ändert sich
    - Wollen schlank sein, 63 % der Mädchen finden dies wichtig, wenn sie einer Influencerin folgen, nur 38 % der Mädchen, die keiner Influencerin folgen
    - 69 % der Mädchen, die Heidi Klum folgen, hellen ihre Zähne auf, aber nur 36 %, die ihr nicht folgen
    - Alle, die Dagi Bee folgen, optimieren ihre Haut
    - Optimierungen von Fotos: 21 % lassen ihre Brüste größer erscheinen, 19 % machen Hüfte und Taille schlanker, 14 % machen Beine länger, 9 % machen Po muskulöser
- Abschluss und Grußformel

| | |
|---|---|
| Dear Chitra, | greeting |
| Thank you for replying to my email. I'm sure you get quite a few emails from people all over the world. You wrote that you are interested in how women are presented in the media in Germany. | **introductory sentence:** reason for writing |
| I've found an article on that topic. I also found some research on how girls present themselves on the social media and thought you might be interested in that, too. | reference to texts |
| Let me start with the way women are presented in traditional media. The article I've found is based on some research which was conducted over a period of six months. During that time 23 media outlets were analysed. It is striking that women are mentioned less often in the media than men. Not even one in five people mentioned in the media is female. When it comes to the economic sector, only five percent of the people mentioned are female. In the science sector it's 12 percent but in the political sector it's 20 %. Among the most prominent politicians it's even 30 %. This is due to the so-called Merkel factor. Our current chancellor Angela Merkel is mentioned very often. Due to her leadership women appear more often in the media and are also said to be perceived differently. | **main part:** presentation of women numbers |
| However, it is obvious that the terms used for women and men are very different. Women are called "femme fatale", which means man-eater or they are depicted as "cunning widows" or, more positively as having a lot of power, often in the sense of endurance. Angela Merkel, although she is the most powerful woman in Germany, is often called mummy. Men, by contrast, are called "leader of the pack" or "alpha male" or are seen as a prototype for the qualities of a manager. | terms used |
| Let me now turn to the self-presentation of girls on social media. Here, research shows that girls who present themselves on Instagram have a very critical view on their appearance. They use all kinds of tricks when staging themselves, for instance they use a variety of filters to edit their photos. They try to look like influencers and therefore follow the norms of what is seen as beautiful. As a result, the variety of different faces reduces, everyone looks very similar, and our idea of what is natural and spontaneous changes. | self-presentation of girls in social media |
| Researchers underline these findings with some statistics. 21 % of the girls make their breasts appear larger, 19 % make their hips and their waistline look slimmer, 14 % make their legs longer and 9 % have their bottom look more muscular. 63 % of the girls who follow an influencer want to be slim, as opposed to 38 % who do not follow one. 69 % of the girls who follow Heidi Klum, a famous German model who hosts the show *Germany's next top model*, make their teeth look whiter. Among those who do not follow her, only 36 % do | numbers |

so. All the girls who follow Dagi Bee, a famous German influencer promoting fashion and cosmetics on YouTube, change the look of their skin digitally.

You are probably not happy with these findings but I'm afraid it is the way it is. Still, I hope that these pieces of information are interesting for you. Let me know if you would like to know more about the situation of girls and women in Germany because it is a topic I'm very much interested in, too. — **conclusion**

I would love to hear from you again. — greeting

Kind regards,
Carla *(582 words)* name

> **Schriftliche Abiturprüfung NRW – Englisch LK**
> **Sprachmittlung – Übungsaufgabe 2**

**Aufgabenstellung**
Your friend from Ireland is involved in a project called "Nourish the world" and is currently working on an article on food prices in Europe. She would like to know how this discussion is led in Germany. You have found the following article by Katharina Schmitz and want to tell your friend about some of its main points. Write an email to your friend in which you point out the different stakeholders in the discussion and their position. Also point out what according to the author must be factored in the price of food.

**Text:**
**Katharina Schmitz: *Pellkartoffeln mit Quark sind gutes Essen***

*Ungleichheit – Cem Özdemirs Forderung zu Lebensmittelpreisen löste links der Grünen Empörung aus. Wer die Debatte differenziert betrachtet, erkennt aber vor allem eines: den Versuch, uns gegeneinander auszuspielen*

Er habe das „Gefühl", uns Deutschen sei gutes Motoröl wichtiger als gutes Salatöl – so garnierte der [...] Argrarminister Cem Özdemir (Grüne) kürzlich seine Forderung, Lebensmittel dürften nicht mehr zu Ramschpreisen angeboten werden. Der Preis von einem Kilo Hackfleisch müsse „die ökologische Wahrheit" besser ausdrücken. Welch
5 ein Hohn, dachten viele, wer kein Geld hat, kann sich diese Wahrheit nämlich nicht leisten. Also weder gutes Motoröl noch kaltgepresstes Olivenöl und schon gar kein Bio-Hack. Die taz schimpfte: Snobistische Oberschichtspartei!
  Es ist zum Mäuse melken, ja, aber auch wenn es uns nicht schmeckt, in der Sache hat Özdemir recht. Denn bei 3,99 Euro für das Kilo Discounter-Hack ist die tierquäle-
10 rische Haltung von Schweinen oder Rindern sowie der exzessive Einsatz von Antibiotika nicht mit eingepreist. Einkalkuliert ist auch nicht der gesundheitliche Preis für fetthaltige, zuckerreiche Lebensmittel, die in Fertigprodukten stecken. Dass die Billigproduktion von Lebensmitteln schamlos auf die Ausbeutung von Niedriglöhnern geht, das ist in diesem Preis enthalten. Oder: Paprika aus der Türkei ist eben auch nur des-
15 halb so günstig, weil der $CO_2$-Preis nicht einberechnet ist. Weitere Posten wären die unsinnigen EU-Subventionen, die Massen- und Überproduktion fördern und gute Lebensmittel konkurrenzunfähig machen. Schließlich fehlt ein Warnhinweis auf den Verpackungen für all diese Schweinereien im Lebensmittelsektor, ganz so wie bei den Zigarettenschachteln.
20  Aber weil das zugegebenermaßen alles sehr komplex ist und außerdem noch das Gewissen weiter belastet, versuchen viele, den Grünen das Etikett „Verbotspartei" anzuhängen. Die dürften den Bürger:innen nicht vorschreiben, was oder wie viel gegessen werde, moserte Bayerns Ministerpräsident Markus Söder (CSU). Ein Rezept, auf das die CSU gerne zurückgreift, insbesondere dann, wenn es ums deutsche Essen geht
25 (Achtung: kann Spuren von Leitkultur enthalten).

Diesmal wollte Söders Attacke aber nicht zünden. Discounter wie Aldi oder Kaufland fühlten sich sogar zu Stellungnahmen verpflichtet. Das sicher auch, weil sie eine zunehmend konsumkritische Klientel bedienen. Erwartungsgemäß meldeten sich auch die Sozialverbände zu Wort. Aber, und bitte jetzt nicht falsch verstehen, auch hier sind
30 die Menschen vielleicht weiter, als es gut meinende Sozial-Lobbyisten manchmal glauben. Lebensmittel müssen bezahlbar bleiben, ja, aber viele Normalkulinariker, auch die mit geringem Einkommen, wollen sich gesünder, nachhaltiger, ethischer ernähren. Was übrigens so manche Studie belegt. Da sind Pellkartoffeln mit Quark eben nicht nur ein günstiges, sondern auch ein gutes Essen.
35 Was ist noch aus der Ramschpreisdebatte zu lernen? Dass jede Person, die nicht gänzlich politikverdrossen ist, natürlich geradezu gehofft hat, ein grüner Agrarminister werde auch mal selbstbewusste Akzente setzen; dass er womöglich auch den grünen opportunistischen Pragmatismus abstellt, denn das neue Tierschutzgesetz, das die Hochleistungszucht weiter ermöglicht, haben die Grünen mitunterstützt.
40 Das eigentliche Leben ist nicht teurer geworden, Schuld an der steigenden Belastung sind explodierende Mieten, gestiegene Energiepreise. Aber weil Essen so zuverlässig die Gemüter erhitzt, kann man uns prima gegeneinander ausspielen. Wir sollten aber genau hinsehen, wer oder was uns auffrisst. *(488 Wörter)*

*Katharina Schmitz: „Pellkartoffeln mit Quark sind gutes Essen". Erschienen in der Freitag – Die Wochenzeitung, Ausgabe 01/2022 vom 06. 01. 2022*

**Anmerkung**
Z. 7  taz: Berliner Tageszeitung

## Lösungsvorschläge

*Der Zieltext ist eine E-Mail an eine Freundin aus Irland. Anrede und Abschluss sollten entsprechend persönlich und der Stil eher informell sein. Inhaltlich geht es um Lebensmittelpreise und wie diese in Deutschland diskutiert werden. Sie sollen darstellen, wer die unterschiedlichen Akteure sind und welche Position diese vertreten. Außerdem sollen Sie beschreiben, welche Kosten nach Ansicht der Autorin in die Lebensmittelpreise eingerechnet werden sollten, um realistische Preise zu erzielen. Bedenken Sie, dass die Freundin die Partei CSU und die Zeitung taz vermutlich nicht kennt und Sie solche Begriffe umschreiben sollten.*

- Anrede: Hi, Hello, Dear ...
- Einleitungssatz
- Akteure und ihre Positionen:
  - Cem Özdemir, Agrarminister, Partei Bündnis 90/Die Grünen:
    - Lebensmittel werden zu Ramschpreisen angeboten.
    - Preise müssen die ökologische Wahrheit ausdrücken.
  - Die taz, Tageszeitung:
    - Viele Menschen könnten sich teurere Lebensmittel nicht leisten.
    - Forderung einer „[s]nobistischen Oberschichtspartei" (Z. 7)
  - Markus Söder, Bayerns Ministerpräsident, CSU: Man darf den Menschen nicht vorschreiben, wie viel sie wovon essen.
  - Sozialverbände: Lebensmittelpreise müssen bezahlbar bleiben
  - Lebensmitteldiscounter Aldi und Lidl: verteidigen sich gegen die Vorwürfe, weil sie konsumkritische Kund*innen haben
- Nach Sicht der Autorin müsste eingepreist werden:
  - „tierquälerische Haltung von Schweinen oder Rindern" (Z. 9/10)
  - „der exzessive Einsatz von Antibiotika" (Z. 10/11)
  - „der gesundheitliche Preis für fetthaltige, zuckerreiche Lebensmittel, die in Fertigprodukten stecken" (Z. 11/12)
  - „Ausbeutung von Niedriglöhnern" (Z. 13)
  - „$CO_2$-Preis" (Z. 15)
  - „EU-Subventionen, die Massen- und Überproduktion fördern" (Z. 16)
- Abschluss

| | |
|---|---|
| Hi Cath, | address |
| How are you? I hope you're well. I'm studying hard for my A-levels and don't have the time for interesting projects like yours. But I found an article published in a German weekly newspaper on 6 January 2022. It was written by Katharina Schmitz and deals with food prices in Germany. So, it fits your topic perfectly. | opening sentence / reference to article |
| Our minister of agriculture, who is a member of the Green Party, triggered the discussion on food prices when he claimed that food is far too cheap. He wants food prices to better express what he calls the ecological truth. That means food prices should also include the | stakeholder: minister of agriculture |

price we all have to pay for environmental damage caused by food production.

Schmitz, the author of the article, lists a couple of things that, according to her, should be included in food prices. She mentions the cruel way in which animals are kept, the excessive use of antibiotics, the expenses that fatty and sweet foods lead to in healthcare, the exploitation of cheap labour, the price that has to be paid for the emission of carbon dioxide during the production and transportation of food and EU subsidies that support mass and excessive production. — the author's view

Journalists from a German daily complained that people are not able to pay higher prices for food. They reproached the Green Party with being snobs and representing just the upper class. Social welfare associations agree that food must be sold at an affordable price. — stakeholders: journalists / social welfare associations

Another participant in the discussion is the governor of Bavaria, who is a member of the conservative party CSU. He says that the Green Party wants to rule by telling people what to do, which he believes to be wrong. — governor of Bavaria

Finally, also discount grocery stores like Aldi and Lidl, which you also know in Ireland, I believe, joined the discussion and defended themselves against the minister's reproaches. Their clients are increasingly aware of problems regarding food production, so they had to counter the accusations. — discount grocery stores

That's as far as the article goes. I hope the information is helpful for your project.

Write soon and please keep your fingers crossed for my exams! — ending

Take care, — salutation
Tobi *(359 words)*

## Schriftliche Abiturprüfung NRW – Englisch LK
## Sprachmittlung – Übungsaufgabe 3

**Aufgabenstellung**

You are spending a year at an American high school. In your social science course, you have discussed the meaning of home within a nation of immigrants as well as the relevance of the Department of Homeland Security. Your teacher has asked you to present the German perspective in an article for the school paper. You want to base your article on the interview with Naika Foroutan, a German professor researching immigration and integration. Present her view on the German "Heimatministerium" and the term "Heimat".

**Text:**
**Auch Einwanderungsländer bieten eine Heimat**

MEDIENDIENST: Frau Foroutan, das bisherige Bundesinnenministerium wird künftig um ein „Heimatministerium" ergänzt. Was halten Sie davon?

NAIKA FOROUTAN: Es kommt darauf an, wie man es mit Leben füllt. Wenn dieses Ministerium die Aufgabe hat, die regionalen Ungleichheiten etwa zwischen Stadt und Land strukturell auszugleichen, dann halte ich das für sehr sinnvoll. Wenn sie an Deutschland denken, dann haben viele nur Metropolen wie Berlin, Hamburg, Frankfurt und München im Kopf. Dabei besteht Deutschland hauptsächlich aus vielen kleinen und mittelgroßen Städten. Durch ein eigenes Ministerium, das dafür zuständig ist, findet eine Aufwertung der Regionen statt und man macht sichtbar, dass Deutschland auch regional gesehen bunt und vielfältig ist. Aber mir ist klar, dass sich hinter dem Heimatbegriff auch die Idee verstecken kann: Wir geben euch euer altes Deutschland wieder zurück. Ein Deutschland ohne diese verwirrende Vielfalt.

MEDIENDIENST: Der Heimatbegriff kam im 19. Jahrhundert auf, als Reaktion auf Verstädterung, Industrialisierung und Migration. Er wurde in der Nazizeit missbraucht, in den 1950er-Jahren durch kitschige „Heimatfilme" popularisiert, jetzt hat er wieder Konjunktur. Ist das nicht Ausdruck von Nostalgie?

NAIKA FOROUTAN: Ja, die Sehnsucht nach einer verklärten Vergangenheit schwingt da immer mit, aber auch eine Sehnsucht nach Verwurzelung und nach dem Gefühl von früher, als man noch ein Kind war. Insofern ist das kein Begriff für eine Bundesregierung, die ein Zeichen für morgen setzen möchte. Aber man kann mit dem Begriff natürlich auch subversiv arbeiten. Wir hatten mal ein großes Forschungsprojekt mit dem Titel „Heymat", da ging es darum, wie sich Identitäten in der Moderne immer wieder neu zusammensetzen, je nach Kontext. Das Y stand bei uns dabei für Hybridität und Hybridisierung von Gesellschaften. Bei vielen Menschen gibt es eine Suche und Sehnsucht nach Identität und dabei greifen sie immer wieder ganz stark auf Erzählungen aus der Vergangenheit zurück. Woher jemand kommt, aus welcher Region, aus welcher Familie, aus welchem Land, aus welcher Schicht, aus welcher politischen Tradition, das sind wichtige Elemente der eigenen Identität. Und dieses

„von irgendwoher kommen" kann auch dazu genutzt werden, um zu erklären, wohin man geht. Der Rückgriff auf eine Vergangenheit, um eine mögliche Zukunft zu beschreiben, kann funktional sein.

MEDIENDIENST: Was könnte denn ein Heimatbegriff sein, der Einwanderer und Alteingesessene verbindet?

NAIKA FOROUTAN: Wenn wir den Anfang unserer heutigen Einwanderungsgesellschaft mit dem ersten großen Anwerbeabkommen der Bundesrepublik von 1955 ansetzen, dann können wir bereits auf eine über 60-jährige Geschichte der Migration zurückblicken. Insofern teilen viele hierzulande bereits eine gemeinsam geteilte Vergangenheit und eine gemeinsame Heimat. Und wenn man mit Einwanderern der ersten Generation redet und bittet, sich selbst zu beschreiben, dann nennen sie ganz oft die Städte, in denen sie leben. Aus diesen Selbstbeschreibungen ist eine starke Verbundenheit mit konkreten Orten oder Regionen wie dem Ruhrgebiet zu spüren. Viele dieser Einwanderer nennen seltener Deutschland als Heimat, sondern sagen: ich komme aus dem Pott, ich bin mit Leib und Seele Hamburger, Rheinländer oder was auch immer.

MEDIENDIENST: Der Sprachforscher Anatol Stefanowitsch meint: Wer Heimat zu einem politischen Begriff macht, teilt die Bevölkerung eines Landes auf in die, die dazugehören, und die, die Fremde sind. Das trifft auf die rechten Gruppen zu, die sich den „Heimatschutz" auf die Fahnen schreiben. Wie sehen Sie das?

NAIKA FOROUTAN: Ich kann dem folgen. Aber wenn man mit Menschen mit Einwanderungsgeschichte spricht, merkt man: Die meisten gehen mit dem Begriff relativ ungezwungen um. Ich finde nicht, dass dieser Begriff nur in einer destruktiven Form gedeutet werden muss. Man muss anderen nicht die Deutungshoheit überlassen, sondern kann sich Begriffe auch aneignen, erobern oder erweitern. Und auch Einwanderungsländer können eine Heimat bieten. In den USA verbindet sich der Begriff mit der Vorstellung von der strahlenden Stadt auf einem Hügel und dem Wissen, dass Millionen Menschen über das Meer zu diesem verheißungsvollen Ort gekommen sind. Das muss nicht automatisch auf „Homeland Security" hinauslaufen.

*(612 Wörter)*

*https://mediendienst-integration.de/artikel/heimat-heimatministerium-einwanderer-einwanderung-deutschland-naika-foroutan-integration-migration.html*

## Lösungsvorschläge

*In dieser Aufgabe müssen Sie für eine amerikanische Schülerzeitung einen kurzen Artikel zum Thema Heimat und Heimatministerium halten. Ihre Zielgruppe sind also amerikanische Jugendliche. Entsprechend braucht Ihre Sprache nicht allzu formell zu sein, darf aber dem Thema angemessen auch nicht zu umgangssprachlich sein. Inhaltlich müssen Sie auf die Aspekte aus dem Interview mit Foroutan eingehen, die deren Einschätzung des Heimatministeriums und des Heimatbegriffs deutlich machen. Die Funktion des Artikels ist es, eine deutsche Perspektive zum Thema zu bieten. Auch wenn in der Aufgabenstellung die deutschen Begriffe zitiert werden, sollten Sie in Ihrem Lösungstext passende englische Umschreibungen finden.*

- *Überschrift*
- *Foroutans Sicht auf das deutsche Heimatministerium*
  - *Sinnvoll, wenn es darum geht, regionale Ungleichheiten z. B. zwischen Stadt und Land auszugleichen*
  - *Kann Regionen Deutschlands aufwerten*
  - *Kann regionale Vielfalt sichtbar machen*
  - *Gefahr, dass der Eindruck entsteht, es gehe darum zu einem alten Deutschland ohne verwirrende Vielfalt zurückzukehren*
  - *Eher rückwärtsgewandt als auf Zukunft ausgerichtet*
- *Foroutans Sicht auf den Heimatbegriff*
  - *Tendenziell rückwärtsgewandt, verklärte Sicht auf die Vergangenheit*
  - *Menschen greifen bei der Suche nach Identität häufig auf Erzählungen aus der Vergangenheit zurück, darauf, woher jemand kommt (Region, Familie, Land, Schicht, politische Tradition)*
  - *Auch Migranten teilen diese Erzählung; starke Verbundenheit mit Orten oder Regionen in Deutschland, in denen sie gelebt haben oder leben; nicht so sehr mit Deutschland als Ganzes*
  - *Menschen mit Einwanderungsgeschichte gehen häufig ungezwungener mit dem Heimatbegriff um*
  - *Im deutschen politischen Diskurs teilt der Begriff häufig in diejenigen, die dazugehören und diejenigen, die fremd sind*
  - *Plädoyer dafür, den Begriff selbst zu deuten und nicht einer destruktiven Deutung den Raum zu überlassen, denn auch Einwanderungsländer können Heimat bieten*
  - *Beispiel für subversiven Umgang mit dem Begriff: „Heymat" mit y um auf Hybridität und Hybridisierung von Gesellschaften zu verweisen; Forschungsprojekt zur Bildung von Identitäten in der Moderne*

## Home and homeland seen from a German perspective | headline

In Mr Janeiro's social science course we have talked a lot about the meaning of the term home and homeland as well as about the relevance of the Department of Homeland Security. Being a German exchange student, I would like to present a German perspective on these issues. To do so, I want to refer to an interview with a German professor on migration and integration who has brought forth some interesting thoughts. First, I'm going to talk about the relatively new German Department of Homeland and then on the term home as seen by Professor Foroutan. Finally, I'll come to a conclusion and will present my view. | introduction

reference to article

give an outline

Let me start with some remarks on the German Department of Homeland, which is part of the Department of the Interior. According to Foroutan it is not quite clear what the function of this new department is. You may have noted that it is not called Department of Homeland Security and therefore Germany's security is not the focus of this new department. She suggests its task could be to balance regional differences within Germany. In Germany there are relatively few big cities like Berlin or Munich. We have more small or medium-sized cities as well as rural areas. The different regions could be strengthened and revaluated. The regional differences could become more visible and appreciated. | German Department of Homeland

chances

However, Foroutan sees the danger that many people get the impression that it is this department's task to bring back good old Germany without its troubling diversity. Then the department would not be apt to prepare Germany for the future. | risks

Now I'll turn to the term home or homeland. Following the argument in the interview, this term is often connected with looking back, and in doing so with glorifying the past. However, people tend to refer to the past when they try to determine their identity. They refer to their roots, which may be the region or the country they come from, their family, their social group or their political tradition. People with a migrational background share this narrative. The towns and areas they have lived in or are still living in in Germany make an important part of their identity, but not necessarily the country as a whole. Foroutan stresses that these people often have a less complicated relationship with the term homeland. | transition – "homeland"

identity

view of people with migrational background

In a political context, in Germany the term is often used to make a difference between those who "belong" to Germany and those who – allegedly – do not. As a consequence, Foroutan suggests that each and everyone fills the term with meaning for themselves in order not to allow certain right-wing groups to use the term in a destructive way because foreign countries can offer a home too. She presents one example of such a different interpretation. In a research project they spelled the German word "Heimat", which means home or homeland, with "ey" instead of "ei", which sounds the same in German. Thus, the word home could be linked to other words spelled with "h" and "y" such as hybridity and hybridization, terms which are meant to show that in our times identities are not fixed but are reinvented again and again.

political context

different interpretations

example: project "Heymat"

I chose to present Foroutan's ideas because to my mind they are worth considering, especially her appeal not to allow right-wing groups to use the term homeland to their purpose. I reckon we all want to feel at home somewhere and right now, this American town and my host family feel a bit like home for me, even though Germany will remain my home country. *(602 words)*

**conclusion**

## Mündliche Abiturprüfung NRW – Englisch LK
## Übungsaufgabe 1

### Prüfungsteil 1: Monologische Präsentation

**Aufgabenstellung**

1. Point out Lewis's views on performing Shakespeare.
2. Analyse how Lewis presents her views to the readers. Focus on her line of argument and her use of language.
3. Comment on Lewis's demand to "do away with Shakespeare altogether – at least on stage" (l. 6). Refer to work done in class and your personal experience.

**Text:**
**Jemima Lewis, Shakespeare is too obscure for the stage, methinks**
*I'd like to do away with Shakespeare altogether – at least on stage. It's just too old*

1 [...] Is there any less convivial feeling than sitting in a theatre surrounded by people pretending to laugh at a Shakespearean gag? "Wahahaha," they squawk, perhaps dabbing at their eyes for extra authenticity. And then, when you ask what's so funny, it turns out to be a 400-year-old pun that means Sir Toby Belch has a tiny willy.

5 [...] I'd like to do away with Shakespeare altogether – at least on stage. It's just too old. The language is so antiquated that, unless you've already studied the play at school, you spend the whole time trying to work out the meaning of one line without missing the next one. It's like trying to pat your head while rubbing your tummy.

There isn't a self-respecting culture vulture in the land who would agree with me, 10 of course. The received wisdom tends to go the other way. Shakespeare, according to those in the know, is only difficult or boring when it hasn't been brought to life. It must be performed on stage to be truly understood.

[...] Dame Judi says children should be encouraged to look beyond the text and think about the big themes: love, anger, jealousy and so on. "That's what Shakes-15 peare's about, all those things. He says it better than anybody else."

I'm sure he does. But you have to leap the hurdle of basic comprehension before you can get to the deeper meaning. The reason I am a Shakespeare philistine is that I was badly educated. I only ever studied – by which I mean line-by-line analysis with a beetle-browed teacher – one play: *Macbeth*. And actually, I loved it. Still do. I can 20 even watch it on stage without undue suffering.

Perhaps Shakespeare does come alive on the stage. But first he must be exhumed in the classroom. *(298 words)*

Jemima Lewis: *Shakespeare is too obscure for the stage, methinks*,
https://www.telegraph.co.uk/culture/theatre/william-shakespeare/11214992/Shakespeare-is-too-obscure-for-the-stage-methinks.html, 07. 11. 2014

**Annotations**
l. 4   *Sir Toby Belch*: a character in a Shakespeare play
l. 4   *willy*: (informal) penis
l. 9   *vulture*: a large bird of prey; (derogatory) a person who preys on others
l. 13  *Dame Judi*: Judi Dench, a renowned actress associated with Shakespeare plays
l. 17  *philistine*: a person who is hostile or indifferent to culture (here, to Shakespeare)
l. 19  *beetle-browed*: strict and serious

## Prüfungsteil 2: Flexibles Prüfungsgespräch

**Mögliche Impulse**

1. Your view on Shakespeare plays is rather negative/positive. What about other literary texts that we have read in class, could you relate to these more easily/as easily? **Explain** why or why not.

2. It is often claimed that Shakespeare's themes are for all times. What about the themes addressed in the play/novel (that you have just talked about), are they relevant for today's society? **Discuss**.

3. **Present** features of a dystopian novel and **analyse** to what extent they can be applied to the dystopian texts we have dealt with in class.

4. **Discuss:** Do you consider dystopias to be a means to make people aware of current trends which might lead to dystopian scenarios if people do not change their ways?

5. One of the topics we have dealt with in class has been "Globalisation and global challenges". Can you **explain** what globalisation is, and **illustrate** some advantages as well as disadvantages of globalisation?

6. Do you think there should be (more or less) global organizations to face challenges of globalisation? Please **state and explain** some.

7. **Name and exemplify** positive effects and/or challenges of cultural encounters in connection with globalisation.

8. **Explain** what globalisation could mean to you yourself in the context of studying and working in a globalised world.

# Lösungsvorschläge

*Allgemeiner Hinweis: Für die Lösungsvorschläge zur mündlichen Prüfung wird bewusst auf ausformulierte Musterlösungen verzichtet. Anhand der Stichpunkte sehen Sie, welche inhaltlichen Aspekte Sie abdecken sollten. Gehen Sie bei Ihrer Vorbereitung ähnlich vor und notieren Sie nur ein Gerüst, das Sie anschließend einem Gegenüber mündlich präsentieren.*

## Prüfungsteil 1

1. *In dieser Aufgabe geht es darum, das eigene Textverständnis zu belegen. Denken Sie daran, mit einem einleitenden Satz zu Titel, Autorin, Erscheinungsjahr/-ort zu beginnen. Fassen Sie danach die Thesen der Autorin zu Aufführungen von Stücken Shakespeares kurz zusammen.*

   - Shakespeare should not be performed on stage, because
     • the plays are too old
     • the language is hard to understand
     • as a result, one cannot enjoy the play
     • seeing a performance without knowing the play is even more difficult
   - however, the themes Shakespeare deals with are important
   - play must be thoroughly studied in school before it can be enjoyed on stage

2. *Hier handelt es sich um eine Textanalyse. Erläutern Sie, wie die Autorin ihren Standpunkt unterstreicht. Achten Sie dabei insbesondere auf ihre Argumentation und auf die verwendete Sprache. Stellen Sie zu Beginn eine Arbeitsthese auf, die Sie dann mit Textbelegen untermauern.*

   - Lewis wants to **convince** the readers **of her hostility** towards Shakespeare's plays on stage.
   - Her argumentative structure is supposed to underline the logic of her argument
     • **provocative thesis** in the headline and subheading
     • offers an **example** that illustrates and proves her point (ll. 1–4)
     • presents typical **counterarguments** but **distances herself** from these (see language) (cf. ll. 9–12)
     • **partly agrees with opponents** as far as importance of Shakespeare's themes are concerned (ll. 13–15)
     • names a **condition under which she can agree**: Shakespeare has to be analysed in detail (at school) before he can be enjoyed (ll. 16–20)
     • this condition leads to a **compromise** (ll. 21/22)
   - The particular use of language underlines her argument
     • **imagery** to make herself understood and to contrast her everyday language with Shakespeare's antiquated English (e. g. ll. 8/9, 16, 19, 21)
     • **makes fun of** those who defend Shakespeare

- negative expressions (e. g. "culture vulture", l. 9; "they squawk", l. 2)
- "of course" (l. 10), "received wisdom" (l. 10) → defending Shakespeare is the thing to do; she calls into question how serious defendants really are; reproaches them with inauthenticity

3. *Bei dieser Aufgabe ist Ihre eigene Meinung gefragt. Wie stehen Sie zu der Forderung, dass Shakespeares Stücke nicht mehr aufgeführt werden sollten? Sie können die Argumente von Lewis und die in ihrem Text genannten Gegenargumente nutzen, um ihre eigenen Gedanken zu strukturieren und zu belegen. Beziehen Sie sich auf Ihre eigenen Erfahrungen sowie auf die Filmausschnitte und Textauszüge und ggf. Theateraufführungen, die Sie im Unterricht besprochen haben.*

- express your opinion on Lewis's view: agreement or disagreement
- refer to aspects discussed by Lewis
  - language
  - themes
  - performances; bringing Shakespeare to life
- give reasons for your view
  - difficult to understand
  - the pictures in the movie helped/didn't help to understand the play (give examples)
  - say if it was easier for you to watch the film scenes before or after having dealt with the text
  - however, important topics, e. g. love in *Romeo and Juliet*, ambition in *Macbeth*
  - ways of bringing Shakespeare to life, e. g. acting out scenes yourself

**Prüfungsteil 2**

1. Ideas for your answer:
   - refer to literary texts dealt with in class (a modern drama and a novel)
   - give a brief **summary** of the play's or the novel's content
   - say what helped you and what made it difficult to understand these texts

2. Ideas for your answer:
   - name the themes dealt with in the novel and the drama
   - say whether you think that they are still up to date
   - **give reasons for** your view and also consider arguments **against** it

3. Ideas for an example answer (additionally you need to apply these features to the specific text you dealt with):
   - set in the future
   - exaggerated worst-case scenario
   - make a criticism about a current trend, societal norm, or political system

- warning of current trends, e. g. lack of freedom
- the manipulation of people
- protagonist
  - questions the existing system
  - helps the audience recognize the negative aspects through her/his perspective
- caste-like organization

4. Ideas for your answer:
   - give arguments for and against dystopias warning of current problems
   - refer closely to the text you dealt with
     - say what warning was included
     - explain whether you think the topic at question is important for society/your life
     - explain how you reacted to it
     - say if it made you think about your actions or even change your behaviour

5. Ideas for your answer:
   - give a definition, e. g. a process characterized by the interaction of people, countries and companies, closely connected with economy, influence on culture and society, enhanced by advances in technology
   - mention some advantages as well disadvantages to you yourself and give examples
     - advantages: e. g. easier access of goods, information, possibility to travel more easily, to cooperate on a wider scale, get quite different new incentives
     - disadvantages: e. g. being forced to be more flexible, in communication, moving geographically, being confronted by different sets and values etc.

6. Ideas for your answer:
   - name and explain e. g. UN, NATO, IMF, but also Commonwealth and/or EU
   - illustrate positive effects and shortcomings of one or more of these organizations
   
   *Example: UN*
   - advantages of the UN: democratic structure, 192 nations are represented, opportunity to discuss and solve problems diplomatically, UN charter proclaims global values
   - shortcomings of the UN:
     - The Assembly's resolutions are not legally binding → they cannot make new international law nor authoritatively interpret existing international law.
     - Before a dispute can be submitted to the Court of Justice its jurisdiction has to be established by both parties (states). Some countries do not accept its jurisdiction at all.
     - the Security Council has no army of its own → relies heavily on member states to respect and carry out its resolutions
     
     = "toothless tiger"

7. Ideas for your answer:
   - illustrate e. g. the advantage of clothes, food, music from other cultures being readily available, the easier exchange of ideas and attitudes, and how something new can be created as an outcome etc.
   - as opposed to e. g. the challenge of being confronted by very different ideas and cultural beliefs and having to reconcile these, or the supposed threat of Americanization felt by many people
8. Ideas for your answer:
   - explain e. g. chances of finding a place to study, and later on to work
   - mention challenges included, e. g. challenge of language(s), having to adapt to new cultural surroundings, being away from family etc.

**Abiturprüfung NRW – Englisch 2020**
**Leistungskurs: Aufgabe 1**

## Teil A: Leseverstehen und Schreiben (integriert)   Inhalt 42 P. / Sprache 63 P.

### Aufgabenstellung                                                                 Punkte

1. Point out what Amy and Archie are each occupied with.
   *(Comprehension)*                                                                    12

2. Analyse how Archie and his state of mind are presented. Focus on point
   of view and use of language. *(Analysis)*                                             16

3. Choose **one** of the following tasks:                                                14

3.1 In the excerpt, the events taking place in the USA in 1963 are described
as an "endless tangle of horror and hope that seemed to define the
American landscape" (l. 15).
Evaluate to what extent this might also be a valid description of the
situation in the USA today. Refer to the text and work done in class on
American myths and realities then and now. *(Evaluation: comment)*

3.2 Having devoted her life to a "cause" (l. 35), Amy, now 73 years old, has
agreed to give an interview to *The New York Times* on crucial causes
young people should fight for in the 21st century. Write the interview,
taking into account the text and work done in class on economic,
ecological and political issues of globalisation.
*(Evaluation: re-creation of text)*

**Text:**
**Paul Auster, *4 3 2 1***

*Archie Ferguson meets Amy Schneiderman, daughter of his parents' friends, at a Labor Day barbecue party at his home in Montclair, New Jersey. It is September 2, 1963.*

1   They were the same age, or very nearly the same age, two hundred months old as opposed to a hundred and ninety-eight months old, but because Amy had been born at the end of 1946 (December 29) and Ferguson at the beginning of 1947 (March 3), she was a full year ahead of him in school, which meant that she was about to start her
5   senior year at Hunter while he was still stuck in the trenches as a lowly junior. College was no more than a nebulous anywhere to him at that point, a far-flung destination that had yet to be given a name, whereas she had been studying maps for the better part of a year and was almost ready to begin packing her bags. She would be applying to several schools, she said.

2020-1

10    Everyone had told her she would need backups, second and third options, but Barnard was her first choice; her only choice, really [...].
  [A]s he sat in the room with Amy and later walked through the streets with her, they talked about any number of things, mostly about the roller-coaster summer that had started with the killing of Medgar Evers and ended with Martin Luther King's speech,
15 the endless tangle of horror and hope that seemed to define the American landscape, and also about the books and records on the shelves and floor of Ferguson's room, not to mention schoolwork, SATs, and even baseball, but the one question he did not ask her, was determined at all costs to refrain from asking, was whether she had a boyfriend, for he had already decided he was going to do everything in his power to make her the
20 *next one*, and he had no interest in learning how many rivals were standing in his way.
  On September fifteenth, less than two weeks after the Labor Day barbecue, which was exactly six days before they were supposed to get together again in New York, she called him, and because he was the one she called and no one else, he understood that there was no boyfriend in the picture, no rival to be afraid of, and that she was with
25 him now in the same way he was with her. He knew that because he was the person she chose to call when she heard the news about the bombing of a black church in Birmingham, Alabama, and the murder of four little girls inside, another American horror, another battle in the race war spreading across the South, as if the March on Washington two and a half weeks earlier had to be avenged with bombs and murder,
30 and Amy was crying into the phone, struggling not to cry as she told him the news, and bit by bit, as she slowly pulled herself together, she began to talk about what could be done, about what she felt had to be done, not just laws passed by politicians but an army of people to go down there and fight the bigots, and she would be the first one to join up, the day after she graduated from high school she would hitchhike to Alabama
35 and work for the cause, bleed for the cause, make the cause the central purpose of her life. It's our country, she said, and we can't let the bastards steal it from us.

*(559 words)*

Paul Auster, 4 3 2 1, New York: Henry Holt 2017, pp. 140–142

**Annotations**
l. 5  *Hunter:* Hunter College High School in Manhattan, New York
l. 10  *Barnard:* Barnard College in New York City, a college for women only
l. 14  *Medgar Evers:* an American civil rights activist in Mississippi
l. 17  *SATs:* Scholastic Assessment Test; standardised tests used for college admissions in the USA
ll. 26/27  *16th Street Baptist Church bombing, Birmingham, Alabama, 1963:* a terrorist act committed by the Ku Klux Klan

**Teil B: Sprachmittlung (isoliert)**  Inhalt 18 P. / Sprache 27 P.

**Aufgabenstellung**

4. Your English friend is a member of a political youth organisation. They are interested in young people's social commitment across Europe. She/He has asked you specifically for information on volunteering in Germany. Based on Julia Emmrich and Theresa Martus' article, write her/him an email in which you present the situation of volunteering and ways to encourage more young people to participate. *(Mediation)*     18

**Text:**
**Julia Emmrich und Theresa Martus, *Wie sinnvoll wäre ein Pflichtdienst für junge Leute?***

1 Raus aus der Schule – rein ins richtige Leben: Für viele junge Deutsche ist der Schritt alles andere als leicht. Ausbildung? Studium? Auslandsjahr? Oder erstmal jobben? Die Politik diskutiert in diesen Tagen über die Einführung eines verpflichtenden Dienstjahrs für Schulabgänger. Aber ist das überhaupt sinnvoll? Rund 100 000 junge Leute
5 leisten derzeit bereits Jahr für Jahr Freiwilligendienste. Und: Es gibt jetzt schon mehr Bewerbungen als freie Stellen. Wäre es nicht besser, den Freiwilligendienst zu stärken?
    Die traditionsreichste Form des freiwilligen Engagements ist das Freiwillige Soziale Jahr, kurz FSJ. Seinen Ursprung hat das Konzept in Aufrufen der Kirchen; sich ein
10 Jahr lang freiwillig in den Dienst der Gemeinschaft zu stellen. Seit 1964 regelt das Gesetz Rahmenbedingungen für die Dienste. 1993 kam das Freiwillige ökologische Jahr (FÖJ) dazu, bei dem sich junge Leute für Natur- und Umweltschutz einsetzen können.
    Die Einsätze, die meist zwölf Monate lang sind, aber auch kürzer oder länger sein
15 können, sind nicht auf das Inland beschränkt: Viele Träger bieten auch im Ausland FSJ-Plätze an. […]
    Rund 100 000 Männer und Frauen leisten derzeit einen der Freiwilligendienste. Etwa 55 000 arbeiten im Rahmen der Jugenddienste. Der Trend geht aber nach Angaben des Familienministeriums seit Jahren nach oben. Die meisten Freiwilligen im Sozialen
20 Jahr seien 18 Jahre alt, sagt Jaana Eichhorn vom Bundesarbeitskreis FSJ, einem Zusammenschluss der Trägerorganisationen. In den letzten Jahren sei zudem die Zahl der Minderjährigen gestiegen. […]
    Vor allem Unionspolitiker hatten Sympathie für die Idee eines Dienstjahrs ausgedrückt. Verbände dagegen sind skeptisch und sprechen sich eher für eine Stärkung der
25 bestehenden Angebote aus. „Wir haben mit den Freiwilligendiensten zeigen können, dass dort, wo Menschen sich freiwillig einbringen, die Zufriedenheit bei allen Beteiligten extrem hoch ist", sagt Jaana Eichhorn vom Bundesarbeitskreis FSJ dieser Redaktion, „bei den Freiwilligen selbst genauso wie bei den Einrichtungen." Es mache

einen Unterschied, ob jemand sich freiwillig für einen Dienst entscheide oder gezwun-
gen sei.
   Sie plädiert deshalb dafür, die existierenden Dienste attraktiver zu machen, zum Beispiel mit besserer Bezahlung. Denn während Zivildienstleistende die gleichen Bezüge erhielten wie Wehrdienstleistende, bekommen Menschen in den freiwilligen Jugenddiensten und im BFD nur ein Taschengeld. „Unsere Freiwilligen können meist nicht von zu Hause ausziehen und sind auf ihre Eltern angewiesen", sagt Eichhorn. Außerdem wünscht sie sich mehr gesellschaftliche Anerkennung, zum Beispiel in Form bevorzugter Studienzulassung.
   Das Deutsche Rote Kreuz, nach eigenen Angaben der größte Träger von Freiwilligendiensten in Deutschland, begrüßt die Debatte um die Dienstpflicht, weil sie dazu beitragen könne, das Engagement zu stärken. Doch auch das DRK will mehr Engagement aus der Politik für freiwillige Optionen. „Wir wünschen uns mehr Anerkennung sozialen Engagements", sagt DRK-Sprecher Dieter Schütz, „denn wir werden in den nächsten Jahrzehnten zunehmend mehr Einsatz brauchen." *(434 Wörter)*

*Julia Emmrich und Theresa Martus: „Wie sinnvoll wäre ein Pflichtdienst für junge Leute?", NRZ vom 08. 08. 2018, http://www.nrz.de/politik/wie-sinnvoll-waere-ein-pflichtdienst-fuer-junge-leute-id215037271.html, © Neue Ruhr / Neue Rhein Zeitung, Zeitungsverlag Niederrhein GmbH & Co. Essen Kommanditgesellschaft*

**Anmerkungen**
Z. 17/18 Freiwilligendienste/Jugenddienste: Im Gegensatz zu Jugenddiensten sind Freiwilligendienste auch offen für Erwachsene über 27 Jahren.
Z. 32/33 Zivildienstleistende/Wehrdienstleistende: Bis 2011 bestand für männliche Jugendliche die Pflicht, entweder Wehr- oder Zivildienst zu leisten.
Z. 34 BFD: Bundesfreiwilligendienst

## Lösungsvorschläge

### Teil A: Leseverstehen und Schreiben (integriert)

1. *In this task, you need to show what the two protagonists, Amy and Archie, are concerned about. This could be done very briefly, but to elaborate a little, you will need to choose further details to include.*
   - *Amy*
     - *her choice of college; currently in her last year at high school, has set her mind on Barnard*
     - *her priorities change after the Birmingham attacks; she intends to become active in the Civil Rights Movement*
   - *Archie*
     - *his relationship with Amy: in love with her, intends to become her boyfriend*
     - *wonders if she already has a boyfriend*
     - *remains preoccupied with this topic even after the attacks; interprets her call only in terms of their relationship, thinks she is interested in him*

| | |
|---|---|
| The excerpt from Paul Auster's novel *4 3 2 1* published in 2017 is set in 1963. In it, two teenagers, Archie and Amy, have two conversations, one at a Labour Day barbecue the other on the telephone after the attacks on a church in Birmingham. | introductory sentence |
| During the conversation on Labour Day Amy is preoccupied with her choice of college. She is in her last year of high school and is determined to attend Barnard College afterwards. Two weeks later, after the attacks on a Black church in Birmingham, Alabama, Amy's focus has changed completely. She now intends to become an active member of the Civil Rights Movement after high school. | Amy's thoughts |
| By contrast, Archie's priorities remain constant. His mind is set on making Amy his girlfriend. He asks himself if she has got a boyfriend already but does not really want to know. When she phones him two weeks later, he interprets her call only in terms of their relationship and believes it to be proof that his feelings are reciprocated. *(171 words)* | Archie's thoughts |

2. *Here the focus is on Archie only. You need to analyse how his frame of mind is presented. In doing so, take into account the point of view chosen as well as the effect of that choice. Also analyse the use of language, e. g. choice of words.*
   - *Archie seems immature, only focused on making Amy his girlfriend*
   - *point of view*
     - *third-person narrator (cf. l. 1)*
     - *Archie's perspective (e. g. ll. 23, 25/26) → limited point of view*

2020-5

- reader gets an insight into the character's thoughts and feelings
- reader also realizes Archie's naivety and self-centredness (cf. ll. 21–26)
- narrator is also judgemental of Archie's disorientation (cf. ll. 5–8)
- distanced and impersonal → rather emotionless description of the encounter on Labour Day (ll. 12–17) and the phone call (cf. ll. 26–36)
- hard for the reader to sympathize with the protagonist
- use of language
  - juxtaposition of the two characters' states of mind (cf. ll. 1–11) → Archie is more immature even though they are almost the same age
  - imagery to describe his current situation, e. g. "stuck in the trenches" (l. 5), "a nebulous anywhere" (l. 6)
  - enumeration of topics discussed (ll. 12–17)
  - repetition of "rival(s)" (ll. 20, 24), Amy is supposed to be "the next one" (ll. 19/20) → love affair as a competition, not very serious
  - long sentences in which he repeats her feelings and thoughts without commenting on them (cf. ll. 26–36)

Whereas Amy undergoes a change and becomes more mature, Archie remains preoccupied with his personal feelings. He only thinks about making Amy his next girlfriend. This makes him appear immature and self-centred, which becomes obvious through the point of view chosen and the linguistic composition of the excerpt.

**introductory sentence:** thesis

The story is told by a third-person narrator (cf. ll. 1–3) who often sees the action from Archie's perspective. Whenever the reader gets an insight into Archie's thoughts, the protagonist is wondering how to win Amy over (e. g. ll. 17–20). Even when Amy calls him to talk about the brutal attacks that took place in Birmingham, he only considers what her calls tell him about her affections for him (cf. ll. 21–26). Thus, it becomes clear that he is very self-centred as well as naïve.

**point of view** limited
Archie as self-centred and naive

In other passages, the narrator remains more impersonal and aloof and, at times, judgemental. For instance, the encounters between the two protagonists on Labour Day and during their phone call are described very unemotionally as the topics of their conversation are merely enumerated (cf. ll. 12–17, 26–36) but not commented on. At the beginning of the excerpt, the narrator chooses imagery to describe Archie's situation at school. He is "still stuck in the trenches as a lowly junior" (l. 5) and college is still "a nebulous anywhere to him at that point, a far-flung destination that [has] yet to be given a name" (ll. 6/7). Here the narrator seems rather judgemental of Archie's immaturity and disorientation. As a consequence, it becomes harder for the reader to empathize with the protagonist.

**narrator** judgemental

→ enumeration

→ imagery
immature, disoriented

2020-6

The impression of Archie's immaturity is further underlined by the way his and Amy's state of mind are juxtaposed (cf. ll. 1–11). Due to the implicit comparison between the two characters, which is stressed by conjunctions such as "but" (l. 2), "while" (l. 5) and "whereas" (l. 7), it becomes obvious that Amy is planning ahead and that she is more grown-up although she is only two months older than him (cf. ll. 1/2).

→ juxtaposition

→ conjunctions
disparity between the characters

Even his infatuation with Amy is superficial because to him it seems to be more of a competition with others than a matter of the heart. The word "rival[s]" is repeated twice (cf. ll. 20 and 24) and Amy is simply meant to be the "next one" (l. 20), which implies that she is neither the first nor the last one but just another girl to be conquered. Also, he never comments on Amy's thoughts and feelings but merely repeats them in extremely long sentences (cf. ll. 26–36). As a consequence, the reader gets the impression that Archie is not really interested in what she says but only focuses on the fact that she has called *him* to discuss what has happened and what she intends to do. This is even more striking as she is talking about the killing of "four little girls" (l. 27) in "the bombing of a black church" (l. 26). Even in the face of such horrible events, Archie can only think about himself and his possible romantic conquest.

**choice of words**
love for Amy = conquest, competition

All in all, the choice of language and point of view stress Archie's state of mind as one of a very self-centered and naïve young man who only considers his chances with a girl although far more serious events are occurring around him. *(566 words)*

**conclusion**

3.1. *Here you are given a quote from the excerpt as a starting point for an evaluation. This suggests that you should present your own opinion on the topic and support it with arguments. Start by explaining the quote and by putting it in its context. Then explain why you think it fits or does not fit the current situation in the USA. Refer to the excerpt at hand and to background knowledge on the American Dream to support your view.*

- meaning of the quote and context
    - excerpt set in 1963 → civil rights movement, race relations
    - reference to killing of civil rights activist Medgar Evers → horror
    - reference to Martin Luther King's speech in Washington → hope
    - a time both of hope and of disastrous setbacks, e. g. attack on Black church in Alabama
- situation today
    - brief explanation of American Dream
    - American Dream still more difficult to achieve for Black people
    - true equality has not been achieved

- *social inequalities, e. g. education in poorer areas is worse, during Corona crisis more Black people and people of colour died*
- *everyday racism, e. g. stopped more often by police*
- *not represented adequately in politics, the media, at universities, etc.*
- *police brutality against BIPOC (Black, Indigenous and people of colour)*
- *President Trump does not seem to aim at reconciling the American people but rather stirs conflicts, e. g. encourages police to react to BLM protestors with great severity*
- *hope: e. g. first Black president, Barack Obama; Black Lives Matter Movement, also White people support BLM Movement*
- *conclusion: quote still appropriate, could also embrace other minorities, e. g. Hispanics*

In the excerpt at hand, the protagonists are discussing the events of 1963 against the backdrop of the civil rights movement. The narrator describes the situation as an "endless tangle of horror and hope that seemed to define the American landscape" (l. 15). The quote indicates that horrific and hopeful events alternated. A Black activist is killed (cf. l. 14), Martin Luther King gives his famous "I have a dream" speech in Washington, a Black church is attacked and "four little girls inside" (l. 27) are killed. Therefore, the description is very fitting for that "roller-coaster summer" (l. 13) but does it also describe the current situation in America appropriately?

**introduction:** explanation and situation of quote relevance of topic

There is certainly hope because Black Americans have come a long way since 1963 and, for instance, segregation has long been abolished. The USA have had their first Black president, Barack Obama, who wanted to heal the rift running through society.

**main part:** **hope:** development since 1963

However, true equality has not been attained. The American Dream, which states that everybody can gain success and prosperity if they only work hard enough, is still more difficult for Black, Indigenous and people of colour than for White people. Social inequality and everyday racism still exist and are apparent, for instance, in the quality of schools depending on the neighbourhood they are in, in the difficulties BIPOC have in finding a home in a predominantly White neighbourhood and in the fact that Black people and people of colour are stopped more often by the police and that the number of Black prisoners is out of proportion, whereas they are not appropriately represented in politics, law or the media, for example. During the Corona crisis, more Black people were affected by Covid 19, indicating that their social status is lower. With a lower level of education, they work in lower-paid jobs like sales assistants or nurses and have been at a greater risk of exposure to the virus.

**horror:** inequality and racism persist

→ examples

Another example of inequality is police brutality. A disproportionate number of Black Americans die at the hands of police officers, the most recent example being George Floyd, who was suffocated during an arrest in 2020. The subsequent protests organised, e. g. by the Black Lives Matter Movement show the dissatisfaction of Blacks and people of colour in the USA. Unlike his predecessor, who had to deal with similar events, Donald Trump, the current president, does not try to calm people down, but rather encourages the police to react with particular severity to the demonstrators.

**horror:** police brutality

Donald Trump

However, these demonstrations can be seen as a sign of hope because White and Black people have been demonstrating together. This is a very significant change compared to 1963. Nowadays, people of all races and from all walks of life are standing together to fight racism and inequality.

**hope:** demonstrations

One can only hope that, in the long run, their fight will be successful so that the quote, which still adequately describes the situation today, will one day be considered inappropriate.

**conclusions**

*(493 words)*

3.2 Here you are to write an interview with Amy Schneiderman, who is expressing her view on the necessity for young people to fight for crucial causes in the 21st century. You need to put yourself into Amy's shoes and consider what her point of view might be and what causes she might consider crucial. The excerpt provides some ideas as to what her opinion might be. For the causes, you need to consider global challenges you discussed in class. Make sure to structure the interview appropriately and to stick to everyday spoken language that is suitable for an interview with a quality paper.
- beginning
    - briefly present her to the readers
    - give reasons for the interview
- main part, global challenges, e. g.
    - racism
    - social equality
    - migration
    - climate change
    - impact of the digital age
- Amy's motivation
    - explain why she became an activist
    - evaluate how successful she has been
- ending
    - thank Amy for the interview
    - Amy might appeal to readers

**NYT:** Hello Amy, thank you for meeting with us.  
**AS:** The pleasure is all mine.  
**NYT:** You've dedicated your entire life to fighting for equality between Black and White people. How did this come about?  
**AS:** When I was sixteen, in 1963, the civil rights movement was at its peak. I'd heard Martin Luther King speak in Washington and I was fascinated. But what really triggered my decision to join the movement was the bombing of a Black church in Birmingham, Alabama, back in 1963.  
**NYT:** Can you tell our readers more about that appalling attack?  
**AS:** It was a White supremacist terrorist attack; the KKK attacked the church and four little girls died. At the time, I was a senior in high school and I had my mind set on going to Barnard College, but then everything changed. All of a sudden, I felt that I couldn't go on as if all of this didn't have anything to do with me. There were Black people dying at the hands of White men, and I needed to show that I was ashamed of the way White people treated Blacks.  
**NYT:** Looking back at your life, would you say that you managed to make a difference?  
**AS:** I think we can all make a difference. Maybe not like Martin Luther King or Malcom X or like Rosa Parks. But it certainly made a difference back in 1963 that White people joined the Black movement. It showed the Black activists that they were supported not only within their own community but also from the outside. I think that made a difference, yes, I do.  
**NYT:** What about your grandchildren and other young people today, what do you think they should fight for?  
**AS:** I'm afraid there is a great deal to fight for these days. Where should I start? For one, racial inequality is still there. And there's social inequality, gender inequality, there is global warming, migration. The list could go on and on.  
**NYT:** So, do you think young people are less active in fighting for a cause they believe in than people were back in the 1960s?  
**AS:** Actually, I don't think so at all. Just think of Black Lives Matter or the Fridays for Future Movement. FFF started with one teenager who was persistent enough to engage young people around the world. And not only young people, even people my age have joined that movement. Climate change is probably THE most important challenge we're facing. If we do not manage to slow global warming, all the other issues will no longer be relevant because we might be facing extinction.  
**NYT:** Now you're being very pessimistic.

| | |
|---|---|
| | **opening sentence** |
| | Amy's motivation, reference to text |
| | achievements |
| | causes to fight for today |
| | → examples |
| | biggest challenge: climate change |

2020-10

**AS:** Yes, you're probably right. That is something I've realized about myself. I'm growing more pessimistic because scientists have been warning us for ages about global warming and yet our president still continues to deny it. I certainly hope that the younger generation will take this more seriously and act accordingly.

**NYT:** So, looking back at your life and at the half a century you've dedicated to civil rights, what would you recommend young people to do? advice for young people

**AS:** What would I recommend? Be persistent, don't stop nagging people, and don't listen to anyone who tells you that things cannot be changed. Connect with each other and make yourselves heard. If there are enough of you and if you keep repeating your demands, eventually, you'll succeed.

**NYT:** That sounds more positive. Your own success with the civil rights movement really does show that change is possible. Thank you for the interview. closing sentences

**AS:** Thanks for having me.  *(584 words)*

## Teil B: Sprachmittlung (isoliert)

4. *In dieser Mediationsaufgabe müssen Sie eine persönliche E-Mail an eine befreundete Person schreiben, die Mitglied in einer politischen Jugendorganisation ist. Der Text kann daher umgangssprachlich verfasst sein. Inhaltlich geht es um die aktuelle Situation des Freiwilligendienstes in Deutschland und die Frage, wie man mehr junge Leute motivieren kann, einen solchen Dienst zu absolvieren.*

   – *Anrede, Bezug zur E-Mail des Freundes/der Freundin*
   – *Aktuelle Situation*
     - *rund 100 000 junge Leute leisten jedes Jahr Freiwilligendienste*
     - *mehr Bewerbungen als freie Plätze*
     - *steigender Trend genauso wie steigender Bedarf*
     - *FSJ und FÖJ als gängige Formen des freiwilligen Engagements*
   – *Möglichkeiten der Motivation*
     - *Überlegung, den Freiwilligendienst verpflichtend zu machen*
     - *Verbände fordern Freiwilligkeit bei besserer Bezahlung beizubehalten (in freiwilligen Jugenddiensten nur Taschengeld)*
     - *mehr gesellschaftliche Anerkennung, z. B. in Form bevorzugter Studienzulassung*
   – *Schlusssatz*
   – *Grußformel, Name*

Hi Sean, — greeting

How are you? Thanks for your mail! How interesting that you've joined a political youth organization. I was thinking of doing so, too, but I haven't made up my mind yet. Maybe you can tell me a bit more about the organization and your work there in your next mail. — introductory sentence, reference to task

You've asked for information on volunteering in Germany, and I've found an article in a regional daily which outlines the situation quite nicely. The authors say that in Germany, the most popular forms of volunteering are in the social or ecological sector. Every year, about 100,000 people volunteer in these areas. There are even more applicants than vacancies, and the number of people who want to volunteer keeps rising. However, organizations like the Red Cross predict that the amount of volunteer work needed will also increase. — current situation

Recently, politicians have been discussing whether to make such social or ecological volunteer work obligatory for young people for one year. According to the article, most organizations dealing with volunteers are against such an obligation. Apparently, they would prefer better pay for volunteers because, at the moment, they only earn pocket money. They also want the work these young people do for society to be better acknowledged. For instance, they could be given easier access to university. — ideas to encourage more young people

That's about it from that article. I hope you can use this information for your work. If there is anything else I can do to help you, just let me know. — closing sentences

Yours,
Karim       (248 words) — closing name

## Abiturprüfung NRW – Englisch 2020
## Leistungskurs: Aufgabe 2

**Teil A: Leseverstehen und Schreiben (integriert)** Inhalt 42 P. / Sprache 63 P.

### Aufgabenstellung
Punkte

1. Outline Hanif Kureishi's views on diversity and discrimination in the British cultural world and in education. *(Comprehension)* — 12

2. Analyse the way the author presents his views. Consider communicative strategies and use of language. *(Analysis)* — 16

3. Choose **one** of the following tasks: — 14

3.1 Hanif Kureishi claims that "real talent has been neglected and discouraged by those who dominate the culture, deliberately keeping schools, the media, universities and the cultural world closed to interesting people" (ll. 31–33). Discuss this statement referring to the text and work done in class on multiculturalism.
*(Evaluation: comment)*

3.2 You are taking part in an international youth conference on the topic *Stronger Together? – Facing Global Challenges in the 21st Century*. Taking Kureishi's claim that we live in a world characterised by a "retreat into panic and nationalism" (ll. 35/36) as a starting point, write a debate statement in which you present your position on the topic of the conference *(Evaluation: re-creation of text)*

### Text:
**Hanif Kureishi, *Diversity in publishing is under attack. I hear the sound of knuckles dragging.***

*Hanif Kureishi, an award-winning British playwright, screenwriter, filmmaker and novelist of Pakistani and English descent, discusses diversity in the British culture industries.*

1 The furore over Penguin's wise and brave decision to "reflect the diversity of British society" in its publishing and hiring output seems to have awoken the usual knuckle-dragging, semi-blind suspects with their endlessly repeated terrors and fears. They appear to believe that what is called "diversity" or "positive action" will lead to a dilution
5 of their culture. Their stupidity and the sound of their pathetic whining would be funny if it weren't so tragic for Britain. You might even want to call it a form of self-loathing; it is certainly unpatriotic and lacking in generosity.

The industries I've worked in for most of my life – film, TV, theatre, publishing – have all been more or less entirely dominated by white Oxbridge men, and they still mostly are. These men and their lackeys have been the beneficiaries of positive discrimination, to say the least, for centuries. The world has always been theirs, and they now believe they own it.

Some of us have been fortunate enough to force a way through the maze and make a living as artists. It was a difficult and often humiliating trip, I can tell you. There was much patronisation and many insults on the way, and they are still going on.

We are still expected to be grateful, though those in charge – never having had to fight for anything – have always been the lucky ones. And these lucky ones, with their implicit privilege, wealth and power – indeed, so much of it they don't even see it – are beginning to intuit that their day is done. Before, with their sense of superiority and lofty arrogance, they could intimidate everyone around them. No more. [...]

It is not coincidental that at this Brexit moment, with its xenophobic, oafish and narrow perspective, the ruling class and its gatekeepers fear a multitude of democratic voices from elsewhere and wish to keep us silent. They can't wait to tell us how undeserving of being heard we really are. But they should remember this: they might have tried to shut the door on Europe, refugees and people of colour, but it will be impossible for them to shut the door on British innovation. We are very insistent, noisy and talented. [...]

The truth is, the conservative fear of other voices is not because of an anxiety that artists from outside the mainstream will be untalented, filling up galleries and bookshops with sludge: it's that they will be outstanding and brilliant. Those conservatives will have to swallow the fact that, despite the success of British artists, real talent has been neglected and discouraged by those who dominate the culture, deliberately keeping schools, the media, universities and the cultural world closed to interesting people.

It is good news that the master race is becoming anxious about whom they might have to hear from. At this terrible Brexit moment, with its retreat into panic and nationalism, and with the same thing happening across Europe, it is time for all artists to speak up, particularly those whose voices have been neglected.

No one knows what a more democratic and inclusive culture would be like. It is fatuously omniscient to assume it would be worse than what we already have. The attempt of reactionaries to shut people down shows both fear and stupidity. But it's too late: they will be hearing from us.   *(554 words)*

*Hanif Kureishi, "Diversity in publishing is under attack. I hear the sound of knuckles dragging", in:* The Guardian, *15 June 2018*
*https://www.theguardian.com/commentisfree/2018/jun/15/diversity-publishing-culture-minority-writers-penguin*

**Annotations**
l. 1   *Penguin:* an important British publishing house
l. 2   *publishing and hiring output: here:* the authors whose works Penguin publishes and the staff Penguin hires
l. 4   *positive action: also:* affirmative action
l. 9   *Oxbridge:* contraction of Oxford and Cambridge, the two most prestigious British universities
l. 15  *patronisation: here:* behaviour that seems friendly but shows that the person acting that way feels superior towards the other person

## Teil B: Sprachmittlung (isoliert)   Inhalt 18 P. / Sprache 27 P.

**Aufgabenstellung**

4. Your English friend is working on a presentation on the role of immigrant culture across Europe. She/He has asked you about information from Germany.
Write an email to her/him in which you sum up what Christoph Manus' article says about the concept of the *Frankfurter Immigrationsbuchmesse* and the impact of immigrant culture on urban life in Germany.
*(Mediation)* 18

**Text:**
**Christoph Manus, *Literatur als Brückenbauer in Frankfurt***

Die Immigrationsbuchmesse ist eine eher intime Angelegenheit. Zwölf Verlage präsentieren sich an Ständen im Leopold-Sonnemann-Saal des Historischen Museums, haben Romane, Erzählungen, Sachbücher dabei, in denen es schwerpunktmäßig um Migration und interkulturellen Austausch geht. Zwei Tage lang lesen Autoren in dem Museumssaal und der Evangelischen Akademie aus ihren Werken vor. Es gibt Vorträge und Diskussionen.

Das Selbstbewusstsein der Organisatoren aber, die die kleine, aber anspruchsvolle Veranstaltung zum achten Mal ehrenamtlich gestemmt haben, ist durchaus groß. Bei der Immigrationsbuchmesse gehe es um Kultur und Kommunikation, bei der großen Frankfurter Buchmesse um Kommerz, sagt Hamidul Khan, der die Bücherschau mit Fokus auf Migration einst ins Leben rief. Die Migrationsbuchmesse sei wichtig, um die literarische Vielfalt in Frankfurt zu zeigen, sagt Mitorganisatorin Susanne Konrad. Man solle den Literaturbetrieb nicht allein den herrschenden Schichten überlassen, sondern auch andere zu Wort kommen lassen.

Die wohl prominenteste Autorin, die die Veranstalter diesmal verpflichtet haben, ist Gretchen Dutschke. Die Witwe des Studentenführers Rudi Dutschke liest aus ihrem Buch „1968: Worauf wir stolz sein dürfen". Inzwischen sei sie deutsche Staatsbürgerin. Sie wisse aber noch sehr genau, wie es ist, ausgeschlossen zu sein, sagt Dutschke am Samstagmorgen bei der Eröffnung der kleinen Messe. Und berichtet, wie sie 1995 ausgewiesen wurde. Sie schrieb an einem Buch, als ihr Visum für Deutschland auslief. Weil sie keine feste Arbeit, kein regelmäßiges Einkommen hatte, musste sie das Land verlassen. [...]

Literatur könne Brücken bauen, etwa zwischen Menschen, die hier schon leben, und solchen, die zuziehen, sagt die neue hessische Ministerin für Wissenschaft und Kunst, Angela Dorn (Grüne), in ihrer Eröffnungsrede. Dazu trage die Immigrationsbuchmesse bei, die selbst ein wunderbares Beispiel für gelebte Vielfalt sei.

Die Einwanderung habe eine neue Kultur in den Großstädten hervorgebracht, dazu beigetragen, dass Frankfurt eine attraktive, multikulturelle Metropole ist, sagt der

Landtagsabgeordnete Turgut Yüksel (SPD). Obwohl es in Deutschland sehr erfolgreiche Schriftsteller und Filmregisseure mit Migrationshintergrund gebe, werde die Kultur der Zugewanderten aber oft noch auf kulinarische Spezialitäten reduziert, kritisiert er.

Die Politik müsse mehr tun, damit mehr Migranten an der Kultur in Frankfurt partizipieren. Der Direktor des Historischen Museums, Jan Gerchow, geht auf die lange Tradition der Buchmesse wie auf die lange Geschichte der Zuwanderung nach Frankfurt ein. Schon bei den ersten Verlegern in der Stadt habe es sich um Zugewanderte gehandelt, sagt er. Die Immigrationsmesse passe daher zu keiner Stadt so gut wie zu Frankfurt.

Der Buchpreis der Immigrationsbuchmesse ging diesmal an die deutsch-ausländische Vereinigung Schwalbach, die das Buch „Zuhause in Schwalbach. Eine Stadt erzählt" herausgegeben hat. In diesem schildern 70 Autorinnen und Autoren, Deutschstämmige wie Immigrierte, ihr Leben in der Kleinstadt. *(423 Wörter)*

*Christoph Manus, „Literatur als Brückenbauer in Frankfurt", in:* Frankfurter Rundschau, *11. März 2019; Frankfurter Rundschau GmbH*

**Anmerkungen**
Z. 16 Gretchen Dutschke: aus den USA stammende Autorin und Aktivistin der Studentenbewegung in der Bundesrepublik Deutschland der 1960er-Jahre

---

## Lösungsvorschläge

### Teil A: Leseverstehen und Schreiben (integriert)

1. *In this comprehension task, you need to present Kureishi's main statements on two aspects, namely diversity and discrimination in the British cultural industries.*
   - *his views on diversity*
     - *supports it, e. g. Penguin's decision to publish and hire more diversely*
     - *it is threatened by people who feel they need to protect "their" culture*
     - *many talents have been wasted*
     - *in the long run, diversity cannot be stopped*
   - *his views on discrimination*
     - *culture industries have been and still are dominated by well-educated white men*
     - *they defend their position against others; they are driven by fear, by xenophobic and nationalistic tendencies*
     - *difficult and humiliating for others*
     - *patronizing and insulting*
     - *people with a migration background are expected to be grateful; however, they are starting to fight back and make their voices heard*

In his article "Diversity in publishing is under attack. I hear the sound of knuckles dragging" published on 15 June, 2018, Hanif Kureishi presents his views on diversity and discrimination in Britain's cultural industries. *(introductory sentence)*

Kureishi fervently supports diversity and praises Penguin's decision to publish and hire more diversely. At the same time, he has the impression that diversity is threatened by people who feel the need to protect "their" culture. According to Kureishi, Britain's cultural industries are largely led and influenced by white men, educated at Britain's elite universities, who appear only to be interested in defending their positions against others. The author believes that they are driven by fear and by both xenophobic and nationalistic tendencies. He claims that their behaviour towards people with a migration background is insulting and patronizing, which makes working in a cultural industry difficult and humiliating for people like the author himself. In addition, he and his colleagues are expected to be grateful for the chances they do get, so Kureishi says. He insists that, as a consequence, many talents are wasted. However, he is convinced that, in the long run, diversity in cultural industries cannot be stopped and that artists of colour are starting to make their voices heard. *(author's view)*

*(206 words)*

2. Here you have to analyse how the author presents the views you outlined in the previous task. In doing so, focus on communicative strategies, for example, use of pronouns. Also focus on the use of language, such as tone and choice of words.
   – communicative strategies
     • pronouns "they" versus "we" and "us" → underline the opposing groups
     • refers to his own experience (e. g. l. 8 and ll. 13–15) → inside knowledge
     • implicit threat (cf. ll. 19/20, 24–27, 40/41) → change will come either way
     • appeal to artists to raise their voices (cf. ll. 36/37) → call to action
   – use of language
     • evaluative adjectives, e. g. "wise and brave" (l. 1), "xenophobic, oafish and narrow" (ll. 21/22)
     • words with a negative connotation, e. g. "fear and stupidity" (l. 40), "pathetic whining" (l. 5), "lofty arrogance" (l. 20), "master race" (l. 34), "knuckle-dragging" (ll. 2/3), "lackeys" (l. 10)
     • words and phrases that threaten or express opposition, e. g. "under attack" (headline), "their day is done" (l. 19), "No more." (l. 20)
     • imagery, e. g. "to force a way through the maze" (l. 13) → stresses just how difficult it is to enter the area of culture; "gatekeepers" (l. 22) and "shut the door" (ll. 25/26) → attempt to protect British culture and Britain in general from diversity
     • tone, partly ironic, e. g. l. 13, often very harsh, e. g. ll. 6/7, 38/39)

2020-17

Kureishi supports his negative view of the lack of diversity and the discrimination that exists within the British cultural industries by using communicative strategies and language; his choice of words is especially telling. He wants likeminded people to see the problem and to act against it. He also threatens the people responsible that the status quo will not remain forever.

**introduction:** thesis

The author harshly attacks those people who try to fight diversity both within and outside of Britain's cultural industries. The use of evaluative adjectives and words with a negative connotation is very striking. For instance, he describes their perspective as "xenophobic, oafish and narrow" (ll. 21/22) and repeatedly refers to their "stupidity" (ll. 5, 40). He states that they act out of a "sense of superiority and lofty arrogance" (ll. 19/20) perceiving themselves as a "master race" (l. 34), a term evoking images of Nazi Germany. Also, their actions are determined by "anxiety" (l. 28) and "panic" (l. 35), which is meant to show that their behaviour is unreasonable and they are weak. Their complaint against what they call "positive action" (l. 4) is called a "pathetic whining" (l. 5) and is seen as "unpatriotic" (l. 7) behaviour because it will damage Britain (cf. ll. 6/7). The author considers these people to be a threat to their country, and he ridicules them. Their actions are not sensible but emotional.

**main part – use of language:**
→ evaluative adjectives, words with a negative connotation

Kureishi also makes use of imagery to show how these people try to protect their domain from diversity. They and their "gatekeepers" (l. 22) "shut the door" (l. 25) both on Europe and on diversity (cf. l. 25), whereas Kureishi and other people with a migrant background have "to force [their] way through the maze" (l. 13). This comment stresses the difficulty that artists of colour have in becoming successful in a cultural field in Britain.

**use of language:**
→ imagery

This opposition between elites working in the area of culture and the artists, especially those of colour, is underlined by the use of pronouns. Kureishi frequently uses the pronouns "they" (e. g. l. 3), "theirs" (l. 11) and "we" (e. g. l. 26) or "us" (l. 13) to make the separation between these two groups more striking and to create the impression that their differences are irreconcilable. The author also uses the pronoun "I" (l. 14) to indicate that he has first-hand experience. He stresses this even further by pointing out that he has "worked in [the culture industries] for most of [his] life" (l. 8) and thus underlines that his observations are based on extensive experience.

**communicative strategy:**
→ use of pronouns

Another communicative strategy he makes use of is the appeal (cf. ll. 36/37). He calls on his fellow artists to "speak up" (l. 37). This is even more effective because it is combined with repeated

**communicative strategy:**
→ appeal

threats to the elite that their rule is coming to an end (cf. ll. 19/20, 24–27, 40/41).

Due to this clash between the cultural elite and the "ruling class" (l. 22) on the one hand and the artists and people supporting diversity on the other, the tone in the article is generally very harsh (e. g. ll. 6/7 and 38/39) but also partly ironic (e. g. l. 13), which fits Kureishi's obvious anger at the way he and other artists as well as people of colour in general are treated (cf. ll. 14/15, 23/24).

*use of language: → tone*

Overall, the author supports his view by making his opponents and their actions appear in a very negative light, whereas he encourages people in favour of diversity to raise their voices by claiming that eventually they will win the upper hand.

*conclusion*

*(611 words)*

3.1 *Here you are given a quote from the article which you have to comment on. Start by explaining the quote in context. You are meant to focus on systematic discrimination in education and culture. As you are asked to discuss the quote, you need to present the pros and the cons and come to a conclusion in which you balance your arguments and state your opinion clearly. In doing so, you need to refer both to the text as well as to your background knowledge.*
  – *meaning and context of the quote*
  – *reference to the text*
    • *the elite (cf. l. 9) tries to keep artists with a migration background out of the cultural industries (cf. l. 11)*
    • *they patronize and humiliate them (cf. ll. 13/14)*
    • *they are afraid that their talents will outshine White British artists (cf. ll. 26–30)*
    • *nationalist tendencies that became apparent in the Brexit referendum (cf. ll. 20–22)*
    • *some have managed to fight their way through despite the obstacles presented (cf. ll. 12/13)*
    • *opponents make themselves heard (cf. l. 25)*
  – *reference to work done in class*
    • *public vs state schools in GB → at the root of inequality in Britain*
    • *only 6% of pupils or students are educated privately; however, they are disproportionally represented in the public → have a great influence on politics and in society*
    • *people of colour are underrepresented in many walks of life, e. g. politics, law, media → if they cannot make themselves heard, their perspective risks being disregarded*
    • *everyday racism and discrimination*

| | |
|---|---|
| In his article, Kureishi claims that "real talent has been neglected and discouraged by those who dominate the culture, deliberately keeping schools, the media, universities and the cultural world closed to interesting people" (ll. 31–33). This quote makes it clear that Kureishi reproaches the "ruling class" (l. 22) with systematic and intentional discrimination, at least in education and culture. | **introduction:** explanation of quote |
| There is quite a lot of evidence to support Kureishi's view. The education system in Great Britain consists of public and state schools. Students attending public schools, which really are private, pay considerable fees. As a consequence, these schools are mainly attended by the children of the rich. As graduates of these public schools and universities disproportionally make their way into politics and law and generally into decision-making positions, they have a tremendous influence on society as a whole. Thus, private education is at the root of inequality in Britain. | **main part:** – **education system:** public schools |
| Kureishi exemplifies this by presenting the situation in the cultural industries, which are "dominated by white Oxbridge men" (l. 9) who fight diversity as the "furore over Penguin's […] decision" (l. 1) to hire and publish more diversely indicates. The author claims that they do not do it because they worry artists with migratory background are less talented but because they are worried that real talent might show itself if given the possibility (cf. ll. 28–30). | reference to text |
| The fact that Kureishi himself has made his way "through the maze" (l. 13) and has become an award-winning author seems to prove that his argument is flawed. However, it must be considered that his way "was a difficult and often humiliating trip" (l. 14) paved with "much patronisation and many insults" (l. 15). Privately educated people and white men in general will seldom face such everyday discrimination. Here it is remarkable that Kureishi's quote does not only include people of colour but all "interesting people" (l. 33) – a term which is far more inclusive and does not depend on gender, race, religion or social status. | **refutation of counter-argument:** reference to text |
| Kureishi's case can also not hide the fact that people of colour are underrepresented in many walks of life, e. g in the law, in politics and in the media, areas in which they might really change something. The problem is that their perspective risks being disregarded if they do not have a voice. Here, however, Kureishi is optimistic. He is sure that the elite cannot "intimidate everyone around them" (l. 20) any longer and that the supposedly "undeserving of being heard" (ll. 23/24) "are very insistent, noisy and | representation of people of colour |

talented" (ll. 26/27). The current protests against racism and discrimination support his optimism.

There is, however, a strong nationalist tendency which became apparent in the Brexit referendum and the on-going discussion about Britain's role in Europe. Kureishi describes the Brexit as a "retreat into panic and nationalism" (ll. 35/36). His use of the term "master race" (l. 34) makes it very clear which mindset is at work here.  `nationalist tendency: Brexit`

Despite all of this, there might be some room for optimism that the situation may change and that more equality will be achieved, but it will be a long and tedious journey with many setbacks. As long as inequality is already entrenched in education, it can truly be described as systematic discrimination. Abolishing public schools and private education in general would be an important but unfortunately very improbable step. As long as the graduates from these universities remain in power, no real change seems possible.  `conclusions`

*(581 words)*

3.2 *In this assignment, you have to imagine you are a speaker at an international youth conference on the topic "Stronger Together? – Facing Global Challenges in the 21st Century". As your audience is young, you may express yourself less formally than a speech would often require. Take into account that certain events might not be known internationally and might need some explanation. In your introduction, you need to set the topic which is global challenges but against the backdrop of Kureishi's quote. In the main part, you should focus on one or two of these challenges; otherwise, you risk remaining too superficial. Make sure to support your arguments with facts or examples from work done in class. To finish off, you will need to come to a conclusion.*
 – *Welcome the audience*
 – *Set the topic: a "retreat into panic and nationalism" (ll. 35/36) does not help solve global problems*
 – *Possible arguments*
   • *Nationalist tendencies can be seen in many countries, e. g. GB, USA, Poland, Hungary, Germany, Brazil*
   • *Populists have an increasing influence on decisions made in politics, e. g. Brexit → decisions are more emotional than reasonable, facts are distorted*
   • *Global challenges cannot be solved within a country, e. g. climate change, migration, international peacekeeping*
 – *Conclusion: make your own position clear, maybe appeal to the audience to act*
 – *End by thanking the audience for their attention*

Dear guests, — greeting

Several days ago, I read an article written by the award-winning British author Hanif Kureishi, in which he names and shames the ongoing discrimination within Britain's cultural industries. At first sight, there doesn't seem to be a connection to our topic but within the article he claims that we live in a world characterised by a "retreat into panic and nationalism" (ll. 35/36) and he takes the Brexit as an example to prove his point. His observation is true but disconcerting because the problems we are facing can only be solved globally and not by individual nations on their own. — introduction: Kureishi's quote, thesis

First let me underline Kureishi's claim that we are observing a "retreat into panic and nationalism". In the last couple of years, we have observed leaders putting a strong focus on the wellbeing and advantages of their own countries. This is true of Great Britain when they voted for the Brexit, and it is still true now even though more people seem to realize that this decision may backfire. The most prominent example is probably Donald Trump, who keeps putting America first, a slogan, which many countries have adopted, even though many probably weren't as serious about it as Trump unfortunately is. — main part: evidence to support quote: nationalism

In many countries, including Turkey, Poland or Hungary for example, we have very conservative leaders, and in many countries we see that populists are enjoying more and more popularity. In my home country, Germany, the AfD, a right-wing party, has found its way into parliament and manages to influence debates in a very negative way. Discussions are becoming more and more emotional and often get personal, for example when politicians insult each other. The problem is that decisions made by our governments must not be personal or emotional, but they must be sensible and based on facts. Take the discussion before the Brexit referendum. It was very often emotional and facts were distorted, which easily leads to panic and wrong decisions. In the end, the British made a decision that at least the younger generation will almost certainly regret. — populism

In Germany, during the so-called "migration crisis" in 2015, one politician from the afore-mentioned AfD seriously asked border patrolmen to shoot women and children crossing the border illegally. This is merely populist opinion-making and makes no sense whatsoever. However, migration is a very serious topic – I am avoiding the word "problem" here on purpose – and it has to be discussed unemotionally to find ways to address it. But it has become very clear that this cannot be done by one nation — demand to discuss unemotionally alone, but rather all countries across the globe must work together.

The existential challenges we are facing, above all climate change, are global ones. If every country only asks how they can profit and is not willing to compromise, we will never be able to solve these existential problems and again it will be the younger generation, namely us, who will have to suffer from this inability or rather this unwillingness.  reason for acting together

We must not let this happen, and we can make a difference if we act together, united. The Fridays for Future movement is a good example of how we can work together across borders. Thanks to social media, we are connected across the globe and ideas travel fast. Let's take this chance and make leaders all over the world hear that we have had enough of their nationalist decisions and that they must work together to ensure that our future will be as good as theirs used to be.  appeal

Thank you.  *(586 words)*  thanks

---

**Teil B: Sprachmittlung (isoliert)**

4. *Der Zieltext für die Mediationsaufgabe ist eine E-Mail, die sich an eine befreundete Person aus England richtet. Die Sprache sollte entsprechend umgangssprachlich sein. In dieser E-Mail sollen Sie das Konzept der Frankfurter Immigrationsbuchmesse darstellen und aufzeigen, welchen Einfluss die Kultur von Immigrant\*innen auf das Leben in deutschen Städten hat.*
   – *Anrede*
   – *einleitender Satz*
   – *Konzept der Messe*
       • *Schwerpunkt: Migration und interkultureller Austausch, Kultur und Kommunikation*
       • *2 Tage mit Lesungen, Vorträgen und Diskussionen*
       • *kleiner als Frankfurter Buchmesse*
       • *Ziel: literarische Vielfalt in Frankfurt zeigen; Literaturbetrieb nicht den herrschenden Schichten überlassen; Brücken bauen zwischen Menschen, die in Frankfurt leben und solchen, die zuziehen*
   – *Einfluss der Kultur von Immigrant\*innen auf das Leben in deutschen Städten*
       • *multikulturelle Metropolen entstehen*
       • *Reduktion der Kultur von Immigrant\*innen auf kulinarische Spezialitäten abbauen*
   – *abschließender Satz*
   – *Grußformel und Name*

| | |
|---|---|
| Dear Ted, | greeting |
| Thank you for your email. It sounds as if you're working on a really interesting presentation there. Of course, I'm glad to give you some information from Germany, and I think I've found an interesting article for you in a German daily. | **introduction:** reference to task |
| It is about a book fair in Frankfurt. It is not about THE Frankfurt Book Fair but about a much smaller event focusing on immigrant literature. Over two days, there are readings, lectures and discussions. The emphasis is on migration, culture and intercultural communication. They want to show how diverse literature in Frankfurt is beyond the literary mainstream. They are also aiming at connecting people who have always lived in Frankfurt with those who have recently moved there. | concept of book fair |
| According to the article, the impact of immigrant culture on urban life in Germany is often reduced to their culinary influence. However, they have much more to offer in transforming German cities, such as Frankfurt, into truly multicultural centres. | impact of immigrant culture |
| That's the information I've discovered for you. I hope it's useful for your presentation. If you need more, let me know and I'll search the net some more. | finishing paragraph |
| I hope to hear from you again soon. | |
| Yours, | closing |
| Harkan                                    *(199 words)* | name |

**Abiturprüfung NRW – Englisch 2021**
**Leistungskurs: Aufgabe 1**

**Teil A: Leseverstehen und Schreiben (integriert)**  Inhalt 42 P. / Sprache 63 P.

## Aufgabenstellung                                            Punkte

1. Outline the speaker's views of Africa. *(Comprehension)*                    12

2. Analyse how the speaker's views are presented. Focus on structure, use of language and poetic devices. *(Analysis)*    16

3. Choose **one** of the following tasks:                                      14

3.1 Assess to what extent Igbinedion's poem can be seen as a comment on social and political realities in Nigeria today. *(Evaluation: comment)*

3.2 For the project course "Africa rising – Africa's role in a globalised world" you have been asked to write an article for the course's website. You decided to take a quote by the African Kumi Naidoo, the former Secretary General of Amnesty International and Executive Director of Greenpeace International, as a starting point: "Economic growth is not sustainable without social and environmental justice."
Write the article, taking into account economic, ecological and political issues of globalisation. *(Evaluation: re-creation of text)*

*Zitat: Africa Renewal Online, "We need a sustainable path for our future"*
*https://www.un.org/africarenewal/web-features/%E2%80%98we-need-sustainable-path-our-future%E2%80%99 (Zugriff: 11. 06. 2020)*

## Text:
## Osayande Igbinedion, *AFRICA*

*Osayande Igbinedion is a male poet from Nigeria.*

1   Africa, my Africa,
    Africa my motherland,
    Africa the land of the black race,
    Torn in a conflict
5   Africa of high and low lands,
    Africa of thick forest and shrubs,
    Africa in which abound many rivers,
    And natural wealth
    Bountiful and splendid
10  Africa, my Africa,
    A race struggling within

For a place in the sky;
Whither do you go now?

When the white race
15 Had lunged upon you
A cloud overshadowed you,
In a wave of cultures
Like the mighty roars of the Atlantic
Across the beaches of Lagos.
20 You were torn apart,
Body and soul,
In bits of disgusting rags …

When believers and ministers of imported religions
Go back to their African roots
25 You are an edifice of tattered cloths
When teachers and students of white knowledge
Go up and down in the mystery of the same
You are an effigy of the past.
When the series of the western trials
30 Have failed us as we have failed them.
You are in chaos.
When orthodox medicine swallowed tradomedics
Struggling to re-emerge.
You strangulate between them.

35 When laws are turned upside down
And jungle justice and witchcraft reign.
You too are turned to rags
Metaphysical science still
Has a place in our wars.

40 When tradition goes on
In the presence of a foreign marriage.
You are in a great confusion.

Africa, my Africa,
Africa, my fatherland,
45 Africa of past proud warriors,
Africa then and now,
Africa of the black race,
Torn in conflict
Knowing not how to mend the rags.

And now, arise, Africa!
Wake up from your slumber, Africa!
You either be up or down the ladder
The present midway takes your breath.  *(273 words)*

*Osayande Igbinedion: Africa, in: GMT Emezue (ed.), New Voices. A Collection of Recent Nigerian Poetry, Oxford: Handel 2008, pp. 135–137*

**Annotation**
l. 32  *tradomedics:* traditional medicine

## Teil B: Sprachmittlung (isoliert)     Inhalt 18 P. / Sprache 27 P.

### Aufgabenstellung

4. Your friend from the UK is doing a school project on the importance of poetry in the 21st century. She/he has asked you for information on current trends and their perception in Germany.
Write an email to your friend, outlining the different views on instapoetry presented in Eileen Breuer's article. *(Mediation)*     18

### Text:
**Eileen Breuer, *Wie der junge Goethe: Warum gerade ausgerechnet auf Instagram Gedichte ganz groß sind***

Poeten haben Instagram für sich entdeckt und teilen ihre Werke mit tausenden Followern. Unter dem Hashtag Instapoetry finden sich dort fast drei Millionen Beiträge, tippt man die deutsche Entsprechung Instalyrik ins Suchfeld ein, werden einem mehr als 6 000 Treffer angezeigt. […] [D]och warum sind die Gedichte auf Instagram so erfolgreich?

Eine der bekanntesten deutschsprachigen Poetinnen auf Instagram ist Clara Louise, 26 Jahre alt. Ihr folgen dort mehr als 166 000 Menschen.

Sie hat mit etwa 13 Jahren begonnen, Gedichte zu verfassen: „Ich habe einfach alles niedergeschrieben, was mich belastet hat oder was in meinem Kopf vorgegangen ist", erzählt sie bento. Die Poetin schreibt meistens über Liebe – die zu anderen und die zu sich selbst.

„Die Gedichte haben mir dabei geholfen, mich selbst zu verstehen."

Clara wollte die Gedanken nicht mehr nur für ihre heimische Schublade aufschreiben, also fing sie an, Ausschnitte auf Instagram zu veröffentlichen. Manchmal in Retrooptik auf der Schreibmaschine getippt, manchmal in verschnörkelter Handschrift. Es sollte ein Testlauf für einen Gedichtband sein. Die Likes und steigenden Followerzahlen gaben ihr recht: Als Clara anfing, lag sie bei gut tausend Followern, heute zählt sie 160-mal so viele.

Obwohl sie ihre Ideen lieber ins Handy tippt als zum Notizblock zu greifen und Verse in den sozialen Medien postet, will Clara nicht als Insta-Poetin bezeichnet werden.

„Ich verstehe nicht, was es für einen Unterschied macht, ob man etwas auf Instagram veröffentlicht oder nicht. Es ist nur ein Medium, wo man sich und das, was man macht, präsentieren kann. Es ist aber keine andere Form von Lyrik", sagt Clara Louise.

Literaturwissenschaftler Niels Penke ist anderer Meinung. Er arbeitet am Germanistischen Seminar der Universität Siegen und setzt sich unter anderem mit Popkultur auseinander. Seiner Ansicht nach zeichnen sich die Gedichte auf Instagram durch andere Charakteristika aus als konventionelle Lyrik. Während Gedichte der zeitgenössischen Lyrik oft irritieren und Fragen aufwerfen, könne dies auf Instagram nicht funktionieren, sagt Penke: „Hier geht es darum, nicht zu irritieren, sondern ohne große Voraussetzungen verständlich zu sein. Nicht formal komplex, sondern formal einfach."

Die Art des Mediums habe Auswirkungen darauf, was dort veröffentlicht wird, so der Wissenschaftler: „Der Erfolg der Instapoetry liegt vor allem darin, dass die Affordanzen des Medium befolgt werden." Affordanzen sind Spielregeln und Funktionsweisen, die ein Medium mit sich bringt.

„Das Formbewusstsein, ob man nun ein Sonett oder eine Ballade schreibt, spielt hier gar keine Rolle. Auf Instagram gilt es, sich möglichst kurz zu halten – es muss auf dem kleinen Bildschirm gut lesbar sein – und den Effekt zu provozieren, geliked, geteilt und kommentiert zu werden."

Außerdem prägen sentenzenhafte Verse die Instalyrik, sagt Penke. Damit werden kurze und prägnante Zeilen beschrieben, die sich dem Leser ins Gedächtnis einbrennen. „Die Lyriker veröffentlichen auf Instagram Sätze, die man sich auch als Kalenderspruch vorstellen, auf ein T-Shirt drucken oder auf den Unterarm tätowieren lassen kann", sagt Penke.

Tatsächlich hat Clara schon oft Bilder von Tattoos ihrer Gedichte zugeschickt bekommen. Sie denkt, dass die Menschen sich aus einem Grund wieder mehr nach Poesie sehnen: „Dieses Bewusstsein dafür, dass Dinge sich verändern, dass wir an einem Maximum angekommen sind und es irgendwann nicht mehr weiter nach oben geht, ist vielleicht ein Grund dafür, warum die Leute sich wieder mehr mit sich selbst befassen anstatt mit allem, was um sie herum passiert."

Niels Penke sieht dabei eine Ähnlichkeit zum jungen Goethe des Sturm und Drang. Dessen Erlebnislyrik handele ebenfalls von Erlebnissen und Empfindungen, die authentisch und glaubwürdig wirken sollten. „Von besonderen Erfahrungen authentisch zu schreiben, das hat immer schon in bestimmten lyrischen Traditionen eine Rolle gespielt", sagt Penke. Die jungen Lyriker heute würden in ihren Gedichten oft Stimmungslagen ihrer Generation aufgreifen – damit könnten sich die Nutzer identifizieren.

*(603 Wörter)*
*aus SPIEGEL.de, (ehemals bento), von Eileen Breuer, 30. 08. 2019*
*https://www.spiegel.de/panorama/instapoetry-warum-auf-instagram-jetzt-gedichte-ganz-gross-sind-a-570d093c-4f8f-48f6-b356-5ccab2d44969*

**Anmerkungen**
Z. 10 bento – Magazin des *Spiegel* für junge Menschen von 18 bis 30

# Lösungsvorschläge

## Teil A: Leseverstehen und Schreiben (integriert)

1. *In this task you briefly need to present Africa's situation as perceived by the speaker in the poem. Also give the reasons for this situation as the speaker sees them. Since the speaker comes to a conclusion about what follows for Africa, you have to also point this out. Note that the speaker may well address "Africa" as one entity, but you should make it clear that you realize that it is a continent consisting of many individual countries.*
   - *Africa's situation*
     - *rich, beautiful and varied landscapes*
     - *in chaos, confused*
     - *smothered by different and contradictory influences*
   - *reasons for this situation*
     - *effects of colonialization manifest themselves in different areas of life*
     - *torn in conflict between the races*
     - *torn between cultures*
     - *western influences mix with African traditions, e. g. religion, medicine*
     - *tries to find a compromise between contradictory influences*
   - *consequence*
     - *needs to wake up and begin anew*
     - *swing to one side or the other but must not remain torn*

The speaker in Osayande Igbinedions's poem "Africa" published in 2008 presents Africa's current situation, explains what causes this situation and what needs to be done. — **introduction:** reference to source, topic

According to the speaker, Africa is a beautiful continent, rich in varied landscapes. But it is also in chaos because it is smothered by different and often contradictory influences. — **main part:** Africa's situation

The speaker claims that this situation is a consequence of Africa's colonialization, which still affects different areas of life. Thus, Africa is torn between the races and between cultures. Western influences mix with African traditions, for example when it comes to religion or medicine. As African countries try to find a compromise between these clashing influences, they cannot develop properly but risk regressing, if they stay stagnant. — reasons

Therefore, Africa needs to wake up and begin anew. It has to swing to one side or the other but must not remain torn. — consequence

*(145 words)*

2021-5

2. *Here you have to analyze how the author employs structure, language and poetic devices like form, rhythm and visual elements to stress the views outlined above.*
   - *speaker is closely connected to Africa and identifies with the continent*
     - *use of personal pronouns and possessive determiners in the first and second person singular (e. g. "my Africa", l. 1; "my motherland", l. 2; "my fatherland", l. 44)*
     - *personification of Africa (e. g. "Body and soul", l. 21)*
     - *repetition of "Africa, my Africa" (ll. 1, 10, 43) and of "Africa" in general (17 times at the beginning and the end), often at the beginning of a line → anaphora*
   - *expresses his/her worries about Africa*
     - *words belonging to the semantic field "struggle and chaos" (e. g. repetition of "torn", l. 20, or "[t]orn in conflict", ll. 4, 48; "struggling", ll. 11, 33; "chaos", l. 31; "strangulate", l. 34; "turned upside down", l. 35; "wars", l. 39; "confusion", l. 42)*
     - *metaphor of the White\* race coming over Africa like a "cloud" (l. 16) or an Atlantic "wave" (l. 17) → turns the continent gloomy and threatens to wash it away*
   - *underlines Africa's disorientation caused by its being torn between rival influences*
     - *no rhyme scheme, no harmonic rhythm*
     - *lines and stanzas of different length*
     - *missing punctuation (e. g. ll. 25, 37)*
     - *words stressing contrasts or contradictions ("the black race", l. 3; "the white race", l. 14; "imported religions", l. 23, and "African roots", l. 24; "orthodox medicine" and "tradomedics", l. 32)*
   - *final appeal is stressed*
     - *end position*
     - *lines of the last stanza are indented → visual emphasis*
     - *ll. 43–49 are a variation of first lines (ll. 1–6)*
     - *question at the end of the first stanza (l. 13) is answered in the final stanza*
       - *use of two imperatives make the appeal more urgent*
       - *the contrast "up or down" (l. 52) stresses that a decision must be made*

*\* The words "Black" and "White" are written in capital letters to signal that they are not natural categories but social ones (for more background information on this topic see e. g. https://www.theatlantic.com/ideas/archive/2020/06/time-to-capitalize-blackand-white/613159/). Quotations from the poem are left unchanged.*

The author uses language and poetic devices to stress the speaker's close connection to and concern for the African continent. S/he uses mainly poetic devices to underline Africa's disorientation. The poem's structure emphasizes the appeal made in the last stanza.

**introduction:** thesis

| | |
|---|---|
| The author uses many personal pronouns and possessive determiners in the first and second person singular. The speaker calls Africa "my Africa" (l. 1), "my motherland" (l. 2) or "my fatherland" (l. 44). This shows his or her close connection to and identification with the continent. Africa itself is personified, as it consists of "[b]ody and soul" (l. 21), which makes the bond between "the land" (l. 3) and the speaker an almost human one. Also, the numerous repetitions of the word "Africa", often as anaphora at the beginning of several lines (e. g. ll. 1–3 and 5–7), stress the importance of the continent for the speaker. | **main part: language** → pronouns, determiners identification language → personification → repetition, anaphora |
| It is striking that the author uses many words belonging to the semantic field of struggle and chaos. The expression "torn" (l. 20) or "[t]orn in conflict" (ll. 4, 48) is repeated. The word "struggling" is used twice (ll. 11, 33). Furthermore, there are the words "chaos" (l. 31), "wars" (l. 39) and "confusion" (l. 42). All these words and expressions emphasize Africa's dire situation as being in "disgusting rags" (l. 22) and serve as proof of the speaker's concern. Additionally, the metaphor of the White race coming over Africa like a "cloud" (l. 16) or an Atlantic "wave" (l. 17) which threatens to crush the continent, stresses the gloomy state Africa is in. This again is cause for the speaker's worry. | → semantic field, repetition expression of the speaker's concern language → metaphor |
| The influences introduced by the White race clash with African traditions and lead to the struggle and chaos mentioned above. The clash is underlined by words stressing contrasts or contradiction: The "black race" (l. 3) is contrasted to "the white race" (l. 14); "imported religions" (l. 23) cannot be reconciled with traditions with "African roots" (l. 24). Apart from conflicts between White and Back races, the speaker also sees a "race struggling within" (l. 11) in Africa. To give the reader an impression of the resulting disorientation, the author does without rhyme scheme and rhythm. Lines and stanzas are of different length and sometimes punctuation is missing (e. g. ll. 25, 37). This may appear rather confusing. | → contrasts disorientation language → poetic devices |
| In the last stanza, the speaker appeals to the continent. This appeal is stressed by its position at the very end of the poem and also because the lines of the last stanza are indented, which emphasizes them visually. The lines leading to this appeal, namely lines 43 to 49 are a variation of the first lines (ll. 1–6), which lead to the speaker's question "Wither do you go now?" (l. 13), which is answered in the final appeal. There, the author uses two imperatives (ll. 50/51) to make the appeal more urgent. | **structure** language → question appeal → imperatives |
| To conclude, structure, language and poetic devices are used to depict Africa's current situation, the reasons for this state of | **conclusion** |

confusion and stagnation and the appeal, which the speaker makes out of concern for the continent, with which he or she identifies. *(526 words)*

3.1. *You need to assess to what extent the poem can be seen as a comment on social and political realities in Nigeria today. This implies that it can definitely be seen as such a statement, the question is to which extent. Therefore, you should briefly point out the poem's message and then refer to Nigeria's present situation regarding politics and society.*
  – *the poem's message: Africa's colonial past still affects the continent today; torn between western and African influences, it needs to start anew*
  – *Nigeria's colonial past: British colony from the mid-19th century to 1960; effects still visible, e. g. faith, language, politics*
    • *after independence: divided into three geographic regions, controlled by different ethnic groups → fight each other, e. g. Biafra War*
    • *four Nigerian republics since colonial rule ended → political instability*
  – *situation in Nigeria today*
    • *deep religious and ethnic differences still visible*
    • *Christians and Muslims distrust each other*
    • *terrorism, Boko Haram*
    • *Nigerian writers and musicians often use English language → often more popular abroad*
    • *social divide between rich and poor, child labour*
    • *high rate of corruption → international investors often shy away*
    • *inadequate education for the poor, situation for girls even more difficult*
  – *conclusion: say how appropriate the speaker's message is*

In the poem "Africa" the speaker explains Africa's difficult present situation with its colonial past. According to the speaker, the effects of colonialism are still present in Africa today and threaten to tear the continent apart. Therefore, the speaker urges Africa not to try to reconcile western and African influences any longer but to start anew. **introduction:** reference to poem and its message

The following text assesses whether that message is also applicable to Nigeria, by far the most populous African country. To do so, the social and political realities in Nigeria today are taken into consideration as well as its past. **approach,** reference to task

From the mid-19th century to 1960 Nigeria was a British colony. The effects of British colonialism are still visible today and manifest themselves for example in faith, language and politics. **main part:** colonial past

2021-8

After its independence the country was divided into three geographic regions, which were controlled by different ethnic groups, who have often fought each other as for example in the Biafra War. Since its independence Nigeria has not seen long lasting political stability. Democratic and military rule have alternated until the current fourth Nigerian republic. There is a very high rate of corruption among politicians and business people, which explains why international investors often shy away, though the country is rich in oil and other resources. *(ethnic diversity; political instability; corruption)*

White colonists introduced Christianity to Nigeria and the religious differences divide the country's society even today. Most people are Muslims, closely followed by Christians and a minority of traditional believers. There is a lot of inter-religious conflict between Muslim and Christian zealots, often resulting in violence. For instance, Boko Haram terrorizes parts of the country to fight for an Islamic state within the country. *(faith: inter-religious conflict; terrorism)*

There is also a social divide between the rich and the poor. Though the country is rich in oil, only few profit from it. The underprivileged often cannot afford adequate education for their children because their offspring often have to work and cannot attend school regularly. This perpetuates the social divide, the results being even more dramatic for girls. If parents cannot send all of their children to school, boys are usually prioritized. *(social divide)*

The English language is also a legacy of colonialism. Nigerian writers and musicians often express themselves in English to spread their ideas. As a result, they are often more popular abroad than within their own country. *(language)*

Nigeria was a colony for a whole century and has been independent for about 70 years. Many of its problems result from colonialism and therefore the speaker's demand to give up the "present midway" between Western and African influences seems convincing. However, I honestly do not see how it can be done as both influences are deeply rooted within the society. *(conclusion)*

*(443 words)*

3.2. *You have to write an article for the website of a project course, dealing with Africa's role in a globalized world. In this article you have to use the given quote as a starting point. You should deal with economic, ecological and political issues of globalization. That means you do not only stick to the African perspective but also reflect on Africa's situation from the point of view of a European student.*
- *headline*
- *present quote and point out its relevance for the present situation and your article*

- *Africa aims for economic growth*
  - *natural resources, e. g. rare earth elements*
  - *oil, e. g. in Nigeria*
  - *tourism due to exceptional landscapes and wildlife*
- *importance of environmental and social sustainability*
  - *oil spills poison water, destroy mangrove forests*
  - *child labour in mines*
  - *large parts of Nigerian population do not profit from the money gained by oil companies*
  - *social divide grows*
  - *African and international enterprises have to act responsibly*
    - *protect environment*
    - *make sure that Africans profit from the wealth generated in their country*
    - *education*
    - *fight corruption*
- *conclusion: summarize your arguments, come back to the quote, appeal to your readers or express a wish for Africa's future*

**Africa's economy should grow responsibly** — headline

The former Secretary General of Amnesty International and Executive Director of Greenpeace International, Kumi Naidoo, pointed out that "economic growth is not sustainable without social and environmental justice". This statement sounds fairly simple and self-evident and it is highly unlikely anyone would contradict Naidoo. Still, too often this statement is not put into action. — introduction: quote as starting point

The African continent aims at economic growth and its preconditions are perfect. The continent is rich in natural resources like rare earth elements, farmland, oil and sun. It also has enough cheap labour to exploit its riches. Furthermore, it also has abundant wildlife and impressive landscapes to attract tourists. It is only normal that the people want to profit from these resources. However, all too often ecological and social sustainability are neglected in the process. — main part: Africa's economic precondition

Take Nigeria as an example. The country is rich in oil. However, the oil companies are often run by international companies which do not invest in the country but take the profits home. If these companies wanted to act in a socially acceptable way, they would employ more Nigerians and invest in the local infrastructure to help the people in the country. Instead, they often bribe politicians and business people and thereby deepen the social gap between the rich and the poor. The companies also tend to exploit low ecological standards in Nigeria to save money. Thus, oil spills happen far too often, and mangrove forests are — one example: Nigeria's oil industry / low ecological standards

2021-10

destroyed. This reality is a far cry from what we understand by ecological sustainability.

International and national companies have a responsibility, which they neglect on a regular basis. They need to fight corruption instead of making use of it in order to ensure that all Africans can profit from the riches their continent provides. They need to invest in education and in a medical infrastructure. As they are probably well-aware of the importance of ecological standards, both international and national companies should apply them to their projects in Africa and not be glad that they have not yet been enforced there.  — responsibility of companies

The results of social and ecological injustice do not stop at the continent's border. Pollution knows no frontiers and people who rally against African immigrants need to acknowledge their own responsibility for the continent's problems.  — consequences

Naidoo's statement really is self-evident and what is more, there is no alternative to social and ecological sustainability because in the end we will all pay the price – one way or another.  — **conclusion**

*(410 words)*

## Teil B: Sprachmittlung (isoliert)

4. In der Sprachmittlungsaufgabe gilt es eine E-Mail an eine befreundete Person in Großbritannien zu schreiben, die für ein Schulprojekt Informationen zur Bedeutung von Lyrik im 21. Jahrhundert sammelt. Auf der Basis des vorliegenden Artikels stellen Sie die verschiedenen Ansichten zu Instapoetry, Lyrik die auf Instagram veröffentlicht wird, dar. Adressat*in und Textsorte verlangen nach einem eher informellen Stil.
   – Anrede
   – Einleitungssatz
   – Aufgreifen des Anlasses für die Mail
   – Information zu Instapoetry/Instalyrik: 3 Millionen Beiträge international bzw. 6 000 deutschsprachige Beiträge → hohe Popularität
   – Sicht von Clara Louise, 26, Lyrikerin, 166 000 Follower
     • keine andere Form der Lyrik
     • nur anderes Medium der Veröffentlichung
     • Grund für Beliebtheit: Menschen befassen sich wieder mehr mit sich selbst
   – Sicht von Niels Penke, Literaturwissenschaftler
     • sieht Unterschiede zu konventioneller Lyrik
     • Gedichte müssen Spielregeln des Mediums beachten
       ◆ leicht verständlich → formal einfach/kein Formbewusstsein
       ◆ möglichst kurz

- ⬥ *prägnante Zeilen, die leicht im Gedächtnis bleiben*
- ⬥ *ähnlich Goethes Erlebnislyrik → authentische und glaubwürdige Erlebnisse und Empfindungen*
- ⬥ *junge Leser\*innen können sich damit identifizieren*
– *Abschluss und Grußformel*

| | |
|---|---|
| Dear Emily, | greeting |
| How are you? It's great to hear from you. Do you like your school project? I'm not too much into poetry myself really, but I've found an interesting article on instapoetry, which might help you. | introductory sentences |
| It seems that poetry is currently quite popular on Instagram. There is even a hashtag instapoetry which links to almost three million posts. The German equivalent still produces 6,000 hits. | main part: popularity of instapoetry |
| One young German poet called Clara Louise, who has 166,000 followers, doesn't like to be called an "instapoet" because she thinks that Instagram is just the medium to publish her poems. The poems themselves aren't any different from those published in books, she claims. According to her, poems are popular on Instagram since people are more concerned with themselves these days because they've realized that times are changing. | Clara Louise's view |
| However, Niels Penke, a literary scholar, sees some differences between conventional poetry and instapoetry. The poems on Instagram have to follow the rules of the medium, which means they have to be easy to understand and short. Therefore, their form is simple. Lines are catchy so that they can be easily remembered. Their content reminds Penke of the young Goethe, one of the most famous German writers, because they are about authentic and believable experiences and feelings. This allows young readers to identify with the poem's speaker and makes the texts popular. | Penke's view |
| I hope this helps you with your project. I for one, found the article quite interesting and I think I will look up some instapoems. If it is easy to understand, it might change my attitude to poetry. | closing sentence |
| I hope to hear from you again soon. | closing |
| Love, Carla *(275 words)* | name |

## Abiturprüfung NRW – Englisch 2021
## Leistungskurs: Aufgabe 2

**Teil A: Leseverstehen und Schreiben (integriert)**  Inhalt 42 P. / Sprache 63 P.

**Aufgabenstellung**  Punkte

1. Outline the controversy about the Colston statue in Bristol as presented in the article. *(Comprehension)*  12

2. Analyse how the author presents his views. Focus on communicative strategies and use of language. *(Analysis)*  16

3. Choose **one** of the following tasks:  14

3.1 According to David Olusoga the toppling of Edward Colston's statue "is one of those rare historic moments whose arrival means things can never go back to how they were" (ll. 69/70). Assess to what extent this view on the incidents in Bristol is a valid description of recent developments in multicultural Britain. *(Evaluation: comment)*

3.2 In the USA, journalists have been fired for criticising the violent tearing down of historical statues in their articles. In response, Jonathan Turley, Professor of Public Interest Law, warns, "We are experiencing one of the greatest threats to free speech in our history and it is coming, not from the government, but from the public." Referring to this statement, write a letter to Turley in which you reflect on the importance of free speech in the USA against the background of American myths and realities. *(Evaluation: re-creation of text)*

**Text:**
**David Olusoga, *The toppling of Edward Colston's statue is not an attack on history. It is history.***

1 For people who don't know Bristol, the real shock when they heard that the statue of a 17th-century slave trader had been torn from its plinth and thrown into the harbour was that 21st-century Bristol still had a statue of a slave trader on public display. [...]
  Edward Colston, the man in question, was a board member and ultimately the deputy
5 governor of the Royal African Company. In those roles he helped to oversee the transportation into slavery of an estimated 84,000 Africans. Of them, it is believed, around 19,000 died in the stagnant bellies of the company's slave ships during the infamous Middle Passage from the coast of Africa to the plantations of the new world. The bodies of the dead were cast into the water where they were devoured by the sharks that, over
10 the centuries of the Atlantic slave trade, learned to seek out slave ships and follow the bloody paths of slave routes across the ocean. This is the man who, for 125 years, has

been honoured by Bristol. Put literally on a pedestal in the very heart of the city. But tonight Edward Colston sleeps with the fishes.

The historical symmetry of this moment is poetic. A bronze effigy of an infamous and prolific slave trader dragged through the streets of a city built on the wealth of that trade, and then dumped, like the victims of the Middle Passage, into the water. Colston lies at the bottom of a harbour in which the ships of the triangular slave trade once moored, by the dockside on to which their cargoes were unloaded. […]

The crowd who saw to it that Colston fell were of all races, but some were the descendants of the enslaved black and brown Bristolians whose ancestors were chained to the decks of Colston's ships. Ripped from his pedestal, Colston seemed smaller: diminished in both size and potency. Lying flat, with his studied pensive pose, he looked suddenly preposterous. It was when the statue was in this position that one of the protesters made a grim but powerful gesture. By placing his knee over the bronze throat of Edward Colston, he reminded us of the unlikely catalyst for these remarkable events.

The fact that a man who died 299 years ago is today on the front pages of most of Britain's newspapers suggests that Bristol has not been brilliant at coming to terms with its history. Despite the valiant and persistent efforts of campaigners, all attempts to have the statue peacefully removed were thwarted by Colston's legion of defenders. In 2019, attempts to fix a plaque to the pedestal collapsed after Bristol's Society of Merchant Venturers, the high priests of the Colston cult, insisted on watering down the text, adding qualifications that, it was felt, had the effect of minimising his crimes. Yet what repulsed many about the statue was not that it valorised Colston but that it was silent about his victims, those whose lives were destroyed to build the fortune he lavished upon the city.

The long defence of the figure and Colston's reputation was overt and shameless, but not unique. In other British cities other men who grew rich through the trafficking of human beings or who defended the "respectable trade" are venerated in bronze and marble. In Edinburgh's St Andrew Square, on a pedestal 150 feet high, stands Viscount Melville, Henry Dundas, another of history's guilty men. His great contribution to civilisation was to water down and delay attempts to pass an act abolishing the slave trade. Historians struggle to estimate how many thousands died or were transported into slavery because of his actions. Already social media is ablaze with calls for Dundas to be thrown into the Forth.

Today is the first full day since 1895 on which the effigy of a mass murderer does not cast its shadow over Bristol's city centre. Those who lament the dawning of this day, and who are appalled by what happened on Sunday, need to ask themselves some difficult questions.

Do they honestly believe that Bristol was a better place yesterday because the figure of a slave trader stood at its centre? Are they genuinely unable – even now – to understand why those descended from Colston's victims have always regarded his statue as an outrage and for decades pleaded for its removal?

If they do not confront such questions they risk becoming lost in the same labyrinth of moral bewilderment in which some of Colston's defenders became entrapped in 2017. That year Colston Hall, Bristol's prime concert venue, and one of the many institutions named after the slave trader, announced that it was to change its name. In response, a number of otherwise reasonable decent people announced that they would be boycotting the hall. Think about that for a moment. Rational, educated, 21st-century people earnestly concluded that they were taking a moral stance by refusing to listen to music performed within the walls of a concert hall unless that venue was named after a man who bought, sold and killed human beings.

Now is not the time for those who for so long defended the indefensible to contort themselves into some new, supposedly moral stance, or play the victim. Their strategy of heel-dragging and obfuscation was predicated on one fundamental assumption: that what happened on Sunday would never happen. They were confident that black people and brown people who call Bristol their home would forever tolerate living under the shadow of a man who traded in human flesh, that the power to decide whether Colston stood or fell lay in their hands. They were wrong on every level. Whatever is said over the next few days, this was not an attack on history. This is history. It is one of those rare historic moments whose arrival means things can never go back to how they were.

*(973 words)*

David Olusoga: "The toppling of Edward Colston's statue is not an attack on history. It is history", in: The Guardian, *8 June 2020, https://www.theguardian.com/commentisfree/2020/jun/08/edward-colston-statue-history-slave-trader-bristol-protest – Copyright Guardian News & Media Ltd 2021*

**Annotations**
ll. 24/25 *By placing his knee over the bronze throat of Edward Colston ...:* reference to the killing of the African-American George Floyd, who became the victim of police violence on 25 May 2020
ll. 30/31 *Society of Merchant Venturers:* society formerly specialised in sea trading from and to Bristol, including slaves from West Africa
l. 44 *Forth:* Firth of Forth, embayment where several Scottish rivers meet
l. 64 *heel-dragging:* reluctant to act

## Teil B: Sprachmittlung (isoliert)  Inhalt 18 P. / Sprache 27 P.

## Aufgabenstellung

4. You are taking part in the international school project *Colonial Heritage – Reconciling with History*. Each participant is expected to contribute an online article to the project's website presenting examples of dealing with the colonial past from their own countries. In your research you came across the initiative *Tear This Down*. Based on the interview with Simone Dede Ayivi, write the article. *(Mediation)*   18

2021-15

**Text:**
*„Die kolonialen Denkmäler und Straßennamen müssen weg"*

*Der deutsche Kolonialismus steckt immer noch in vielen Straßennamen. Die Berliner Künstlerin Simone Dede Ayivi hat das Projekt „tearthisdown.com" mit initiiert und fordert, Geschichte endlich sichtbar zu machen. Der Sender „radioeins" hat ein Interview mit Ayivi geführt.*

**Die BVG plant, den U-Bahnhof Mohrenstraße umzubenennen. Den Schritt begründen die Berliner Verkehrsbetriebe auch mit der aktuellen Diskussion um die Black Lives Matter Proteste. Ist das eine PR-Aktion, die den Schwung von Black Lives Matter mitnimmt, oder finden Sie das sinnvoll?**

Sinnvoll finde ich es allemal. Und es ist ja auch nicht was, was aus dem Nichts kommt, sondern viele Schwarze Initiativen oder Expertinnen zum Thema Postkolonialismus und Erinnerungskultur haben schon sehr, sehr lange darauf hingewiesen, dass der U-Bahnhof umbenannt werden muss und natürlich auch die dazugehörige Straße. Und die BVG ist eigentlich mit der Diskussion vertraut. Dass das jetzt passiert, hat natürlich damit zu tun, dass das Thema gerade so groß in den Medien ist und dass da auch viel Druck auf der Straße ist.

**Die digitale Karte *tearthisdown.com* markiert diese Orte zunächst. Was ist das Ziel?**

Das ist eine Initiative vom Peng Kollektiv und der Initiative Schwarze Menschen in Deutschland. Und beide arbeiten schon lange zu dem Thema. Interessant daran fanden wir, die Möglichkeit zu schaffen, erst all diese Orte zu sammeln und einen Überblick zu bekommen. Und vor allem die Menschen dazu anzuregen, denn das ist ja ein partizipatives Projekt. Jeder kann Straßennamen oder Denkmäler eintragen, aus der eigenen Nachbarschaft zum Beispiel. Wir wollten die Menschen dazu anhalten, mit offenen Augen durch die Stadt zu gehen und sich zu überlegen: Wie viel Kolonialismus steckt eigentlich in meiner Nachbarschaft?

**Wie groß ist denn das Ausmaß des Problems? Jetzt hat man es ja zahlenmäßig in der Karte mal sichtbar. Hat Sie das überrascht?**

Nein, ich beschäftige mich jetzt schon eine Weile mit dem Thema. Positiv überrascht und erfreut hat mich, dass es tatsächlich so viele Rückmeldungen gibt, dass es so viel positives Feedback auf die Karte [gibt] und so viele Menschen die [Karte] nutzen. Wir hatten 275 neue Eintragungen innerhalb der ersten 24 Stunden. [...]

**Jetzt ist die Sichtbarmachung wahrscheinlich ja nur der erste Schritt. Was sollte darüber hinaus passieren?**

Die Denkmäler und die Straßennamen müssen weg. Und es muss um ein „Um-Erinnern" gehen, um einen Perspektivwechsel. Sie sollen nicht ersatzlos verschwinden, sondern im Gegenteil: Geschichte soll endlich sichtbar gemacht werden, indem wir zum Beispiel an Stelle eines Kolonialverbrechers jemanden ehren, der in dieser Region antikolonialen Widerstand geleistet hat, oder Menschen, die sich um antirassistische Belange verdient gemacht haben. Das ist die Forderung, und die hat ja zum Beispiel

sehr gut geklappt in Berlin-Kreuzberg, am May-Ayim-Ufer. Das hieß ja irgendwann mal Groeben Ufer, da erinnert sich kaum noch wer dran. Und da ist es ja nicht nur so, dass die Straße nach einer afrodeutschen antirassistischen Aktivistin und Lyrikerin umbenannt wurde. Es gibt ja auch eine große Stele, auf der erklärt wird, warum umbe-
40 nannt wurde, was die Geschichte dieses Ufers ist und wie die Zusammenhänge sind. Das heißt vorher, mit dem einfachen Namen von der Groeben, war die Geschichte eigentlich nicht wirklich sichtbar. Was blieb, war die Ehrung eines Kolonialverbrechers. […]

**Lüderitzstraße, Walderseestraße: Ohne die Karte wüssten die meisten von uns ja**
45 **gar nicht, dass das Namen mit Bezug auf die deutsche Kolonialgeschichte sind. Ist das nicht das eigentliche Problem, dass man das nicht in der Schule lernt?**
Das ist ein Riesenproblem, und das ist auch etwas, was sich dringend verändern muss. Es gab einfach sehr lange keinen Fokus auf der deutschen Kolonialgeschichte. Es gibt diese Erzählung, Deutschland hätte ja nicht so viele Kolonien gehabt, die außerdem
50 nach dem Ersten Weltkrieg ja direkt verloren, es sei also nur eine kurze Zeit gewesen … Dass Deutschland aber tatsächlich ein wichtiger und auch brutaler kolonialer Akteur war, ist irgendwie etwas, was jetzt erst so ins Bewusstsein kommt.

*(591 Wörter)*
*o. V.: „Die kolonialen Denkmäler und Straßennamen müssen weg", in: rbb24, 6. 7. 2020*
*https://www.rbb24.de/panorama/beitrag/2020/07/berlin-kolonialismus-umbenennung-strassen-karte-tearthisdown.html (Zugriff: 23. 09. 2020)*

**Anmerkungen**
Z. 1   BVG: Berliner Verkehrsbetriebe
Z. 1   Mohrenstraße – Mohr: veraltet, heute abwertend für dunkelhäutige Afrikaner
Z. 14 Peng Kollektiv: Berliner Gruppe von Aktivistinnen und Aktivisten aus Kunst, Handwerk und Wissenschaft
Z. 37 Groeben – Otto Friedrich von der Gröben (1657–1728): Offizier und Forschungsreisender im Dienste Brandenburg-Preußens, der auch eine zentrale Rolle im Sklavenhandel spielte

## Lösungsvorschläge

### Teil A: Leseverstehen und Schreiben (integriert)

1. *You have to outline the different parties' attitude towards the Colston statue. You should consider the attitude to the statue itself and to the fact that it has been torn down.*
   - *attitude towards statue*
     - supporters
       * *have honoured his great contributions to Bristol's economic wealth for 125 years*
       * *averted all attempts to remove statue peacefully*
       * *remain silent about his victims*
     - opponents
       * *people of all races*
       * *have rallied against the statue for decades*
       * *have regarded statue as an outrage*
       * *reminds them of the crimes against humanity their ancestors had to suffer*
   - *attitude towards toppling of the statue*
     - supporters
       * *are shocked*
       * *feel like victims*
       * *see it as an attack on history*
     - opponents
       * *inspired by people protesting against police violence against Black\* people in the aftermath of George Floyd's killing in the USA*
       * *see it as historical event → possible turning point → Black and Brown\* people in Bristol make themselves heard*

   *\* The words "Black" and "Brown" are written in capital letters to signal that they are not natural categories but social ones. Quotations from the original text are left unchanged.*

| | |
|---|---|
| In his article "The toppling of Edward Colston's statue is not an attack on history. It is history.", published in *The Guardian* on 8 June 2020, David Olusoga presents the controversy about the Colston statue in Bristol. | **introduction:** reference to article and task |
| This controversy has been going on for a long time because supporters of the statue have honoured Colston, a notorious slave trader, for his great contributions to Bristol's economic wealth for 125 years. They have averted all attempts to remove the statue peacefully and remained silent about his victims. | **main part:** a long lasting controversy |

Opponents have rallied against the statue for decades because they have regarded it as an outrage. Descendants of slaves were

2021-18

constantly reminded of the crimes against humanity their ancestors had to endure.

When the statue was violently toppled by people of all races in June 2020 its supporters were shocked and felt like victims themselves. They saw the event as an attack on history. — toppling of the statue

By contrast, opponents of the statue see its removal as a historical event. They believe it could be a turning point in the way Black and Brown people have a say in how Bristol deals with its colonial past. Their act was inspired by people protesting against police violence against Black people in the aftermath of George Floyd's death in the USA. *(211 words)*

2. *In this task you have to analyse how the journalist uses communicative strategies and language to present his views you have outlined above. Don't forget to explain what effects the different strategies and the language employed have on the reader.*
   – *author's overall view: toppling of Colston's statue was long overdue, has historic implications*
   – *vivid description of Colston's deeds → prove that he is not a person to be honoured*
     • *gives numbers (cf. ll. 6/7) → facts*
     • *evaluative adjectives, e. g. "infamous", "stagnant" (l. 7) → depict situation on board; "infamous" (l. 14), "prolific" (l. 15) → characterize Colston as shameless slave trader*
     • *gruesome details (cf. ll. 9–11) → evoke pictures*
     • *choice of words: "mass murderer" (l. 45)*
     • *enumeration: "bought, sold and killed human beings" (l. 61)*
   – *stresses long protest against glorification of Colston in Bristol*
     • *evaluative adjectives: "valiant and persistent" (l. 28) → positive image of campaigners*
     • *reference to former attempts to put Colston's relevance into perspective in 2017 and 2019 (cf. ll. 29–35, ll. 53–61)*
   – *presents Colston's defenders in a negative light*
     • *choice of words: "legion of defenders" (l. 29), "the high priests of the Colston Cult" (l. 31) → campaigners are outnumbered by more powerful supporters; mocking tone; "overt and shameless" (l. 36) → defense of Colston*
     • *tone: "has not been brilliant" (l. 27) → mocks defenders*
   – *emphasizes that the toppling of the statue is long overdue*
     • *time phrases: "299 years ago" (l. 26), "first full day since 1895" (l. 45) versus "dawning of this day" (ll. 46/47); "yesterday" (l. 49), "even now" (l. 50), "always" (l. 51), "for decades" (l. 52)*
     • *indirect appeal, cf. ll. 46–48*
     • *rhetorical questions, cf. ll. 49–52 → stress a need for change of perspective → supporters' view is outdated*

- *moral reprobation of defenders*
  - *choice of words: "lost in [...] labyrinth of moral bewilderment" (ll. 53/54)*
    → *creates image*
  - *enumeration: "[r]ational, educated, 21st-century people" (ll. 58/59)*
    → *makes their behaviour even more unbelievable*
  - *"contort themselves into some new, supposedly moral stance, or play the victim" (ll. 62/63)*
  - *Direct appeal to reader (cf. l. 58)* → *asks reader to consider the enormity of their standpoint*
- *points out that implications of toppling the statue are "historic" (l. 70)*
  - *repetition of the word "history": headline, ll. 28, 40, 69 (varied repetition of headline)*
  - *parallel sentence structure: (cf. ll. 64–68)* → *supporters believed that Black people and people of colour (BPoC) could be ignored*
  - *short sentences, e. g. "They were wrong on every level." (l. 68), "This is history." (l. 69)* → *very effective/powerful in contrast to otherwise complex sentence structures*
  - *Black and Brown people demand their say and will do so in the future*

In his article Olusoga tries to persuade the readers that the toppling of the Colston statue was long overdue and has historic implications. He uses communicative strategies and language to make his point more convincing.   **introduction:** reference to task

To start with, Olusoga points out very clearly what kind of man Colston was. He uses evaluative adjectives like "infamous" (ll. 7, 14) and "prolific" (l. 15) as well as an enumeration (cf. l. 61) to characterize him as a shameless slave trader and "mass murderer" (l. 45). To prove his point, he uses facts (cf. ll. 6/7) and shows his accurate knowledge of Colston's deeds by presenting gruesome details (cf. ll. 9–11). These details evoke pictures that will be hard to forget and raise feelings of indignation.   **main part:** characterization of Colston
→ evaluative adjectives
→ facts
→ details evoking pictures

The journalist emphasizes that the toppling of the statue was long overdue. He uses many time phrases like "299 years ago" (l. 26), "for decades" (l. 52) and "the first full day since 1895" (l. 45) to show for how long Colston and his statue have been prominent in Bristol and for how long campaigners have rallied against it.   act long overdue
→ time phrases

The campaigners are described as "valiant and persistent" (l. 28) to put them in a positive light. References to former attempts to put Colston's relevance into perspective stress the fact that the protests have been going on for years peacefully (cf. ll. 29–35, 53–61).   **positive image of campaigners** former attempts

Colston's defenders, on the other hand, are presented in a negative light. This is mainly achieved by a certain choice of words. Thus, they are called a "legion of defenders" (l. 29) and "the high priests of the Colston Cult" (l. 31). These expressions mock the defenders but also show that the campaigners are outnumbered by more powerful supporters. The word "cult" also implies that honouring Colston is not sensible or rational, which appears even more absurd, when Olusoga uses an enumeration to describe them as "[r]ational, educated, 21st-century people" (ll. 58/59). The author even reproaches them with a lack of moral integrity when he says that they are "lost in [a] labyrinth of moral bewilderment" (ll. 53/54) and "contort themselves into some new, supposedly moral stance, or play the victim" (ll. 62/63). To stress that he believes this way of looking at the facts is absurd, the journalist appeals directly to the readers and asks them to "[t]hink about that for a moment" (l. 58).

**negative image of defenders**
→ choice of words
→ mocking tone

→ enumeration

lack of moral integrity

→ direct appeal

The defenders are only addressed indirectly, when prompted to "ask themselves some difficult questions" (ll. 47/48). These questions are then raised rhetorically (cf. ll. 49–52) and stress that the supporters' view is outdated and that they need to consider the point of view of the slaves' descendants.

→ indirect appeal
→ rhetorical questions

Consequently, the author perceives the toppling of the statue as "historic" (l. 70). He points out that the supporters believed that Black and Brown Bristolians could be ignored. To stress this point, he uses a parallel sentence structure (cf. ll. 64–68) presenting the supporters' misconception. This complex sentence structure is followed by a short but all the more powerful sentence: "They were wrong on every level" (l. 68), which emphasizes that their view really is just a misconception. In the headline, in lines 28 and 40 and at the very end in line 69 the word "history" is repeated to show that what happened is in fact history because it proves that Black people and people of colour demand their say and will also do so in the future.

historic act

→ parallel sentence structure

→ repetition

All in all, Olusoga shows that Colston's defendants are in the wrong and are old reactionaries, whereas the campaigners have accomplished a historic act. *(600 words)*

**conclusion**

3.1 *You are given a quote from Olusoga's article and have to assess to what extent his view on what happened in Bristol can be applied to Britain as a whole. That means you need to explain the quote first and then show which recent developments in multicultural Britain support his view and which ones contradict it. Finally, you need to come to a conclusion.*
  – *introduction*
    • *explanation of the quote and thesis*
      ◆ *toppling of Colston statue is historic*
      ◆ *sign of a change in society and politics*
      ◆ *ethnic minorities demand their say and will keep doing so*
    • *express disagreement or agreement*
  – *arguments opposing Olusoga's view*
    • *ethnic minorities still underrepresented in many areas, e.g. law, politics, media → their view is not represented appropriately*
    • *Brexit shows strong nationalist tendencies → immigration is an important and controversially discussed topic*
    • *Muslims in particular feel that Britain has become less tolerant recently, especially in social media*
    • *ethnic minorities still often live in separate areas*
  – *arguments supporting Olusoga's view*
    • *Sadiq Khan is reelected Mayor of London (British-Pakistani origin, Muslim)*
    • *Black Lives Matter movement has influenced people of colour in Britain → stand up for their rights and fight against discrimination*
    • *English football players and clubs boycott social media because of racism*
  – *conclusion: some reason for hope but still a long way to go; toppling of statue is a single act which does not fix the greater problem*

In his article Olusoga claims that the toppling of Colston's statue "is one of those rare historic moments whose arrival means things can never go back to how they were" (ll. 69/70). He sees this act as a symbol of a decisive change in society and politics as ethnic minorities demand their say and, according to the author, will keep doing so. I only partly agree with Olusoga's view because I think that he is too optimistic and overestimates the long-term effects of the symbolic force of the toppling of a statue.

**introduction:** reference to quote

The author makes much of the expression of opinion that is inherent in the act of throwing Colston from his pedestal. Campaigners who have not been able to make themselves heard for decades have finally acted according to their conviction. However, he fails to see that they were not able to convince a majority of people to remove the statue or even better to change it in a way that gives a voice to Colston's victims.

**main part:** first argument (and counter-argument)

2021-22

Ethnic minorities are still underrepresented in many walks of life in Britain, for example in law, politics and the media. These domains are vital to expressing one's opinion and making a change. Although it is true that Sadiq Khan, a British politician of Pakistani origin and Muslim belief, was reelected Mayor of London, this is not enough to truly give ethnic or religious minorities a real influence.  *second argument (and counter-argument)*

Muslims, in particular, feel that Britain has recently become less tolerant and racism is very prominent, especially in social media. This even caused English football players and clubs to boycott social media. Again, this can only be a start but, in my view, it has no lasting effects.  *third argument (and counter-argument)*

Brexit has proven very clearly how strong nationalist tendencies in Britain really are. Immigration remains a controversially and ferociously debated topic and although the Black Lives Matter movement has strongly inspired people of colour in Britain and encouraged them to fight for their rights, the sheer fact that they still have to do so, shows that single acts will not change the general situation, at least not permanently.

I come to the conclusion that toppling the statue of a notorious slave trader is a strong symbol and certainly reason for hope but as long as people of colour are not represented more appropriately in politics, law and the media their voices will not get heard loud and persistently enough to really make a fundamental and lasting change.  *conclusion*

*(410 words)*

3.2 *This task is only loosely connected to the text as the focus is now on the USA. Due to the fact that US journalists who had written critically about the violent tearing down of historic statues lost their jobs, the question whether free speech is under threat from the public is raised. Taking the given quote by Jonathan Turley as a starting point you need to write a letter to him, in which you express your point of view on the importance of free speech in the USA. Take into account what you have learned about American myths and realities, basically the American Dream. You are supposed to write a letter to a person unknown to you, so you need to express yourself politely and rather formally.*
 – *address Professor Turley by his name and title*
 – *opening paragraph*
   • *present yourself*
   • *refer to the quotation*
   • *explain why you are writing*
 – *main part: say whether you think that freedom of speech is threatened by the public in the USA or not, give reasons*

2021-23

- America is seen as land of the free; American Dream promises liberty, equality and the pursuit of happiness
- freedom of expression is guaranteed in the First Amendment to the Constitution → Bill of Rights prohibits the state to limit the freedom of speech
- example of journalists: freedom is threatened by private people → the public opinion acts as censor
- one important aim of American foreign policy is to promote freedom and democracy (examples from the past: Iraq, Afghanistan)
- freedom of speech is under attack in the USA itself
- Donald Trump kept blaming the press for promoting fake news → distrust
- social media allows everyone to express themselves, sometimes limits are crossed, e. g. racist or abusive posts → freedom of expression has its limits
- ending: one or more of the following
  - draw a conclusion
  - present ideas how the situation could develop
  - thank the author for his time
- closing
- your name

Dear Professor Turley, — greeting

As a German student of English preparing for my A-level examinations I follow quite closely what is going on in Great Britain and the USA. Of course, I have heard about the violent tearing down of historical statues, like the Colston statue in Bristol or statues of Christopher Columbus, George Washington and Thomas Jefferson in the USA. I also came across your warning that the USA is "experiencing one of the greatest threats to free speech in [its] history and [that] it is coming, not from the government, but from the public". I am writing to express how much I agree with your statement. — introduction: present yourself / reference to quote, reason for writing

The freedom of expression is guaranteed in the Bill of Rights and it is remarkable that the statues of two of the founding fathers have been toppled in the aftermath of the killing of George Floyd. This goes to show that the perception of people and their deeds can change in history. The people who tore down the statues obviously saw in them the slave owners and not the founding fathers of the United States. Both perspectives are correct and it should be legal to express both views freely. — main part: Bill of Rights / different perspectives

As a consequence, to my mind, firing journalists who do just that, expressing their opinion on the violent tearing down of those statues, is not correct. Indeed, it goes against their freedom of expression, which should be guaranteed, as stated in the First Amendment. Unfortunately, the opinion of the furious people seems to outweigh the journalists' rights. I strongly disagree with — expression of your own view these people. Everybody must have the right to express their view, be it in the streets, in the press or on social media, as long as they respect other people's rights and do not post racist or abusive statements.

The USA is a democracy and claims to spread democracy and freedom around the world, for example by sending troops to Iraq or Afghanistan. How can Americans try to limit the freedom of expression in their own country? One reason might be the influence of the former President of the USA, Donald Trump. He did not tire of shouting fake news whenever he did not like what the press said about him or his policy. He kept shouting betrayal when he lost the last election. In doing so he sowed the seed of distrust in the media and democracy. Americans now have to pay the price. — limits to freedom of expression / Donald Trump's influence

I sincerely hope that your country and its people will understand what an important accomplishment freedom of expression is. We should not deny it to anyone, not to those who feel tearing down statues helps them to express their frustration and anger and to make themselves finally be heard. But certainly neither to those who express their view peacefully in words. — conclusion

Yours sincerely,
Dimitri Ziegra                    *(467 words)*    closing / name

## Teil B: Sprachmittlung (isoliert)

4. *Hier gilt es einen Artikel für die Webseite eines Schulprojekts zum Thema „Koloniales Erbe" zu verfassen. Basis für den Artikel ist das Radiointerview des Berliner Senders rbb. Der Artikel enthält viele Namen deutscher Straßen, Personen und Initiativen. Hier müssen Sie überlegen, welche davon erwähnenswert sind und dann Informationen liefern, die Menschen im Ausland bei der Einordnung helfen.*
   – *Überschrift*
   – *Projekt „tearthisdown.com"*
       • *digitale Karte → partizipatives Projekt zur Sammlung der Orte, die an die deutsche koloniale Vergangenheit erinnern (275 Eintragungen in den ersten 24 Stunden)*
       • *deutlich machen, dass auch Deutschland ein brutaler kolonialer Akteur war*
   – *Ziele des Projekts*
       • *Menschen anregen, mit offenen Augen durch die eigene Umgebung zu gehen → Zeichen kolonialer Geschichte entdecken*
       • *Geschichte sichtbar machen*

- *Straßen und öffentliche Orte umbenennen (ggf. ein illustrierendes Beispiel geben)*
- *Ersetzen durch Ehrung für Menschen, die antikolonialen Widerstand geleistet haben oder Menschen, die sich um antirassistische Belange verdient gemacht haben*
- *Perspektivwechsel, „um-erinnern"*

**Tear This Down**  headline
*A project to change the way we remember our colonial past.*  subheading

Germany's colonial past is not well known to many people and although many Germans think that their country did not have many colonies and not for a long time, it actually took an active and brutal part in colonialism.   **introduction:** Germany's colonial past

*Tearthisdown.com* aims at changing this lack of understanding. It is a digital project inviting people to walk through their neighbourhoods eyes wide open. Whenever they find a place that is reminiscent of Germany's colonial past, they can mark this place on a digital map. That way, history is made visible. In the first 24 hours that the site was online, there were 275 new entries.   **main part:** presentation of project

The goal is to rename streets and places and to replace memorials that honour people who were colonial agents or that otherwise make proof of an uncritical attitude towards Germany's colonial past. They want to replace these names or memorials with the names or faces of people who put up resistance against colonialism or who fight against racism in our days. For example, one street that was named after a slave trader is now named after an Afro-German anti-racist activist and poet. But instead of merely changing the names, a big plaque which explains why the names were changed and which tells the history of the place has been put up. The idea is not to forget our colonial past but to change perspective and to remember that time differently, namely from the point of view of the victims or opponents.   the project's goal / one example

*(259 words)*

## Abiturprüfung NRW – Englisch 2022
### Leistungskurs: Aufgabe 1

**Teil A: Leseverstehen und Schreiben (integriert)**   Inhalt 42 P. / Sprache 63 P.

### Aufgabenstellung                                                                     Punkte

1. Summarise what we learn about Carole's family background as well as her mother's expectations as presented in the extract. *(Comprehension)*   12

2. Analyse how Carole is presented. Focus on narrative perspective and use of language. *(Analysis)*   16

3. Choose **one** of the following tasks:   14

3.1 Journalist and historian David Olusoga states that many people in Britain deny the existence of structural racism and consider it as "a minor, if regrettable, fact of life – one that black people have to tolerate and learn to live with". Assess to what extent David Olusoga's statement can be seen as a valid description of an attitude prevailing in British society today. *(Evaluation: comment)*

   *Zitat: David Olusoga, "Harry and Meghan interview: This is not just a crisis for the royal family – but for Britain itself", in: The Guardian, 9 March 2021*
   *https://www.theguardian.com/commentisfree/2021/mar/09/harry-and-meghan-interview-this-is-not-just-a-crisis-for-the-royal-family-but-for-britain-itself*

3.2 In the evening after the conversation with her mother on whether to return to university or not, Carole goes back to her room reflecting on her mother's advice. Write an interior monologue expressing her hopes and fears. *(Evaluation: re-creation of text)*

### Text:
**Bernardine Evaristo, *Girl, Woman, Other***

*The story is set in present-day UK. Carole arrives at the university where she is about to start her studies.*
*Please note: The text presented is in the form of the original print version.*

1   her mother couldn't get the day off work and anyway, it was just as well because she'd wear her most outlandish Nigerian outfit consisting of thousands of yards of bright material, and a headscarf ten storeys high, and she'd start bawling when she had to leave her only child for the first time
5   Carole would forever be known as the student with the mad African mother
   that first week she counted on one hand the number of brown-skinned people in her college, and none as dark as her

2022-1

in the baronial dining hall she could barely look up from her plate of revolting Stone Age food, let alone converse with anyone

she overheard loud reminiscences about the dorms and drugs of boarding school, Christmas holidays in Goa, the Bahamas, gap years spent climbing Machu Picchu, or building a school for the poor in Kenya, about haring down the M4 for weekends in London, house parties in the countryside, long weekenders in Paris, Copenhagen, Prague, Dublin or Vilnius (where *was* that, even?)

most students weren't like that but the really posh ones were the loudest and the most confident and they were the only voices she heard

they made her feel crushed, worthless and a nobody

without saying a word to her

without even noticing her

nobody talked loudly about growing up in a council flat on a skyscraper estate with a single mother who worked as a cleaner

nobody talked loudly about never having gone on a single holiday, like *ever*

nobody talked loudly about never having been on a plane, seen a play or the sea, or eaten in a restaurant, with waiters

nobody talked loudly about feeling too uglystupidfatpoor or just plain out of place, out of sorts, [...]

people walked around her or looked through her, or was she imagining it? did she exist or was she an illusion? if I strip off and streak across the quadrangle will anyone notice me other than the porters who will no doubt call the fedz, an excuse they've been waiting for ever since they first set eyes on her

when a student sidled up after a lecture to ask for some ecstasy, Carole almost texted her mother to say she was on the next train home

at the end of her first term she returned to Peckham informing her mother she didn't want to return to university because although she liked her studies and was managing to stay on top of most of it, she didn't belong there and wasn't going back

I'm done, Mama, I'm done

eh! eh! which kain nonsense be this? Bummi shouted, am I hearing you correctly or you wan make I clean my ear with matches?

listen to me good, Carole Williams

firstly – do you think Oprah Winfrey (V I P) would have become the Queen of Television worldwide if she had not risen above the setbacks of her early life?

secondly – do you think Diane Abbott (V I P) would have become Britn's first black woman M P if she did not believe it was her right to enter politics and represent her community?

thirdly – do you think Valerie Amos (V I P) would have become the first black woman baroness in this country if she had burst into tears when she walked into the House of Lords and seen it was full of elderly white gentlemen?

lastly, did me and Papa come to this country for a better life only to see our daughter giving up on her opportunities and end up distributing paper hand towels for tips in nightclub toilets or concert venues, as is the fate of too many of our countrywomen?

you must go back to this university in January and stop thinking everybody hates you without giving them a chance, did you even ask them? did you go up to them and say, excuse me, do you hate me?

you must find the people who will want to be your friends even if they are all white people there is someone for everyone in this world

you must go back and fight the battles that are your British birthright, Carole, as a true Nigerian

Carole returned to her college resolved to conquer the place where she would spend the next two and a half years of her life

she would fit in, she decided, she would find her people, as her mother had advised not with the misfits who skulked about the place with scowls on their faces, their hair gelled up into purple Mohicans

or those with multi-coloured dreadlock extensions, people who were going nowhere fast, as far as Carole was concerned, as she watched them walk through town with placards and loudspeakers, people who would horrify her mother if she brought them home

to have come this far? did your Papa sacrifice his health so that you could become a punky Rasta person who smells?

nor was she interested in the boring ordinaries, as Carole began to think of them, students who were so bland they disappeared, even to her

certainly not the cliques of the elite, now that she knew they existed, who were unreachable, [...]

she studied the inmates to find the best match for her, approached those with the most friendly demeanours, was surprised when people responded warmly once she actually started talking to them

by the end of her second term she had made friends and even got herself a boyfriend, Marcus, a white Kenyan whose family owned a cattle ranch there, who unashamedly had a thing for black girls, which she didn't mind because she was delighted to be desired and he treated her considerately

she knew she could never tell her mother about him, who'd made it clear she had to marry a Nigerian, not that Carole was even thinking of marrying Marcus, they were only nineteen, her mother would then ask her why she was courting someone who did not respect her enough to marry her

it would be lose-lose *(998 words)*

*Bernardine Evaristo*, Girl, Woman, Other, *London: Penguin Books 2019, S. 131–135*

**Annotations**
l. 8 *baronial: here:* elegant, grand
l. 12 *M4:* motorway connecting London with Wales
l. 29 *fedz: slang:* security officers
l. 33 *Peckham:* part of London where many Nigerians live
l. 37 *kain: Nigerian English pidgin:* kind of
l. 37 *Bummi:* Carole's mother
l. 38 *wan: Nigerian English pidgin:* to want to
l. 62 *Mohicans: here:* a hairstyle created by shaving the hair on each side and leaving a strip of longer hair in the middle

## Teil B: Sprachmittlung (isoliert)   Inhalt 18 P. / Sprache 27 P.

**Aufgabenstellung**

4. Your school takes part in a virtual exchange on *European Youth Culture*. In your group, you want to find out about young people's lifestyles across Europe. You have come across Sharma's article and have decided to present it to your fellow group members. Based on the article write them an email in which you outline a current trend in Germany. *(Mediation)*   18

**Text:**
**Mayank Sharma, *Warum wir zu unserem Neo-Spießertum stehen sollten***

*Während eines gemeinsamen Urlaubs in einer Selbstversorgerhütte im Schwarzwald stellte sich der Autorin und ihrem Freundeskreis die Frage nach der Spießigkeit ihres Lebensstils.*

„Wie spießig bin ich eigentlich!?" Als ich die Frage auch meinen Freunden stellte, während wir versammelt in der braun getäfelten Stube am Kachelofen saßen, fühlten sie sich ertappt. Spießig!? Auf keinen Fall. Diesen Vorwurf lässt sich wohl kaum ein junger Mensch widerstandslos gefallen. Spießig sind immer nur die anderen. Doch seit diesem Hüttenurlaub bezeichnen wir uns im Freundeskreis immer wieder spaßeshalber als „Neo-Spießer" – und wenn wir ehrlich zu uns sind, fühlen wir uns auch so.

Der Begriff des Neo-Spießertums kursierte zuletzt vor ein paar Jahren in den Medien. Bereits damals hatte man insbesondere bei Studierenden eine neue Bürgerlichkeit entdeckt. Und bis heute hat er nicht an Aktualität verloren – denn er steht nicht für eine kurze Modeerscheinung, sondern für die Werte und Einstellung einer Generation. Meiner Generation.

Unter „Spießern" stellen sich die meisten engstirnige, kleinkarierte und konformistische Personen mit Bausparverträgen vor, die in Reihenhäusern mit gepflegten Vorgärten wohnen. Werte wie Sicherheit, Familie und Tradition gelten als spießig. Ist nicht genau das die Antithese zu all dem, wofür wir zu stehen glauben, wovon wir uns immer abgrenzen wollten? Machen wir nicht alles anders als unsere Eltern und Großeltern? Oder machen wir uns nur etwas vor und das „Neo", das wir dem „Spießer" voranstellen, gaukelt eine Pseudo-Emanzipation vor, die es gar nicht gibt?

Dass für meine Freunde und mich, genauso wie für viele andere junge Menschen, Dinge zu unserem Lifestyle gehören, die wir selbst mit Spießigkeit verbinden, lässt sich nicht verleugnen. In der Selbstbeobachtung kann das schizophren wirken, Selbstanspruch und Wirklichkeit klaffen auseinander, wenn das eigene Kleingärtner- und Heimwerkertum der Forderung des gesellschaftlichen Wandels gegenüberstehen. Aber ist diese Selbstkritik wirklich berechtigt? Übernehmen wir mit Omas und Opas Vorlieben auch ihren Wertekanon?

Teilweise. Das hat zumindest die Shell-Jugendstudie von 2019 ergeben, für die zwölf- bis 25-Jährige befragt wurden. Die Ergebnisse zeigen eine klare Tendenz: Soziale Eingebundenheit gehört zu den wichtigsten Wertorientierungen. Den meisten sind Familie und soziale Beziehungen sogar wichtiger als Eigenverantwortlichkeit und Unabhängigkeit. Großen Wert legten die Befragten auch auf traditionelle Tugenden, wie den Respekt gegenüber Gesetz und Ordnung, der Orientierung an der Leistungsnorm und dem Streben nach Sicherheit insgesamt. Dieses Bild bestätigt die SINUS-Jugendstudie, die im Juli dieses Jahres veröffentlicht wurde. Untersucht wurden 14- bis 17-Jährige. Die Autoren stellten fest, dass die bürgerliche Normalbiographie das Leitmotiv vieler Teenager ist. In der Mitte der Gesellschaft ankommen. Das scheint den meisten Jugendlichen erstrebenswerter zu sein als ein hoher Lebensstandard oder die eigenen Wünsche und Bedürfnisse durchzusetzen. […]

Bleibt die Frage, ob wir der althergebrachten Spießigkeit tatsächlich zumindest einen neuen Dreh geben. Ich finde: Das tun wir sehr wohl.

Und damit kommen wir zur anderen Seite der Medaille der Spießigkeit, auf der groß „Neo" geschrieben steht. Die Forscher der Shell-Studie haben herausgefunden, dass vier von fünf Befragten ein hedonistisches Streben aufweisen, das Leben also in vollen Zügen genießen wollen. Dabei betonen die meisten weder den Beruf noch die Freizeit übermäßig. Sicherheit und Genuss schließen sich für die junge Generation also nicht gegenseitig aus, sondern scheinen sich eher gegenseitig zu bedingen. Gut in dieses Bild passt, dass wir großen Wert auf eine insgesamt bewusste Lebensgestaltung legen. Wir verhalten uns deutlich achtsamer gegenüber der Umwelt, dem Klima und letztlich uns selbst, als es noch unsere Eltern und Großeltern taten. Das läuft auf einen Kompromiss hinaus. […]

So kommt auch die Jugendstudie zu dem Schluss, dass für die meisten jungen Menschen eine idealistische, sinnstiftende Werteorientierung an Bedeutung gewonnen hat. Mit engstirniger Spießigkeit hat das wenig zu tun. Auch nichts mit Kleinkariertheit.

Es ist eher so, dass wir alte Formen mit neuen Inhalten füllen. Wir lehnen das Alte nicht kategorisch ab, sondern geben ihm einen neuen Anstrich. *(596 Wörter)*

*Mayank Sharma, „Warum wir zu unserem Neo-Spießertum stehen sollten",*
*in: jetzt, 26. Dezember 2020*
*https://www.jetzt.de/kultur/neo-spiessertum-junge-menschen-uebernehmen-alte-werte-vorstellungen*
*(Zugriff: 9. 3 2021)*

## Lösungsvorschläge

### Teil A: Leseverstehen und Schreiben (integriert)

1. *Summarize what you can find out about Carole's family background and what her mother wants her to do.*
   - Family background:
     - Daughter to a single mother who works as a cleaner
     - Father probably died
     - Parents immigrated to Britain from Nigeria
     - Only child
     - Mother adheres to Nigerian traditions
     - Grew up poor in a council flat
   - Her mother wants her to ...
     - have a better life
     - overcome difficulties and fight for her rights
     - make use of the opportunities offered to her
     - take successful Black* women as an example
     - stick to Nigerian values by marrying a Nigerian man

   * The words "Black" and "White" are written in capital letters to signal that they are not natural categories but social ones. Quotations from the original text are left unchanged.

   In the extract from Bernardine Evaristo's novel *Girl, Woman, Other* published in 2019, the reader gets to know Carole, who is new at college. — introductory sentence

   Carole grew up poor in a council flat. Her parents immigrated to Britain from Nigeria. She is an only child to a single mother, who works as a cleaner and adheres to Nigerian traditions. Her father seems to have died. — Carole's family background

   Carole's mother, who is called Bummi, expects her daughter to do better in life than she and her husband did. To make use of the opportunities offered to her, Carole is supposed to overcome difficulties and to fight for her rights. She is meant to take successful Black women as an example, to stick to Nigerian values and to marry a Nigerian man. — her mother's expectations

   *(127 words)*

2. *In this task you need to analyse how the protagonist is presented. Basically, this implies writing a characterization, in which you focus on the use of language and the effects of the choice of narrator and point of view. In this case it is interesting to note how Carole changes throughout the excerpt. She undergoes a significant change from beginning to end.*

2022-6

- At the beginning:
  - Feeling of discomfort: "out of place" (l. 25), like she doesn't belong to university (cf. l. 35), "uglystupidfatpoor" (l. 25)
  - Stressed by language:
    - exaggeration of her mother's dress (cf. ll. 2–4): Carole is ashamed of her mother
    - enumeration (cf. ll. 10–14): list of activities and experiences made by her fellow students
    - anaphora (cf. ll. 20–25): emphasizes her poverty and her being different in that respect
    - "uglystupidfatpoor" (l. 25): four words contracted into one by leaving out blanks → four adjectives with a negative connotation; stresses how she feels that all these qualities refer to her
    - no full stops at the end of a sentence, no capitals at beginning of a sentence → narration gathers speed, leaves reader breathless and emphasizes how overwhelmed Carole is by her experience at university → new environment and different people
  - Supported by narrative perspective
    - third-person narrator with a limited point of view, Carole's perspective
    - reader only gets to know her perspective, can identify with her and her feeling "out of sorts" (l. 26)
    - narrator also makes comments and asks questions either supporting Carole's view (cf. l. 14) or also questioning it (cf. l. 27) → raises doubts about whether Carole's perception is correct, draws attention to her being biased
- In the middle: long insertion of direct speech, her mother tells Carole off for giving up too quickly (cf. ll. 37–57) → throws a different light on Carole's perception → turning point
- At the end: "resolved to conquer the place where she would spend the next two and a half years of her life" (ll. 58/59) → no longer doubtful but determined
  - Stressed by language
    - parallelism: "she would spend […] she would fit in […] she would find" (ll. 58–60)
  - Emphasized by narrative perspective
    - insertions emphasize that it is Carole's view, e. g. "as far as Carole was concerned" (l. 64), "as Carole began to think of them" (l. 69) → she still judges her fellow students but now focuses on finding "the best match for her" (l. 73)
    - narrator comments that she "was surprised when people responded warmly once she actually started talking to them" (ll. 74/75) → puts her former impression that she does not belong into perspective
- Conclusion: protagonist is coming of age; behaves more maturely, stops sulking and withdrawing, becomes more open

Throughout the excerpt, the main character undergoes a fundamental change. Carole comes of age and behaves more maturely. This change is emphasized by the narrative perspective chosen and language employed.

At the beginning of the excerpt, Carole feels "out of place" (l. 25) at university and has the impression that she does not belong there (cf. l. 35). This feeling of discomfort is stressed by language. To start with, the dress Carole's mother might have worn to send her daughter off to university is described in an exaggerated way as an "outfit consisting of thousands of yards of bright material, and a headscarf ten storeys high" (ll. 2/3). Her behaviour would have marked Carole "as the student with the mad African mother" (l. 5). This shows that Carole is ashamed of her mother and her origin because she is different from everybody else.

She feels that way because she does not share the same experience as her fellow students. Here, an enumeration is used to list all the places where the other students have been (cf. ll. 10–14). Furthermore, anaphora is employed to emphasize her poverty (cf. ll. 20–25), which sets her apart from the other students.

As a consequence, she feels "uglystupidfatpoor" (l. 25). Here, four adjectives with a negative connotation are contracted into one by leaving out all the blanks. This underlines that she sees herself in an entirely negative light. Also, there are no full stops at the end of a sentence and no capitals at the beginning of a sentence throughout the excerpt. As a result, the narration gathers speed and leaves the reader breathless and at times confused about what to make of the narration. This emphasizes how overwhelmed Carole is by her experience at university, mainly by the new environment and the people she cannot adapt to.

The novel is told by a third-person narrator with a limited point of view. The reader only gets to know Carole's perspective and therefore can identify with her and her feeling "out of sorts" (l. 26). In the first 36 lines the reader only sees things through Carole's eyes and follows her train of thoughts.

However, the narrator also makes comments and asks questions either supporting Carole's view (cf. l. 14) or questioning it (cf. l. 27). This last example raises doubts as to whether Carole's perception is correct and draws attention to her being biased.

---

introduction:
thesis: character undergoes change

main part:
feeling of discomfort, outsider

→ exaggeration

ashamed of her mother, her origin

poverty
→ enumeration

→ anaphora

negative self-image
→ no blanks

→ no full stops

overwhelming experience

third-person narrator
Carole's perspective

→ questions

bias

In the middle of the extract Carole's perspective is followed by a long passage of direct speech, where her mother tells Carole off for giving up too quickly (cf. ll. 37–57). This passage throws a different light on Carole's perception and can be seen as a turning point. After her stay with her mother, Carole returns to university "resolved to conquer the place where she would spend the next two and a half years of her life" (ll. 58/59). She is no longer doubtful but determined. This change is stressed by language. There is a parallelism stressing her determination; "[…] she would spend […] she would fit in […] she would find" (ll. 58–60).

turning point
→ direct speech

character changes: determination
→ parallelism

There are some insertions by the narrator that emphasize that what is related is Carole's view, e. g. "as far as Carole was concerned" (l. 64), "as Carole began to think of them" (l. 69). These phrases underline the fact that Carole still judges her fellow students, but now she is focusing on finding "the best match for her[self]" (l. 73). Carole "was surprised when people responded warmly once she actually started talking to them" (ll. 74/75). This comment puts her former impression that she does not belong into perspective and hints at the possibility that Carole did not really try to belong.

narrative technique
→ insertions

→ comment

All in all, it can be said that Carole has come of age during the extract. At the beginning she distanced herself from the other students and was willing to give up her chance to improve her life. In the end she behaves more maturely, stops withdrawing, becomes more open towards her fellow students and even enjoys herself at university. *(688 words)*

conclusion

3.1. *You are given a quote which you first have to explain. Be careful not to take the quote for David Olusoga's personal opinion but rather as his perception of British society. Then assess if it is a fitting description of the attitude most Britons have towards Black people and towards racism. Consider whether racism occurs because of individual racist assumptions or if it is deeply rooted within society and its policies, laws and institutions.*
– *Introduction: explanation of the quote*
– *Individual racism: based on the assumptions of individuals and on the resulting behaviour towards Black people and people of colour*
– *Examples of individual racism: wide range, from unconscious bias, insulting glances, nasty remarks, discrimination on the housing and labour market to openly racist violence*
– *More than "a minor, if regrettable, fact of life"*
– *No one should "have to tolerate and learn to live with it"*

- *Structural racism: inequalities are rooted in society as a whole, there are rules and laws that make sure White people have advantages and Black people are excluded from significant participation in major social institutions, e. g. politics, law, the media → their views are not represented and not heard, not addressed*
- *Examples of structural racism: Blacks are more often stopped and searched by police than Whites, more likely to be poor*
- *Border between individual and structural racism is fluid*
- *Individuals act and think racist because that is what society teaches them*
- *Children are taught to see the difference in skin colour*
- *Brexit has shown clear nationalist tendencies*
- *Black Lives Matter movement helps to raise awareness*
- *Conclusion: no quick solutions, but we must not stop trying; the individual can force themself not to think and act racist; if the structural problem is not accepted it will not be addressed*

| | |
|---|---|
| David Olusoga believes that the majority of the British people pretend that structural racism does not exist in Britain. According to them, racism merely depends on the way individuals act and is "a minor, if regrettable, fact of life – one that black people have to tolerate and learn to live with". To assess Olusoga's statement one needs to have a closer look at the difference between both individual and structural racism. | **introduction:** explanation of quote |
| | approach |
| Individual racism is based on the assumptions of individuals and on the resulting behaviour towards other people. White people might think and act racist unconsciously or openly. They make hurtful or nasty remarks, throw insulting glances – or much worse. These (micro)aggressions make BPoC feel uncomfortable and can even lead to health problems. Individual racism also leads to problems on the housing or labour market because Whites may not want to rent their flat to Blacks or offer them a job. As one can see this is definitely more than "a minor, if regrettable, fact of life" and no one should "have to tolerate and learn to live with" such behaviour. | **main part:** individual racism examples |
| | problems |
| What is more, individual racism could not exist if the attitude was not deeply rooted within society. Children are taught to see the difference in skin colour and Black children realize that they are underrepresented in books and films. Probably due to their colonial past, the British have learned that Whites are considered superior. | society |
| | colonial past |

From here on, it is a small step to structural racism, which means that inequalities are rooted in society as a whole, firmly established in its rules, policies and laws. Blacks are excluded from significant participation in major social institutions, e. g. politics, the law and the media. Obviously one can easily find BPoC in all walks of life and this fact is often used to argue that there is no structural problem. But the number of BPoC represented in influential positions does still not represent their number within society as a whole. As a consequence, their views are not visible enough, not heard loudly enough and therefore their needs too rarely addressed. | structural racism

examples

consequence

Brexit and the campaign leading towards it has proven that there are strong nationalist tendencies, which certainly enhance structural racism, even though people may want to close their eyes to it. For instance, Black people are more often stopped and searched by the police, and they are more likely to be poor. Movements like Black Lives Matter would not be necessary if there was no structural racism. However, it also shows that at least some people are willing to open their eyes and to address the problem. | nationalist tendencies

examples

Black Lives Matter

To conclude, I would like to point out how important it is to accept the fact that racism is a structural problem because else it will not be addressed as such. Claiming it is only an individual problem puts the blame on the individual alone although society as a whole must take responsibility if the situation is really supposed to change.  *(497 words)* | conclusion

3.2. You have to write an interior monologue in which Carole considers her mother's words. An interior monologue gives insight into a character's feelings and thoughts. It does not include direct speech or quotation marks, but may be introduced by expressions like, "she thought", "she sighed". Depending on the context it can be told by a first or third-person narrator and be written in simple present or simple past. Content-wise, you're meant to express both Carole's hopes and fears. It will help if you reread your notes on tasks one and two. The task tells you where and when to set the monologue (in Carole's room, after the conversation with her mother), so you'll know how to start off.
 – Carole is in her room
 – Replays her mother's words and advice
 – Expresses her feelings at her mother's advice: maybe anger, but also agreement, in the end she comes to the conclusion that she has to return and to succeed at university

- *Possible fears:*
  - *Remain lonely*
  - *Be laughed at by others*
  - *Make a fool of herself*
  - *Not manage to do well in classes*
  - *Disappoint her mother*
- *Possible hopes:*
  - *Make a fresh start*
  - *Make friends*
  - *Be successful*
  - *Make her mother proud*

In the evening Carole returned to her room. She sat down on her bed and looked around the room. This had been her home for the last ten years. She had grown up here and there still were posters, photos and souvenirs of her childhood. When her mother had talked to her, no, reprimanded her really, Carole sighed, she had basically told her to grow up. **introduction:** presentation of situation<br><br><br><br>Carole's thoughts

How dare she, Carole hissed, she didn't know what it was like to be with these posh students who had seen everything, been everywhere. She didn't know what it was like to sit in this baronial dining hall, eating food that she wasn't used to. She didn't know what it was like to walk across the campus and be asked for drugs. angry at her mother

But maybe she had a point, Carole conceded. She hadn't addressed anyone, quite the contrary, she had more or less avoided everybody for fear of making a fool of herself. The only times she had enjoyed herself was in class. She actually liked studying, she realized. Well, well, she thought, that was true, she did enjoy learning and exercising her mind. So, maybe her mum was right after all, she admitted to herself, she should not let them take that away from her. She shouldn't be defeated. Her parents had sacrificed so much for her, she thought with a pang of guilt. Surely, they could expect her to at least give it a try, to put in a little fight. Well, she grinned, she wouldn't exactly ask them if they hated her, now, would she? But she could return to university more open-minded, she could watch out for those students who were a bit like her, she could observe who was interested in the same subjects as her. Yes, she sighed with relief, she could do that, and she would do that. She would find her place and prove that she belonged. accepts her mother's view

Reassured, she got up again, went back to the kitchen and embraced her mother. *(334 words)* **closing**

## Teil B: Sprachmittlung (isoliert)

4. Sie müssen hier eine E-Mail an vermutlich gleichaltrige Personen verfassen. Arbeiten Sie aus dem Ausgangstext heraus, welcher Trend unter Jugendlichen und jungen Erwachsenen in Deutschland gerade vorherrscht.
   - Informelle Anrede an eine Gruppe
   - Einleitender Satz: Bezug zum gemeinsamen Thema herstellen
   - Neo-Spießertum als aktueller Trend
     - Neue Bürgerlichkeit: Werte und Einstellungen einer ganzen Generation
     - Geben der althergebrachten Spießigkeit aber einen neuen Dreh
   - Dazu gehörten folgende Tendenzen:
     - Soziale Eingebundenheit, z. B. Familie, als wichtigster Wert
     - Eigenverantwortung und Unabhängigkeit
     - Traditionelle Tugenden, z. B. Respekt gegenüber Gesetz und Ordnung, Orientierung an Leistungsnormen, Streben nach Sicherheit
     - In der Mitte der Gesellschaft ankommen
     - Zusätzlich und anders als frühere Generationen: hedonistisches Streben, das Leben genießen wollen ohne Bedürfnis nach Sicherheit zu vernachlässigen; Achtsamkeit gegenüber der Umwelt und sich selbst

| | |
|---|---|
| Hello everyone, | greeting |
| How are you doing? Have you made some progress on our project? I've found an interesting article which describes a current trend among Germany's youth. The author calls it the "new bourgeoisie". Apparently young people adapt traditional values and attitudes of their parents' and grandparents' generations but give them a slightly new turn. | **introductory sentences** reference to task  values and attitudes |
| According to a study among teenagers and young adults, we still consider social inclusion as the most important value. For instance, family is very important to German youth. Other values which we share with our parents are taking responsibility for oneself and being independent. We still adhere to traditional virtues, as we respect law and order, strive to be part of the middle class by working enough in order to be financially secure. However, unlike our parents, we aim to take better care of the environment and of ourselves. We are far more hedonistic in that we would like to balance work and life far better than older generations did. | similarities with / differences to older generations |
| That's as far as the article goes. Do you think that this is true for young people in your countries, too? I still need to figure out if I fit into the image created. Please let me know what you think. | **closing sentences** |
| Bye, | salutation |
| Sajida                                      *(208 words)* | name |

**Abiturprüfung NRW – Englisch 2022**
**Leistungskurs: Aufgabe 2**

## Teil A: Leseverstehen und Schreiben (integriert)     Inhalt 42 P. / Sprache 63 P.

### Aufgabenstellung                                                                Punkte

1. Describe Kosoko Jackson's experiences with the literary world. *(Comprehension)*     12

2. Examine how Jennifer Senior conveys her attitude towards "cancel culture" and its consequences for authors. Refer to line of argument and language. *(Analysis)*     16

3. Choose **one** of the following tasks:     14

3.1 In 1921, Nobel Peace Prize winner Christian Lous Lange said, "Technology is a useful servant, but a dangerous master." Using this statement as a starting point, assess to what extent technology truly has already become the master rather than the servant in our modern world today. Refer to work done in class on global challenges and ethical issues of scientific and technological progress. *(Evaluation: comment)*
   Zitat: Christian Lous Lange, Nobel Peace Prize 1921 Acceptance Speech
   https://www.nobelprize.org/prizes/peace/1921/lange/lecture/

3.2 Your creative writing course at school has set up its own website *Making Our Voices Get Heard*. After reading Jennifer Senior's text about Kosoko Jackson's case, you have decided to write an article for this new website reflecting on the role of freedom of speech and creativity in society. Write the article. *(Evaluation: re-creation of text)*

### Text:
### Jennifer Senior, *Teen Fiction and the Perils of Cancel Culture*

1  Late last month, a young man named Kosoko Jackson became the second young adult author in five weeks to pull a debut work just before it hit the shelves. His book, "A Place for Wolves," ran afoul of the sensibilities of the Twitter gatekeeping class, which deemed it insensitive to Muslims and unduly focused on people of privilege.

5  There was an obvious irony to his story, a karmic boomerang: Jackson, who is black and gay, often worked as a "sensitivity reader" for major publishing houses, which meant his job was to flag just the sort of problem content for which he was now being run out of town. He was Robespierre with his own neck in the cradle of the guillotine. One of the captains of "cancel culture" – which urges people to shun the insensitive,
10 the oppressive, the morally questionable – got canceled himself.

As often happens with these things, the online pile-on was mainly led by people who hadn't read Jackson's book. It did start with someone who had – a reader who'd written an intemperate, if highly impassioned, review of an advance copy for the community website Goodreads. But it most likely would have remained just that, a pan from a citizen critic, had the review not been noticed by that corner of Twitter that's obsessed with Y. A. fiction. Even by Twitter standards, it's a hothouse subculture – self-conscious, emotional, quick to injure. Not unlike teenagers themselves.

I have read Jackson's book. Before I get to the actual contents, let's get this out of the way: What happened to Jackson is frightening. Purity tests are the tools of fanatics, and the quest for purity ultimately becomes indistinguishable from the quest for power. In the Twitterverse, ideologues have far more power than moderates. They have more followers; their tweets get more traction (studies have shown that emotional tweets pretty much always have more traction); they set the terms of their neighborhood's culture and tone.

But this does not mean they have better judgment.

This episode is proof of nothing if not of Twitter's asymmetrical power: A semi-anonymous mob (the leader of the charge was someone with the handle @flightofstaz) can sufficiently scare an author into withdrawing his book, even though it received a starred review from Booklist and was a Kids' Indie Next pick. (Not a small deal, that.) The die-hards in this army of crusaders will argue they're doing it in the name of diversity, but it's really just the opposite: If Twitter controls publishing, we'll soon enter a dreary monoculture that admits no book unless it has been prejudged and meets the standards of the censors.

What Jackson's case really demonstrates is just how narrow and untenable the rules for writing Y. A. literature are. In a tweet last May, Jackson himself more or less articulated them: "Stories about the civil rights movement should be written by black people. Stories of suffrage should be written by women. Ergo, stories about boys during life-changing times, like the AIDS epidemic, should be written by gay men. Why is this so hard to get?"

In a live Q. and A. for an online children's literature conference in January, Jackson explained that he was at one point tempted to write tangentially about immigration, but his Latino friends talked him out of it: He'd be encroaching on their turf, poaching their spot on the shelves. So he didn't. But his first novel, "A Place for Wolves," is not exclusively populated by gay African-Americans. His two protagonists are gay teenagers, yes, and one of them is black. But his secondary characters are ... Serbs and Albanians. The book takes place in Kosovo, during the early days of its civil war in the late '90s.

Let's stop to contemplate this for a moment. When Jackson was left to his own devices to create and dream – rather than to simply read books for possible cultural violations – his natural, irrepressible reflex was to write about something that went beyond his own experience. Because that's what novelists do: conjure other worlds, imagine their way into other realities, guess at the texture of other people's consciousness. It's part of the pleasure of inventing stuff for a living. [...]

What raised people' hackles was that an Albanian Muslim is one of the book's villains, when it was the Albanian Muslims who suffered disproportionately during the

Kosovo war. That, and the idea that two comparatively privileged American teenagers could be the focus of the book

Did Jackson do this out of malice? No. It was his explicit intention, according to an author's note, to complicate the reader's picture of a tragic ethnic war. There's nothing wrong, per se, with making a victim a villain, or a hero a jerk: Art is filled with anti-heroes with redeeming qualities, whether they're Humbert Humbert or Tony Soprano. Nor are two American teenagers in a war-torn country, on the face of it, a bad premise for a Y.A. book.

The book's real sin is that Jackson didn't do what he set out to do. Though he can write with charm and the authentic sass of an American adolescent, much of the book is painfully clumsy and poorly paced – which makes it a fairly typical debut novel, by the way. His job as a sensitivity reader also shows: "Sounded a little Eurocentric to me," is a not unrepresentative observation by the narrator.

If the book-buying public had found "A Place for Wolves" as criminally distasteful and insensitive as Twitter did, it would have sunk the novel in slower, more deliberate ways. Librarians would have read it and taken a pass. Bookstore owners would have decided it wasn't worth the space. Book critics would have savaged it – or worse, ignored it.

It should have failed or succeeded in the marketplace of ideas. But it was never given the chance. The mob got to it first.                                  *(974 words)*

*Jennifer Senior, "Teen Fiction and the Perils of Cancel Culture",*
*in:* The New York Times, *8 March 2019*
*https://www.nytimes.com/2019/03/08/opinion/teen-fiction-and-the-perils-of-cancel-culture.html*
*(Zugriff: 7. 4. 2021). From* The New York Times*. © 2019 The New York Times Company. All rights reserved. Used under license*

**Annotations**
l. 2   *to pull work: here:* to withdraw a new book
l. 5   *karmic:* resulting from one's actions; reference to the Buddhist concept of karma
l. 8   *Robespierre with his own heck in the cradle of the guillotine:* key figure in the French Revolution responsible for killing many people and finally being killed himself by guillotine
l. 14  *pan: here:* very strong criticism
l. 16  *Y. A. fiction:* short for Young Adult Fiction
l. 29  *Booklist:* book review magazine published by the American Library Association
l. 29  *Kids' Indie Next pick:* books for children and young adults recommended by the American Booksellers Association in corporation with independent bookstores
l. 40  *Q. and A.: here:* short for Question-and-Answer session
l. 61  *Humbert Humbert:* controversial protagonist of the novel *Lolita* by Vladimir Nabokov
l. 61  *Tony Soprano:* main character in the TV drama series *The Sopranos* about a mafia family

# Teil B: Sprachmittlung (isoliert)

Inhalt 18 P. / Sprache 27 P.

## Aufgabenstellung

4. As an exchange student at an American high school, you work on a project *News for Youth*. You are supposed to give a talk about the situation in Germany.
Based on the article at hand, write the script for your talk in which you outline the findings of the study and the implications for journalism. *(Mediation)*      18

**Text:**
*Studie: Jugendlichen fehlt bei Nachrichten Alltagsbezug*

Vielen Jugendlichen in Deutschland geht einer Studie zufolge das Nachrichtenangebot an ihrer eigenen Lebenswelt vorbei.

„Die Hälfte der Jugendlichen hält es nicht für wichtig, sich über Neuigkeiten und aktuelle Ereignisse zu informieren. Bei journalistischen Nachrichten fehlt ihnen oft der Bezug zu ihrem persönlichen Alltag", heißt es in der am Mittwoch vorgestellten Studie als ein Kernergebnis zur Nachrichtenkompetenz Jugendlicher und junger Erwachsener in der digitalen Medienwelt.

Die Studie mit repräsentativer Befragung ist Teil des Projekts #UseTheNews. Das bundesweite Projekt ist von der Deutschen Presse-Agentur (dpa) und der Hamburger Behörde für Kultur und Medien initiiert und koordiniert, zahlreiche Partnerinstitutionen unter anderem aus Medien und Wissenschaft beteiligen sich. Das Leibniz-Institut für Medienforschung erstellte die Studie.

Weitere Kernergebnisse, die die Autoren auflisten: Journalistische Angebote sind demnach nur noch eine von vielen genutzten Informationsquellen. 46 Prozent der 14- bis 17-Jährigen widmen sich mehrmals pro Woche journalistischen Angeboten, 58 Prozent schauen auch auf nicht-journalistische Akteure.

Die Studie beschreibt auch, dass für junge Leute der wichtigste Grund, sich auf dem Laufenden zu halten, ist, sich an Gesprächen und Diskussionen im Freundes- und Familienkreis beteiligen zu können. „Auffällig ist zudem, dass die Jugendlichen, die das Gefühl haben, politisch etwas bewirken zu können, deutlich mehr Interesse an Informationen über das aktuelle Geschehen äußern."

Der Medienforscher und Studienleiter Uwe Hasebrink vom Leibniz-Institut betont, dass es innerhalb derselben Altersgruppe sehr unterschiedliche Typen bei der Nachrichtenorientierung gebe. [...]

Studienautor Sascha Hölig teilte zur Studie unter anderem dies mit: „Insgesamt stellen wir fest, dass vielen Jugendlichen bei journalistischen Nachrichten der Bezug zu ihrem eigenen Alltag fehlt. Auch das Wissen über Funktionen und Arbeitsweisen des Journalismus ist begrenzt, und dass dieser sich dadurch von anderen Informationslieferanten unterscheidet." Hölig schlussfolgerte: „An beiden Stellen sollten sowohl Bildungsinitiativen als auch Nachrichtenanbieter ansetzen. In der Medienbildung sollten

Aufgaben mit Funktionen des Journalismus in einer Demokratie verständlicher gemacht werden und was die von ihm erbrachten Leistungen mit dem eigenen Leben zu tun haben." Für den Journalismus werde es wichtig sein, sich von anderen Akteuren abzugrenzen und einen tatsächlichen Mehrwert zu liefern. „Dazu gehören solides Handwerk und die Lieferung von relevanten und zuverlässigen Informationen."

Hasebrink betonte bei der Vorstellung der Studie auch, dass Journalismus zwar in den Sozialen Medien präsent, aber dort als solcher erkennbar sein müsse. Er sollte Strategien der zahlreichen nicht-journalistischen Akteure in den Sozialen Medien nicht vorschnell übernehmen.

Aus dem Kuratorium von #UseTheNews gaben Mitglieder Einschätzungen. So sagte etwa die Aufsichtsratsvorsitzende der Funke Mediengruppe, Julia Becker: „Gerade weil Jugendliche die sozialen Medien so intensiv nutzen, braucht es solide recherchierten, verlässlichen Journalismus, der auf Fakten und Vielstimmigkeit setzt, nicht auf eine Agenda, die Algorithmen oder Influencer festgelegt haben." Mehr denn je leisten Verlage diese demokratiebewahrende Arbeit. „Wir müssen bei aller Verlässlichkeit und Glaubwürdigkeit jedoch auch die Wellenlänge junger Menschen treffen – etwa durch digitale Formate wie Podcasts, Videos oder Online-Beiträge direkt aus der Lebenswelt dieser Generation."

Der Senator für Kultur und Medien der Freien und Hansestadt Hamburg, Carsten Brosda, betonte: „Ziel professioneller Redaktionen muss es sein, den Wert guter journalistischer Arbeit gerade auch für das Leben junger Menschen deutlich zu machen. Zugleich muss die Vermittlung von Nachrichtenkompetenz und der Rolle des Journalismus für die demokratische Öffentlichkeit besser gelingen." ZDF-Chefredakteur Peter Frey verwies hierauf: „Besonders wichtig ist, dass wir eine noch bessere Übersetzungsleistung erbringen und erklären, welche konkreten Auswirkungen Nachrichten aus Politik und Wirtschaft auf den Alltag von jungen Menschen haben."

*(551 Wörter)*
*Studie: Vielen Jugendlichen fehlt bei Nachrichten Alltagsbezug vom 28. 4. 2021,*
*© dpa Deutsche Presse-Agentur GmbH*

**Anmerkung**
Z. 41 *Funke Mediengruppe*: deutscher Medienkonzern mit zahlreichen Beteiligungen an gedruckten und elektronischen Medien

## Lösungsvorschläge

### Teil A: Leseverstehen und Schreiben (integriert)

1. In the first task you have to describe the different experiences Kosoko Jackson made with the literary world. Take into account his role as critic and as author.
   - Jackson as critic:
     - Worked as a "sensitivity reader" for important publishers → warned publishers if novels might be seen as insensitive
     - Took an active part in literature conferences
     - Argues that authors should only write about characters from their own cultural, racial or sexual community → only write about their own experiences
   - Jackson as author:
     - Was about to publish his first Young Adult novel
     - Gained some positive book reviews and recommendations
     - Many negative posts on social media, mostly by people on Twitter who had not read the novel
     - Scared to publish his work, withdrew it before its release

   The article "Teen Fiction and the Perils of Cancel Culture" written by Jennifer Senior and published on 8 March 2019 in *The New York Times*, is about Kosoko Jackson, a young author and critic.  —  opening sentence

   Jackson has worked as a "sensitivity reader" for important publishers to warn them of novels which might be seen as hurtful to the feelings of minority groups. He has also taken an active part in literature conferences, where he argued that authors should only write about topics within their own world of experience.  —  Jackson's experience as critic

   As an author Jackson was about to publish his first Young Adult novel, which gained some positive book reviews and recommendations. However, it also generated a number of negative posts on social media, mainly by people on Twitter who had not read the novel themselves but just read about it. In the end Jackson was too frightened to publish his work and withdrew it before it was even released.  *(156 words)*  —  Jackson's experience as author

2. In the second task you need to examine what attitude Jennifer Senior, the author of the given article, adopts towards "cancel culture". You need to show how she conveys this attitude to the reader. You should take into account her line of argument and the language she chooses. To examine the line of argument it is helpful to subdivide the text into sense units and to note what effect each unit has on the reader.

- *Author's attitude: Senior is wary of "cancel culture", it is dangerous, brutal and unfair*
- *Line of argument*
  - *Headline → sets the tone*
  - *Presents one example to show the problem (ll. 1–10)*
  - *Explains how it came to the withdrawal; focus on social media (ll. 11–24)*
  - *Cancel culture threatens diversity and literary creativity (ll. 25–47)*
  - *Assesses if the criticism is appropriate; presents her own view on the novel in question (ll. 48–68)*
  - *Concludes that books must prove themselves on the market (ll. 69–75)*
- *Language*
  - *Words with a negative connotation*
    - *e. g. "perils" (headline), "fanatics" (l. 19), "mob" (ll. 27, 75) → dangerous*
    - *"dreary monoculture" (l. 32) → boring; only one perspective is accepted*
  - *Imagery:*
    - *"[one] of the captains of 'cancel culture'" (l. 9), "army of crusaders" (l. 30) → a few individuals lead the movement, many others follow orders*
    - *"Robespierre with his own neck in the cradle of the guillotine" (l. 8) → brutal, other opinions are not accepted*
  - *Enumeration*
    - *e. g. l. 17: "self-conscious, emotional, quick to injure" → description of Twitter subculture dealing with Y.A. fiction*
    - *e. g. ll. 51–53 → lists what authors usually do; stresses creative process*
  - *Parallelism, e. g. ll. 71–73 → stresses test books usually have to pass, namely get past librarians, bookstore owners and book critics*
  - *Insertions, e. g. ll. 27, 29, 66/67 → underline the author's preceding statement*
  - *Question and answer (l. 58), direct addresses to the reader (ll. 18, 48) → guide readers and convince them of her line of argument*

The author Jennifer Senior is very wary of what she calls "cancel culture" because she thinks that it is dangerous, brutal and unfair. To convey her attitude she uses a convincing line of argument and language that stresses her view.  **introduction**
**thesis**

Right from the start, Senior's choice of headline makes it clear that she rejects "cancel culture". Thus, the headline sets the tone for what is to come. Then she presents Kosoko Jackson and his debut novel as an example to show the problem (cf. ll. 1–10). In lines 11 to 24 she explains why Jackson chose to withdraw his novel. In her explanation she focuses on the influence social media had on his decision. In the next passage (cf. ll. 25–47) she claims that cancel culture threatens diversity and literary creativity. She then assesses if the criticism brought forth in the social media is appropriate and presents her own view on the novel  **main part:**
**line of argument**

2022-20

in question (cf. ll. 48–68). Finally, she concludes that books must prove themselves on the market (ll. 69–75). So, Senior's line of argument points out the problems and offers an alternative way of dealing with insensitive or otherwise questionable literature. The example she chooses helps the reader to understand her line of argument. [effects]

Her negative attitude towards "cancel culture" is further underlined by language, specifically by her choice of words. She uses a number of words with a negative connotation, e. g. "perils" in the headline, "fanatics" (l. 19) and "mob" (ll. 27, 75). All these words indicate that "cancel culture" is dangerous. The expression "dreary monoculture" (l. 32) indicates that literature will get boring and only represent one perspective if censorship becomes more common. [**language** → choice of words]

Senior also uses imagery to support her view. She depicts Jackson as one of the "captains of 'cancel culture'" (l. 9). In doing so, she warns that only a few individuals have a say while the others have to follow more or less blindly. She also compares him to "Robespierre with his own neck in the cradle of the guillotine" (l. 8), which illustrates how brutal censorship is and that dissenting opinions are not accepted. [→ imagery]

The author makes use of enumerations to stress that the Twitter subculture dealing with Y.A. fiction is highly subjective. She describes it as "self-conscious, emotional, quick to injure" (l. 17). Another enumeration is employed to refute Jackson's claim that authors should only write about their own world of experience. In ll. 51–53 she lists what authors usually do when writing a novel and thereby stresses the creative process. [→ enumerations]

In lines 71–73 a parallelism supports Senior's claim that censorship is not needed because books have to assert themselves on the market. The parallelism stresses that they need to get past librarians, bookstore owners and book critics. [→ parallelism]

Finally, the author also uses insertions to stress her preceding statement. For instance, she adds the nondescript name of a Twitter user (cf. l. 27) to prove that we are dealing with a "semi-anonymous mob" (ll. 26/27). She comments on the reviews Jackson's novel got to show that they were "[n]ot a small deal" (l. 29) and downplays the failures in Jackson's novel as "fairly typical" of a "debut novel" (l. 66). All these examples show that Senior uses insertions and comments to make her point even clearer. [→ insertions and comments]

To conclude, one can say that the author makes use of a clearly structured line of argument and several linguistic devices to convey her attitude that censorship or "cancel culture", as she calls it, will impoverish the literary market and that that market is quite capable of regulating itself. *(604 words)*  — conclusion

3.1 *You are given a quotation, which you first need to situate and then evaluate from your point of view. Take into account global challenges and ethical issues connected with scientific and technological progress. You may want to think of the way artificial intelligence influences our life.*
- Quotation: Lange warns that technology must remain a tool; mankind must not be governed by technology
- Historical perspective, maybe influenced by WW I
- Nowadays the challenges are slightly different → artificial intelligence
- Advantages, e. g.
  - Automation → hard and boring labour can be done by robots
  - Knowledge is accessible to everyone
  - Many things can be done from home, important during pandemic
  - Fast development → can be adjusted to needs
- Challenges, e. g.
  - Loss of jobs
  - Cybercrime
  - Bots influence elections → democracy under threat
  - less diversity through algorithms
  - Technological waste, e. g. storage batteries, mobiles
- Conclusion: Lange's warning is still up-to-date; man must remain master over technology

Lange's statement that "[t]echnology is a useful servant, but a dangerous master" is a warning that technology must remain a tool controlled by human beings. Mankind must not be governed by technology. Though the statement dates from 1921 it is still up-to-date. — introduction: explanation of quote

Lange's warning may well be influenced by World War I, when technological progress led to innumerable deaths. Nowadays the technological progress we can observe and the challenges resulting from it are slightly different. We are much more concerned with the advantages and disadvantages of artificial intelligence. — thesis

To start with the advantages, I would like to point out that automation has rid mankind of much hard, dangerous and boring labour, which can now be done be robots. One example is the reduction of monotonous assembly line work, for example in the — main part: advantages automation

2022-22

car industry. Another example is that robots are used to explore dangerous areas before people dare to enter them.

What is more, through the internet and websites like Wikipedia knowledge is accessible to everyone. At least in democratic countries everyone has access to knowledge from all kinds of sources and can obtain information independently. This is a huge advantage because it democratizes the access to knowledge and makes it harder to influence and bias people. *(internet, access to knowledge)*

Thanks to the internet many things can be done from home nowadays. We can communicate via Teams or Zoom, we can work from home and still collaborate with our colleagues, we can learn at home and do the shopping online. This was very important during the pandemic. Technological progress is extremely fast so that it can be adapted to our needs. *(digital communication and work)*

Obviously, all these advantages also have their drawbacks. Automation leads to a loss of jobs or rather to the creation of entirely different jobs. There are less jobs for unskilled workers, but this again means that people will earn higher wages. **(disadvantages / loss of jobs)**

Cybercrime is a far bigger challenge. There will always be people who use technological progress in a destructive way or to harm others. The internet offers a certain kind of anonymity, which is one reason why people publish things on the net that they would probably not say to someone's face. Unfortunately hate speech is a common phenomenon. Also, the darknet is used to buy and sell weapons, pornography and stolen data. *(cybercrime)*

More dangerous for democracy may be bots that are used to influence people and their opinion. It is said that Russia took enormous influence on the election of Donald Trump through bots. Furthermore, algorithms make sure that people get more of the information they usually search for. So, the diversity of information is reduced through algorithms. *(bots as threat to democracy / less diversity through algorithms)*

The extremely fast development of technological devices also encourages people to buy new smartphones, TV sets or computers before the old ones are broken just to make sure that they have the latest features. This causes ecological problems. Many resources are used to produce the devices and there is a huge amount of technological waste which needs to be disposed of. *(ecological challenges)*

To sum up, one can say that Lange's warning is still fitting. Though the advantages and challenges may be different to a hundred years ago, the danger that man is controlled by technology rather than the other way round, still exists. *(539 words)* **(conclusion)**

3.2 *In this task you have to write an article for a school website of a creative writing course. For this reason, your readers will probably be mostly students your age. In your article you must deal with the role of freedom of speech and creativity in society. You can use the aspects mentioned in Senior's article as well as ideas of your own. You could also show how a certain novel or drama has influenced you.*
- *Headline*
- *Reference to Senior's text and Jackson's experience*
  - *Jackson withdrew his novel because it was discussed negatively on social media*
  - *Jackson was scared by the reactions*
  - *Censorship*
  - *"Cancel culture" limits creativity and the literary market*
- *Further ideas*
  - *Literary works explore alternative ways of living → allow people to get an insight into other people's lives*
  - *Important to develop empathy for others*
  - *Freedom of speech ensures democratic processes*
  - *Investigative journalism uncovers political, economic, ecological or social scandals, e. g. Panama Papers, WikiLeaks*
  - *Life is never black and white but mostly grey → we need to deal with ambiguous problems → we need different perspectives to form our own opinion*
- *Conclusion: importance of freedom of speech and creativity to enrich our lives and to protect democracy*

| | |
|---|---|
| **Creativity and freedom of speech must not be limited** | headline |
| Just imagine you have written your first novel and even found a publisher for it. But before people really have the chance to read your story and form their own opinion about it, you get so much negative feedback on social media that you feel too scared to put the book on the market. Unbelievable? That's exactly what happened to Kosoko Jackson, a young American writer. Due to an unfavourable review of an advance copy of his novel *A Place for Wolves*, a Twitter mob verbally attacked Jackson. | **opening paragraph** reference to Jackson |
| Jennifer Senior, who wrote an article about this case calls this "cancel culture". In this case, "cancel culture" means that a literary oeuvre is cancelled before it even gets the chance to prove itself on the literary market. Senior's article made me think of the importance of creativity and freedom of speech. | reference to Senior's article |
| Literary works explore alternative ways of living. In doing so, they allow their readers to get an insight into other people's lives, which is important to develop empathy for others. For instance, when I read the novel *Girl, Woman, Other* by Bernardine Evaristo, I could walk in the shoes of various Black female characters; a chance I would otherwise never have had because I | exploring alternative ways of living |

identify neither as Black nor as female. It gave me an idea of the problems people face when discriminated against because of their gender and/or skin colour. But it also showed me that one cannot simply talk about "the Black women" because each person has their individual biography, faces different problems and finds different ways to cope with them.

Furthermore, freedom of speech ensures democratic processes in providing us with information and, very important, with different perspectives on an issue. Important issues like migration or global warming are far too complex to be seen as black or white. There is never the one and only correct solution. Therefore, we need different perspectives to form our own opinion and argue for it. Without freedom of speech, we only get one perspective. This can be observed during the war in Ukraine, when people in Russia only get to know Putin's version of the truth. — ensure democratic processes

Journalism and especially investigative journalism play an important part in maintaining our democracy. Journalists uncover political, economic, ecological or social scandals. Just take WikiLeaks as an example. Seeing what happened to Julian Assange or Edward Snowden shows how dangerous it can be to do investigative work. — role of journalism

As a consequence, it can be said that creativity does not only enrich our life, freedom of speech protects our democracy and therefore we should all be ready to fight for it and to speak up against all attempts at limiting it. *(454 words)* — **conclusion**

## Teil B: Sprachmittlung (isoliert)

4. *In der Mediationsaufgabe geht es darum eine mündliche Präsentation in einer amerikanischen Schule zu halten. Ihre Zuhörerschaft besteht also aus gleichaltrigen amerikanischen Schüler\*innen. Dies bedeutet, dass Sie sich nicht sehr formell ausdrücken müssen, aber natürlich dem Thema angemessen. Inhaltlich sollen Sie eine Jugendstudie über den Mediengebrauch deutscher Jugendlicher vorstellen und dabei auf die Ergebnisse der Studie sowie auf deren Auswirkungen auf den deutschen Journalismus eingehen.*
   – *Anrede*
   – *Eröffnung: zum Thema hinführen, ggf. Gliederung vorstellen, Bezug zum Unterricht herstellen*
   – *Ergebnisse der Studie*
     • *Jugendliche haben den Eindruck, dass das Nachrichtenangebot keinen Bezug zu ihrem Alltag hat*
     • *50 % finden es unwichtig, über Neuigkeiten und aktuelle Ereignisse informiert zu sein*
     • *46 % der 14–17-Jährigen nutzen mehrmals pro Woche journalistische Angebote, 58 % nutzen auch nicht-journalistische Angebote*
     • *Wichtigster Grund, sich auf dem Laufenden zu halten: adäquate Beteiligung an Gesprächen und Diskussionen im Freundes- und Familienkreis*
     • *Größeres Interesse an Nachrichten bei Jugendlichen, die den Eindruck haben, politisch etwas bewirken zu können*
     • *Wissen über Funktionen und Arbeitsweisen von Journalismus ist begrenzt, z. B. Unterschiede zu anderen Informationslieferanten*
   – *Auswirkungen auf Journalismus*
     • *Von anderen Akteuren abgrenzen; z. B. auf sozialen Medien nicht vorschnell die Strategien nicht-journalistischer Medien übernehmen; weiter auf Fakten, Vielstimmigkeit, Verlässlichkeit, Glaubwürdigkeit setzen*
     • *Mehrwert liefern, z. B. solides Handwerk, Lieferung relevanter und zuverlässiger Informationen*
     • *Digitale Formate nutzen, die junge Menschen ansprechen, z. B. Podcasts, Videos, Online-Beiträge aus deren Lebenswelt*
     • *Wert guter journalistischer Arbeit deutlich machen*
     • *Vermittlung von Nachrichtenkompetenz*
     • *Rolle des Journalismus für die demokratische Öffentlichkeit vermitteln*
     • *Auswirkungen der Nachrichten aus Politik und Wirtschaft auf den Alltag junger Menschen erklären*
   – *Schluss:*
     • *Kurzes Fazit oder Ausblick*
     • *Für die Aufmerksamkeit danken; Möglichkeit geben, Fragen zu stellen*

| | |
|---|---|
| Hello everybody, | address |
| As we are dealing with News for Youth in our project, I would like to present to you the situation in Germany. To do so, I will first talk about a study carried out among German teenagers and then I will tell you how journalism might react to the findings. | **introduction:** reference to topic outline |
| According to this study, teenagers have the impression that news do not concern their everyday life. About half of the participants think that it is not important to be informed about the news and current events. 46 % of the teenagers aged 14 to 17 use journalistic services several times a week. 58 % also use services by non-journalists. Those who keep themselves informed do so mainly because they want to be able to take part in discussions among friends and within their family. Those teenagers who feel they can make a difference in politics are more interested in keeping themselves informed. The study also showed that young people know little about the way journalists work and about the differences between journalistic and non-journalistic players. | findings of the study |
| Let me now turn to the implication of these findings for journalism. A number of high-ranking German journalists offered the following ideas: The differences between journalism and non-journalistic media must be emphasized. Journalism must not simply adopt strategies of non-journalistic players in social media. It must continue to rely on facts, offer different perspectives, be reliable and credible. It must also show the added value of solid journalistic work, for example by offering relevant and reliable information. However, it should also use digital formats that particularly are attractive for young people, for example podcasts, videos and online contributions that address young people's reality. News literacy must also be taught and the role of journalism within a democracy must be explained. Journalism must help young people understand the consequences political and economic news have on their everyday lives. | implications for journalism |
| As you can see, there is a lot to be done to get more young Germans interested in journalistic news. Thank you for listening. Now I'm curious to hear your questions or comments. | conclusion |

*(348 words)*

**Abiturprüfung NRW – Englisch 2023**
**Leistungskurs**

Um Ihnen die Prüfung 2023 schnellstmöglich zur Verfügung stellen zu können, bringen wir sie in digitaler Form heraus.

Sobald die Original-Prüfungsaufgaben 2023 freigegeben sind, können sie als PDF auf der Plattform **MyStark** heruntergeladen werden (Zugangscode vgl. Umschlaginnenseite, vorne im Buch).

## Aktuelle Prüfung

www.stark-verlag.de/mystark